Living Time
Festival Discourses for the Present Age

MAGGID

Rabbi Shagar

LIVING TIME
FESTIVAL DISCOURSES
FOR THE PRESENT AGE

EDITED BY
Alan Brill

TRANSLATED BY
Levi Morrow

Maggid Books

Living Time
Festival Discourses for the Present Age

First English Edition, 2024

Maggid Books
An imprint of Koren Publishers Jerusalem Ltd.

POB 8531, New Milford, CT 06776–8531, USA
& POB 4044, Jerusalem 9104001, Israel
www.korenpub.com

Cover photo: Eliyahu Yanai

The publication of this book was made possible
through the generous support of *The Jewish Book Trust*.

ISBN 978–1-59264–612–8, *hardcover*

Printed and bound in the United States

Contents

Preface

The Institute for the Advancement of Rabbi Shagar's Writings is proud to present another collection of teachings from Rabbi Shimon Gershon Rosenberg (Rabbi Shagar) in translation for his English-speaking audience. This volume takes its place alongside its predecessor, *Faith Shattered and Restored,* enabling readers to engage more deeply with the breadth of Rabbi Shagar's teachings.

Faith Shattered and Restored, published by Maggid in 2017, was met with enthusiastic interest and acclaim from its audience. The intervening years have seen intense debate among the book's readership regarding the original ideas it contained, as well as their applicability to Diaspora Jewry. We at the Institute take great joy in this discussion, because we believe that Rabbi Shagar's teachings carry considerable meaning and relevance even outside the narrow borders of Israeli Jewry within which they took shape. We hope to continue putting out translations of Rabbi Shagar's writings, making his ideas ever-more accessible to all readers.

Faith Shattered and Restored's introduction contains a detailed description of Rabbi Shagar's life and personality, of the broad horizons and varied textures of his teachings, and of the Institute's continuing efforts to edit and publish these teachings. Readers seeking more information in those areas should look there. Additionally, this present volume begins with an introduction by Rabbi Professor Alan Brill wherein he lays out a broad, rich perspective on Rabbi Shagar's thought, its intellectual context, as well as the way it developed over time. This introduction, therefore, focuses on the novel contributions of the sermons contained in this volume for Rabbi Shagar's English-speaking audience.

This book began as a project of Rabbi Dr. Alan Brill and Rabbi Levi Morrow, who reached out to the Institute with a proposal to translate a selection of Rabbi Shagar's holiday sermons into English. The essays chosen set out in a direction distinct from those in *Faith Shattered and Restored*, which were written in the style of philosophical essays attempting to grapple with the challenge modern and post-modern ideas create for Judaism. The texts contained herein portray a different facet of Rabbi Shagar's thought, and they take a different form as well – they are sermons, written and taught in tandem with the holidays of the Jewish calendar.

Rabbi Shagar was not a philosopher pursuing abstract, timeless ideas. His thought grew organically out of learning and teaching Torah in the *beit midrash* and out of his experiences with real educational challenges. He was driven by his existential reality as a Jew, as a servant of God, and by his lived experience of the Jewish calendar – the holidays, fasts, and the days that have become part of the calendar since the founding of the State of Israel.

Preparing for the holidays was an essential part of Rabbi Shagar's Torah study and spiritual work. He would often say that each holiday has its own unique "illumination," which we must study and prepare for in order to be able to experience it. In his holiday sermons, he sought to express each holiday's unique illumination by exploring relevant texts, analyzing the mitzvot and customs of the holiday, and revealing its underlying ideas. Simultaneously, Rabbi Shagar used the platform provided by the sermons to give each holiday's characteristic attributes new interpretations which would speak to contemporary Jews. In the introduction to *Lottery is Destiny* (*Pur Hu Hagoral*), a book of his Purim sermons that was published during his lifetime, Rabbi Shagar described this practice in the following way:

One of my goals is to create relevant, substantive meanings for the holidays and seasons which are meant to be times of depth and renewal. Each holiday has its own light and color. It is toward this end that I have integrated modern ideas into hasidic lines of thought, in order to translate these hasidic ideas into our world.

The genre of the sermon is well-fit for this purpose. Anyone who reads Rabbi Shagar's sermons will find the ideas similar to what he explores in his more philosophical essays, but in a form that enables different elements of the ideas to emerge. In contrast to the essays in *Faith Shattered and Restored*, the festival sermons have a briefer, more evocative style, reminiscent of a speech presented orally. The sermons do not aim to fully and clearly convey the discussed ideas or to explain the quoted texts, but to awaken the reader to the existential questions inherent in the illumination of each holiday. They seek to go beyond the realm of the intellect and address the heart, and they should therefore be read with openness and attention to the melody behind Rabbi Shagar's words. Great effort and consideration went into making sure that this melody is audible even in the translated version of the sermons.

The management of the Institute for the Writings of Rabbi Shagar appointed me to coordinate the work on this volume, and to oversee the process of selecting and translating the sermons. As a representative of the Institute, I want to express our whole-hearted gratitude to the book's editor, Rabbi Dr. Alan Brill, and to the translator, Rabbi Levi Morrow, for the incredible amount of work they have put into the book, and for their commitment to the spreading of Rabbi Shagar's teachings to the English-speaking world. Rabbi Dr. Brill's initiative and patience were a constant presence while we worked on the book – from start to finish – and Rabbi Morrow's deep comprehension and sensitivity to language created a translation that is clear and accessible while also being precise and faithful to the original.

The original versions of the sermons were edited by Yishai Mevorach, Zohar Maor, Odeya Zuriely, Elhanan Nir, Netanel Lederberg, and myself, and these editors have our grateful appreciation. A note at the beginning of each sermon identifies the sermon's original editor and place of publication.

Our thanks as well to the members of the book's broader editorial team: Professor Tamar Ross, Rabbi Yehoshua Engelman, Rabbi Zach Truboff, and Dr. Zohar Maor, whose many incisive comments throughout the process of working on the book contributed to the exactitude of the translation.

Thank you to Rabbi Shimon Deutsch, chairman of the publication committee, for his involvement in the work and publishing of the book. Thank you as well to Rabbanit Miriam Rosenberg, Rabbi Shagar's widow, for the great efforts she has put into publishing Rabbi Shagar's writings. Finally, thank you to Matthew Miller, Rabbi Reuven Ziegler and Maggid Books for publishing another volume of Rabbi Shagar's teachings in English, and to Maggid's outstanding professional staff: Aryeh Grossman, Caryn Meltz, Ita Olesker, David Silverstein, Tani Bayer, Aryeh Sklar, and Rachel Miskin.

Eitan Abramovich

Editor's Introduction

The Essence of
Rabbi Shagar

Rabbi Dr. Alan Brill
Seton Hall University

Rabbi Shimon Gershon Rosenberg (1949–2007), better known by the acronym formed by the initials of his name ShaGaR (henceforth, Rabbi Shagar), was arguably the first native Israeli religious thinker. He was an introvert, and in his lifetime was mainly known to a small group of students; however, his importance has grown exponentially since his premature death in 2007. He was ardently religiously Orthodox, yet he lived with an existential chaos – a chaos that created an empty space of "existential absurdity" within him. He often spoke about it and posited that it created an anarchistic feel to parts of his thought. Rabbi Shagar left behind decades of drafts of personal reflections and unpublished lectures. His ideas, however, were always in the process of development and not conclusions, part protest and rebellion, and part revealing his own heart in order to encourage others also to be themselves. Therefore, we can say little to clarify the loose ends of

Rabbi Shagar's thought, or resolve the tensions of his thinking. Nevertheless, his lectures as compiled and edited into essays by his students, have created a new post-modern Hasidism, opening up new vistas of religious Jewish thought.

BIOGRAPHY

Rabbi Shagar was born in Jerusalem to Holocaust survivor parents, and attended the Hesder yeshiva Yeshivat Kerem B'Yavneh, afterward studying at Mercaz HaRav and with Rabbi Shlomo Fischer of Itri. After his marriage, he learned in the Kollel of Yeshivat HaKotel. He fought in the 1973 Yom Kippur War. His tank took a direct hit at the very start of the fierce tank battles in the Golan Heights; two of his comrades were killed instantly, and he was wounded and badly burned. This event, along with the subsequent Israeli political trajectory of events – from the withdrawal from Sinai to the disengagement from Gaza – elicited within Rabbi Shagar a sense that the Religious Zionist narrative of messianic redemption through return to the land was broken.

The 1970s and 1980s were a time for Rabbi Shagar – then teaching at Yeshivat HaKotel – to forge his own unique path of education, during which he integrated hasidic thought into the yeshiva and sought to make personal meaning a part of Talmud study. In 1984 he briefly established the yeshiva Shefa, together with Rabbi Adin Steinsaltz and Rabbi Menachem Froman, as a place to explore new ways of understanding within Judaism. During this period, he also taught at the successful high school Yeshivat Makor Haim, established by his close student Rabbi Dov Singer under the auspices of Rabbi Steinsaltz. In 1988–1989, he taught at Beit Midrash Maaleh. In 1990, Professor Benjamin Ish-Shalom established the Beit Midrash of Beit Morasha and appointed Rabbi Shagar to lead it together with Rabbi Eliyahu Blumenzweig (later head of Yeshivat Yeruḥam). At the end of 1996, Rabbi Shagar established Yeshivat Siach Yitzhak (originally Yeshivat Siach) together with his lifelong colleague Rabbi Yair Dreifuss, where he served as head of the yeshiva until his death. On June 11th, 2007 (25th of Sivan, 5767), Rabbi Shimon Gershon Rosenberg died of a rapidly-spreading pancreatic cancer.

There are currently over twenty-five published volumes of Rabbi Shagar's lectures, which could potentially double, or even triple, in number, considering the vast range of topics in his lectures on Jewish philosophy, Kabbala, Hasidism, and talmudic analysis. Much of the posthumous fanfare surrounding Rabbi Shagar focuses on the published lectures he gave in the last decade of his life; however, to put his thought in perspective, we need to turn the clock back to the formation of his ideas in the 1970s and 1980s, as well as his application of these ideas in the 1990s.

CONTEXT: THE NEW RELIGIOUS ZIONISTS

In the early 1990s, the Religious Zionist world in Israel started undergoing tremendous changes, when various groups, collectively called "the New Religious Zionists" (*HaDati'im HaHadashim*), sought to reformulate Religious Zionism away from the messianic ideology of the prior decades toward a greater sense of individualism.[1]

During the 1970s and 1980s, the Religious Zionist yeshivas were swept up into the nationalistic Gush Emunim (Bloc of the Faithful), with its vision of a messianic settling of the West Bank. By the 1990s, much of the Israeli Religious Zionist world followed the teachings of Rabbi Tzvi Yehuda Kook (d. 1982), son of Rabbi Abraham Isaac Kook, in which the individual was to subjugate himself to the collective project of building the nation. One cannot understate the importance of this trend of messianic nationalistic collectivism, ideologically centered at Yeshivat Merkaz HaRav, for Religious Zionist education. Merkaz Harav ideology was against individualist Western culture, secular studies, and political liberalism, and it created an intense sociopolitical and theological pressure to view everything through the lens of immanent messianism, in which its teachers generally offered absolute and certain answers.

This trend intensified under the influence of Rabbi Zvi Yisrael Tau, which culminated in his founding of Yeshivat Har HaMor in 1998. His students created the Hardal ("National Haredi") ideology and community, which follow a straight and constrained path, the *Kav*. They emphasize complete faith in the acute messianic import of the State of Israel and reject any secular studies and secular influences. They are also against any academic influence by teachers and colleges, ultimately

---

1. See Yair Sheleg, *The New Religious Zionists* (Jerusalem: Keter, 2000) (Heb.).

rejecting the influence of modern educational psychology and modern approaches to the study of the Bible. They are especially notable for rejecting individualism, modern personal independence, or the thinking of the New Religious Zionists.

The response of the New Religious Zionists was a turn toward individualism and independence. Instead of prioritizing the collective and the national, they emphasized creativity, academics, filmmaking, neo-hasidic enthusiasm, journeys to India, and poetry writing. These "New Religious Zionists," as they called themselves, freely rejected many traditional elements of the ideology of collective state building by seeking answers in pluralism, social analysis, tolerance, critical thinking, feminism, philosophy, and autonomy. This, in turn, created a wave of new institutions including, but not limited to, those started by Rabbi Shagar. These new Religious Zionist institutions integrated into the yeshiva, a place of traditional Talmud study, a kaleidoscope of new perspectives including New Age thought, creative writing, yoga, philosophy of religion, poetry and academic study of Bible and Talmud. Finally, there was a revivalist Neo-Hasidism of a distinct Religious Zionist nature focusing on experiential Judaism, such as the trend of Habbakook (Chabad, Breslov and [K] Carlebach/Kook) which was characterized by ecstatic prayer, turning to Hasidism instead of Talmud, and wearing sidecurls (*peyot*).[2]

The New Religious Zionists sought to embrace the fullness of the secular world, Western culture, and normal life. Unlike the certainties of the older ideology of prior decades, they acknowledged doubt, questions, and a pluralism of truth. They wrote articles announcing that the older religious language was no longer adequate and that a new religious language was needed; they wanted new answers and new philosophies.

When such Religious Zionists use the term "post-modern," they include anything that emphasizes individualism and uncertainty, including Kafka, Buber, Freud, and Sartre, as well as Elie Wiesel and Soloveitchik's *Lonely Man of Faith*. Even though these authors, whom they cite, wrote during the height of modernism, the New Religious Zionists instead define modernism as the state building and rationalism of the

---

2. Semadar Cherlow, *Who Moved My Judaism? Judaism, Post-Modernism and Contemporary Spiritualities* (Tel Aviv: Resling, 2016) (Heb.).

Merkaz worldview. Their definition of the post-modern, contrastingly, is characterized by the individual and the existential.

Rabbi Shagar was not the leader of this shift in understanding, nor of the attendant social changes, but he became the thinker who gave this new Religious Zionist world the religious language it sought. Not only did Rabbi Shagar advocate for changes in education and religious society, he also connected the post-modern loss of the grand narrative with the breakdown of the former collectivist ideology. Many of his Israeli readers simply saw him as a needed move beyond Merkaz, because for them, he was the first person whom they ever heard say that history, metaphysics, ethics, and social problems do not have absolutes, or who advocated for the importance of subjectivity.

Rabbi Shagar's contribution in the 1980s and 1990s reflected in this volume included a new approach to Torah study, a turn to Hasidism, a use of existential themes, and a unique interpretation of concepts such as repentance and self-acceptance. In the last decade of his life, he integrated post-modern language and worked on the concept of faith for a world without foundations, as well as welcoming the multiplicity of ideas. Finally, in the last years of his life he turned more to the thought of the existentialist Jewish philosopher Franz Rosenzweig and the psychoanalyst Jacques Lacan, and also to the problems of Post-Zionism and the Disengagement from Gaza. We will now conceptually look at these listed topics, explaining their importance to his thought.

TORAH STUDY

Rabbi Shagar's greatest influence on the Israeli scene was setting a new agenda for Torah study as a quest for meaning (*mashmaut*). How does the text speak to you? What do you hear in the text? In asking these types of questions, he was clearly rejecting the widespread focus almost solely on the analytic approach of Talmud study, generally called the approach of Brisk. Instead, he believed, we need to ask human questions, seek personal answers, and look for religious meaning, not just formalism. In Torah study, we need to use not just intellect but also imagination, emotions, and desire.

For Rabbi Shagar, non-legalist Aggada, Hasidism, and Jewish thought need to inspire Talmud study. We need to bring Western culture, philosophy, and literature into dialogue with the Talmud. For Rabbi Shagar, there needs to be individual creativity in interpretation of the Talmud, as well as individual projects and group discussions.

This shift, one of Rabbi Shagar's lasting accomplishments, is the inspiration behind an entire new wave of educators, and the creation of new institutions in which students spend significant time engaged in spiritual quest. These educators and institutions have brought academic studies, Western philosophy, and Eastern spirituality into the study hall (*beit midrash*), which is the crucial place of spiritual formation and religious life. Rabbi Nahman of Breslov, Plato, Franz Rosenzweig, yoga, and poetry writing workshops are made part of the curriculum. The study hall is a place to find one's individuality and relevance to contemporary issues, to hear the eternal voice of God in the authentic self. It should not be a place of submission to an absolute Torah. The novelty in Rabbi Shagar's thought is that these other fields cannot – and should not – be explored in the university or in the secular realm, but in the rabbinic study hall. Discussions of this phenomenon are found in the writings of the generation of rabbis of the yeshivas of Tekoa, Othniel, Maaleh Gilboa, and the institutions Herzog College and Beit Morasha, but the acknowledged theologian of this new approach is Rabbi Shagar.

For Rabbi Shagar, in order for the study of Talmud to be existential, we need to instill a sense of the study hall as a place of personal formation and the Gemara as one's world, the culture in which one lives and plots one's inner life. Rabbi Shagar describes this quality as "*beitiyut*," which we might translate as "at-homeness." This at-homeness allows the study hall to function as a place that allows freely chosen self-identification, a self-affirmed covenant (*brit*), which is also in continuity with one's parents, family, ancestry, and community. The *beit midrash* is one's place because it creates meaning in one's life; it offers experiential contact with the Infinite as both personal and primal. Torah study is creative and individualistic in that anyone can construct his or her own meaning of Torah, which makes space for holiness and the Divine Presence. "This is the Jew's refuge from the alienation and estrangement of the outer world, and it is here that he finds his place and feels at home."[3]

---

3. See below, "Face to Face," p. 279.

For Rabbi Shagar, someone who requires justification of the tradition is already outside of it because tradition, according to its own definition, is a function of self-identity and self-definition, which is composed and sustained by experience.[4] Torah must be studied out of love, not as an outsider. Not only do you have to be a participant in the covenant in order to understand the Torah, but rather the whole sense of Torah study is this revelation of personal meaning.[5]

Alternatively, Torah study serves as a means to ward off existential meaninglessness by lending meaning to one's activities that are grounded in the infinite divine. In Rabbi Shagar's non-foundational existential theology, we construct our world of Torah by means of personal commitment, creativity, and finding meaning, thereby blurring "the lines between discovery and creation" – and by extension, between God and the human. In the encounter with Torah, the student gains the truth of existence and the inner unity that rests in the declaration "I am who I am."[6]

In his later thought, after his post-modern turn, Rabbi Shagar claims that the Torah is not a static body of knowledge, but rather a subjective language game in which a *lamdan* (a talmudic scholar) engages in the activity of *lamdanut* (conceptual understanding of the Talmud). By creating Torah language, Torah continuously creates meaning.[7] Despite this lack of certainty and foundation, Rabbi Shagar requires strict halakhic adherence and thinks laxity would undermine the system. Nevertheless, he states that the concept of halakha is not coherent or determined, but rather includes different genres with different arguments, creating different worlds to inhabit.[8]

---

4. See below, "The Name of the Father," p. 178–180. The idea is from Zygmunt Bauman, *Liquid Modernity* (Cambridge: Polity, 2000), but Rabbi Shagar cites it from Avi Sagi, *The Challenge of Returning to the Tradition*, (Jerusalem-Ramat Gan, 2003), 92 (Heb.).
5. See below, "Face to Face," p. 282.
6. Ibid., pp. 283–284.
7. Rabbi Shagar, *Kelim Shevurim* (Efrat: Yeshivat Siach Yitzhak, 2004), 32.
8. Ibid., 43–44.

HASIDISM

Rabbi Shagar gave talks on hasidic thought in general and on Rabbi Nahman, specifically, as a text and pretext for larger issues of contemporary religious experience, personal meaning and transience. This activity of bringing Hasidism into the Yeshiva canon was a significant departure from previous Religious Zionist culture.

By means of these talks on Rabbi Nahman, Rabbi Shagar was able to advocate for the greater integration of song and poetry, silence, prophecy, meditation and contemplation, the seeking of higher wisdom, and of course, injecting the study of Kabbala and Hasidism into the yeshiva. He also used these talks to emphasize the need to give up seeking a rational explanation and instead, seek faith without a philosophic foundation. A theme that runs throughout these lectures is the impotence of a rational language and the need to move beyond the discursive.

Especially important was Rabbi Shagar's private Thursday night study group of hasidic texts with his core followers. Rabbi Shagar's vision was not to retrieve the eighteenth-century meaning of the texts, but rather, to grapple with the spiritual demands of today. These talks, which form the core of his later thought, are the way his older students fondly remember him.

These early talks already contain the ideas that one must constantly bring oneself to God, overcome egocentrism through giving oneself up to God, treat the Torah as bearing a plurality of meaning, and recognize the importance of prayer. From these talks, Rabbi Shagar developed his idea that providence means personally seeing the workings of the infinite divine in the complexity of one's life, as opposed to the Merkaz emphasis on seeing providence as a predetermined national plan.

I especially want to note Rabbi Shagar's use of Rabbi Nahman for his critique of capitalism, in that capitalism causes greed and prevents knowledge of God. According to Rabbi Nahman, desire for money is a debased transferred desire for God, which leads to depression, alienation, unkindness, and harshness. For Rabbi Shagar, having to live with the power structures of capitalism makes it impossible to lead a life of purity. His utopic vision is to exist beyond our culture of money and move toward one of generosity and openness.

Two decades later, Rabbi Shagar retells many of his earlier teachings with a post-modernist phrasing. In his earlier thought, melody (*nigun*) was a way of moving beyond word and the cerebralism of the yeshiva. In his later thought, under the influence of his popular reading of Derrida's ideas, he formulates the concept of melody as an act of deconstruction, showing that meaning does not inhere in the words, but rather, in a mystical opening to God beyond the text.[9]

Rabbi Shagar especially loved to recount the long allegorical tales of Rabbi Nahman and explicitly called them absurd folktales that convey a dreamlike present beyond time and space, beyond rationalism and talmudic analysis. For Rabbi Shagar, Rabbi Nahman told fantastic tales "of kings and princesses, fantastic lands and wondrous creatures, including giants, spirits, men of the woods, and a prince made entirely of precious stones" in order to empty the world of its certainty, thereby allowing us to reincorporate dream, miracle, play, and ecstasy into our religious lives. For Rabbi Shagar, these non-Jewish folktales expose "the listener to a world of experiences, which is entirely disconnected from the religious experience and its normal, accepted, forms in the traditional Jewish world."[10] As a contemporary application, Rabbi Shagar would use science fiction for his understanding of religious reality.

A note should be made of his use of hasidic language: it is not a translation of Hasidism into post-modernity or vice-versa, but rather theologically pregnant hasidic terms and select passages that he uses to create his original thought. One of these essential terms that he uses as

---

9. Rabbi Shagar, *The Remainder of Faith: Post-Modern Sermons on Jewish Holidays* (Tel Aviv: Resling Publishing, 2014), pp. 41–44 (Heb.).

10. See below, "On Translation and Living in Multiple Worlds," p. 119. On his creating a parallel of tales to science fiction, see Roee Horen (ed.), *Life of Yearning: New Interpretation to the Tales of Reb Nachman of Breslov* (Tel Aviv: Yediot Aharonot – Sifre Hemed, 2010), 21 (Heb.). On his discussion of folktales, see "The Secret of Unity, the Resentment of the Shekhina, and the Divine Hidden in Sin," in Roee Horen (ed.), *Baal Shem Tov: The Man Who Came from the Woods* (Rishon LeZion: Yediot Aharonot – Sifre Hemed, 2017), 227–240 (Heb.). For a broader discussion of Rabbi Shagar's ideas on the topic, see Levi Morrow, "Why Theology Should Always Be Fantasy: Imagination, Fantasy, and Science-Fictional Messianism in the Writings of Rabbi Shagar," in Austin M. Freeman, Andrew D. Thrasher, and Fotini Toso (eds.), *Fantasy, Theology, and the Imagination* (Lanthan, MD: Lexington Press, 2023).

one of his fundamental ideas is Rabbi Nahman's concept of the *ḥalal hapanui* – the empty space, the void or absence of God (*Likkutei Moharan* 64). The world appears devoid of the Divine, yet since the Divine created the void, then the infinite Divine is still found in the void.[11] Rabbi Shagar treats this void as the *ayin* – the nothing, the absurd and meaninglessness of Existentialism, as well as the post-modern lack of grand narrative.[12]

Sometimes, Rabbi Shagar adopts the opposite approach, that the world is filled with the infinite of the Divine and that everything we do is a playing out of the infinite Divine will. The mitzvot give access to this infinite Divine, in that they are a closed symbolic system that signifies the infinite. In these cases, he will especially cite Chabad sources, especially from Rabbi Shneur Zalman of Liady, the Alter Rebbe (1745–1812), R. Yitzchak Eizik Epstein of Homel (d. 1857) and Reb Hillel Paritcher (1795–1864). There is a tension between his turning to the empty void of Rabbi Nahman of Breslov and his use of the immanent infinite Divine from Chabad sources. In general, Rabbi Shagar conflates the infinite of God, the absence of God, and the all-encompassing of God, and thus, the post-modern absence becomes a hasidic omnipresence, and achieving mystical oneness is equated with the notion of reaching the inner-most self and with the nullification of the modern self. For Rabbi Shagar, living with the void of *ayin* affords a life fully lived without the limits that bind others.[13]

From his readings of hasidic texts, Rabbi Shagar creates what he calls a post-modern Torah view, a way to live with doubt and without certain knowledge, yet still affirm a life of Torah study and mysticism. For example, according to Rabbi Shagar, modern rationalism has killed prayer, but post-modernity may bring prayer back.[14] Modern man was like Prometheus, challenging God with his belief in his own powers. In

---

11. As a point of contrast, the Neo-Hasidic heterodox thinker Arthur Green, *Tormented Master* (University of Alabama Press, 1979), 285–336, uses this Rabbi Nahman text to say that we live in a world of modernist doubt disconnected from the theistic God of the past. Instead, Green thinks that now God is known as a spiritual inner-voice within ourselves as well as a panentheism of God in the world.
12. See below, "Story of the Palace," pp. 140–144.
13. See below, "A Screen for the Spirit, a Garment for the Soul," pp. 92–100.
14. R. Shagar, *The Remainder of Faith*, pp. 41–44.

contrast, in the post-modern period, we learn how to turn completely toward God despite the doubt with prayer, ecstasy, meditation, and religious experience.

It is important to note that despite his use of hasidic texts, Rabbi Shagar taught that the actual historical phenomena and practices of Hasidism, as well as the conventions of the current *ḥaredi* hasidic community, are not the correct path for the Religious Zionist world which, in contrast to the Hasidim, embraces the world. This new approach to hasidic thought is called "Israeli Hasidism" or "Religious Zionist Hasidism," specifically using hasidic works for their ideas but without embracing the sectarian version of *ḥaredi* hasidism. At the same time, Rabbi Shagar also didn't want his followers to solely follow the anti-intellectual emotionalism of some forms of Neo-Hasidism.

EXISTENTIALISM AND THE ABSURD

In *Touching the Heart*, written by Rabbi Shagar's colleague, Rabbi Yair Dreifuss, Rabbi Shagar is portrayed as a hasidic existentialist. Indeed, they had founded a yeshiva together whose very name, Yeshivat Siach, means existential dialogue. Rabbi Shagar used the hasidic texts to teach individualism of expression, decision-making, life journeys, and how to live in the moment. Rabbi Shagar recognized that these elements of individualism are inevitable in that we live in an age where there is a breakdown of the hierarchical patriarchal society and children are encouraged to be themselves; we now have the freedom to create our own reality, decide whom we marry, and accept responsibility for our life choices. For much of his teachings, Rabbi Shagar was a modern existentialist and romantic, with an emphasis on individuality in the micro narrative of our lives.[15]

Rabbi Shagar used ideas from Camus suggesting that life is absurd and a person can choose to embrace his own absurd condition. According to Camus, one's freedom – and the opportunity to give life meaning – lies in the recognition of absurdity. If the absurd experience is truly the realization that the universe is fundamentally devoid of absolutes, then we as individuals are truly free. For example, Purim for

---

15. Yair Dreifuss, *Touching the Heart* (Tel Aviv: Yediot Books, 2013) (Heb.).

Rabbi Shagar is when we realize that all of our plans and projects are naught and empty; we never reach the goal of our desires. For Freud, the transience of the everyday leads to a sense of melancholy. In contrast, for Rabbi Shagar, transience lets us live in the moment and reach the infinite beyond the finite rules of the rest of the year. He equates laughing at one's absurdity as a form of hasidic nullification (*bitul hayesh*).[16]

It is worth noting that when Buber, Rabbi Heschel, and Rabbi Soloveitchik turn to Existentialism, they all see faith as an answer to the absurdity, meaningless, and futility of life. In contrast, Rabbi Shagar accepts that our existential situation is indeed absurd, similar to Rabbi Nahman's depiction of the void. Rabbi Shagar's goal is to explain this absurdity as our religious life, then to channel it back to a religious perspective. For Rabbi Shagar, "The *tzaddik* exists in crisis, sensing the deep falsity of his existence.... His ability to turn his crisis into a joke expresses the divine infinitude much more than any attempt to shrink the gap between human and divine through serious service of God."[17] In origins, Rabbi Shagar's ideas reach down to his own existential absurdity of watching his two tank partners die in an explosion and his arbitrary survival of the attack. Later, it becomes the basis for defining the rupture between the Merkaz vision of national divine providence and the post-modern life.

Rabbi Shagar's ethics are a mixture of a Buberian dialogue of I-Thou and the existential decision-making of Camus and Sartre. We trust our human finite truth, our lived experience and our personal judgments as an individual faith. The fact that we cannot substantiate our values and can always doubt them should not hinder our faith; we should have faith in our own faith and that of others. Rabbi Shagar places the emphasis on formation of self through commitment to Torah, on our at-homeness in the study hall, and on hasidic mysticism.

RABBI SHAGAR ON POST-MODERNISM

Rabbi Shagar came to the modern formal aspects of post-modernism in the last eight years of his life. In 1999, Rabbi Shagar read David Gurevitz's

16. See below, "The Joke of the Megilla," pp. 148–151.
17. See below, "The Story of the Palace," p. 140.

Post-Modernism: Culture and Literature at the End of the 20th Century,[18] a general work describing the application of post-modernism to Israeli literature by writers such as Etgar Keret, as well as Jean-François Lyotard's *The Postmodern Condition.*[19] These works opened up a new language for him, which he embraced and applied to his prior project – one that included twenty years of prolific thought. From this start, he quickly read anything written in Hebrew on the topic. In the end, however, he remained an eclectic autodidact who could not read any language but Hebrew, and therefore was dependent on the random publications of the newly emerging translations of twentieth-century European thought.

Throughout many of his talks, the primary meaning of post-modernism for Rabbi Shagar consists of the shift from Rav Kook's approach to the study of a post-modern appropriation of Rabbi Nahman of Breslov. For Rabbi Shagar, Rabbi Nahman was the paradigm of post-modernism in that his Hasidism taught that we have no answers – meaning no grand narrative, or foundational knowledge. For Rabbi Shagar, there were three ways Rabbi Nahman's ideas teach about the breakdown of the narrative. First, that we often have religious problems without answers. Second, that we live with the unresolved paradox of the absence of God in the world, yet His glory fills the earth. Third, that the world is a contradiction of experiences, yet the infinite divine is behind all reality.

Rabbi Shagar asks: what is the Archimedean point of the postmodern era? For Rabbi Shagar, it reveals the hasidic concept we mentioned above of metaphysical nothingness, *ayin.* This is an age of no metaphysics above, no ideology below. Rabbi Shagar writes, "I am of the opinion that post-modernism and deconstructionism constitute a shattering of the vessels. Yet this very shattering is what grants us wide-ranging freedom...to believe, even without absolute proofs and evidence."[20] Furthermore, post-modernism can lead to mysticism and spiritual renewal, because we are beyond language.

---

18. Tel Aviv: Dvir, 1997 (Heb.).
19. English translation was published by the University of Minnesota Press, 1984; Hebrew translation by Tel Aviv: Hakibbutz Hameuḥad, 1999.
20. Rabbi Shagar, *Tablets and Broken Tablets* (Alon Shevut: Mekhon Kitvei Harav Shagar, 2013), 431 (Heb.). See also "Mysticism, Post-Modernism, and the New Age," in *Faith Shattered and Restored* (Jerusalem: Maggid Books, 2017), 119–130.

To understand what Rabbi Shagar calls post-modernism, it is important to bear in mind the difference between post-modernity and post-modernism. Post-modernity is the sense of our era, a *zeitgeist*, when there is a breakdown of modernism. There is a questioning of rationality, science, ethics, and progress. In contrast, post-modernism is an academic and philosophic movement with a canon, similar to Hegelianism, existentialism, and Kantianism, dealing with the current theoretical issues in hermeneutics, cultural theory, literary theory, psychology, and social science. In general, Rabbi Shagar deals with post-modernity as a cultural social moment and not as a philosophy of post-modernism.

Rabbi Shagar's thought is not philosophic post-modernism, according to which the self is socially constructed and bound by language and epistemic ruptures. He generally has no post-modern rejection of self, no reading for power, and no post-structural turns. Rabbi Shagar retains the notion of the existential self and hasidic experiential elements, sometimes downplaying modern subjectivity, as well as maintaining a sense of God's presence and a belief in God as behind all reality. In many places, he connects post-modernism with the spirituality and holism of New Age culture: "I foresee in the footsteps of post-modernism, and in the 'New Age Culture' that comes on its heels, an entry point to a new world, one in which there will occur a real change in human consciousness." He envisions "societal changes, greater social justice, and much deeper interpersonal relationships. A world where the Divine Presence will be tangible."[21]

Rabbi Shagar portrays the intellectualist Talmud study of the twentieth-century yeshivas as a modernist project of rationality to make Torah study scientific and analytic; the goal being to make Torah methodical, rational and orderly. Now in the post-modern world, Torah study is an act of playfulness as well as a study of language, similar to the multi-vocal subversive play of the carnivalesque as presented by Mikhail Bakhtin – an open performance, speaking in different registers and different languages. There is no singular true way to read a text in our age of broken vessels and shattered tablets.

---

21. *Tablets and Broken Tablets*, p. 440.

Avichai Zur, in his important article on what he terms Rabbi Shagar's "Deconstruction of Holiness,"[22] argues that Shagar sought and balanced between existentialism and post-modernity, as well as between concepts of the relative and the absolute, through his complete commitment to God and Torah. To Zur, Rabbi Shagar was not a relativist, nor even that much of a pluralist; rather, he was a modernist in his understanding that different truths are merely different perspectives with tensions, paradoxes, and adaptations. Rabbi Shagar's deconstruction of holiness was a call to create a new religious language, and to remove the obstructions from older formulations. His earliest formulations in Hasidism were rearticulated in different forms, including Existentialism, Post-modernism, and Lacanian thought.

Rabbi Shagar prefers a "soft" post-modernism, which denies the possibility of knowing truth but does not deny the existence of truth itself, as opposed to relativist "hard" post-modernism, which does deny the existence of truth. For Rabbi Shagar, there is still the unknown divine lurking behind everything.[23] When Rabbi Shagar was expressing existentialism, the peak moment was authenticity, a readiness to be oneself. However, in his later thought as a soft post-modernist, he claims that there is no instant of authenticity, and so it is a more difficult freedom.

Rabbi Shagar also extends Chabad texts to teach a post-modern equanimity (*hishtavut*), applying the two Chabad concepts of "*sovev kol almin*" and "*memale kol almin.*" *Sovev* surrounds and has no hierarchy, no good or bad, no sense of absolute – the world is all of God's will. For Rabbi Shagar, post-modern negation is *sovev kol almin*, which shatters the categories that prevent one from maintaining an openness with God and thus allows one to find God in new places. The post-modern innovation is to turn the perspective of God of *sovev kol almin* into a human perspective; nevertheless, for Rabbi Shagar a person cannot live for long

---

22. Avichai Zur, "Deconstruction of Holiness: An Introduction to Rav Shagar's Thought," *Akdamot* 21 (Bet Morasha, 2008), 110–139 (Heb.).

23. See Gurevitz, *Post-Modernism.* The distinction is also found in Ilan Gur-Zeev, *Toward a Diasporic Education: Multi-Cultural, Post-Colonial, and Education in a Postmodern Age* (Tel Aviv: Resling, 2004), 16–24 (Heb.). The soft/hard distinction is generally used in Evangelical Christian thought to say that there is no certain truth in the post-modern world and therefore one turns to Christianity.

on the level of surrounding *sovev,* but can, rather, live in *memale kol almin* of hierarchy, categories, and halakha.[24]

TESHUVA AS SELF-ACCEPTANCE

How do these ideas play out in Shagar's reading of texts? We will look at *teshuva* (repentance), faith, and language, three important topics in his thought, to present his application of ideas.

In Rabbi Shagar's first book, *Shuvi Nafshi*, he offers a distinction between a *teshuva* of freedom (*ḥerut*) and a *teshuva* of compassion or grace (*ḥesed*). He associates the *teshuva* of freedom with Maimonides' demand for autonomous free will and with Rabbi Soloveitchik's approach in which *teshuva* through self-transformation creates a new person. In contrast, he associates the *teshuva* of grace with Bahya ibn Pakuda, according to whom everything should be seen as stemming from God. For Rabbi Shagar, *teshuva* should be about compassion for the self; we have to accept our lives as well as our personal and situational religious challenges. We need to embrace God in the midst of our lives, however messy, even if we do not see a pattern or clear path. In his later post-modern works, he might rhetorically ask: when we "return" in *teshuva*, where are we returning to? His response is that there is no direction to which to return; rather, *teshuva* is the radical acceptance of the self. In the 21st century version, he reframes the repentance of compassion and grace as a post-modern lack of a clear narrative or a clear idea of the future.[25]

Already in the 1980s, Rabbi Shagar advocated a hasidic approach based on the writings of Rabbi Zadok HaKohen of Lublin (1823–1900), in which repentance means understanding that sin is the will of God, since "there is nothing but God." From this hasidic perspective, the will

---

24. Rabbi Shagar, "Living with Nothingness," in *Faith Shattered and Restored*, 95–96. An important article showing how these readings of Nothingness are Existential and absurdist, and definitely not post-modern, is Beverly J. Lanzetta, "Three Categories of Nothingness in Eckhart," *Journal of Religion* 72, no. 2 (1992), 248–268. Rabbi Shagar could have used Michel de Certeau's post-modern reading of mysticism as presented by David Gurevitz, but he chose not to.
25. Rabbi Shagar, *Shuvi Nafshi: Grace or Freedom* (Efrat: Yeshivat Siach Yitzhak, 2000) (Heb.).

of God inheres in the soul of every Jew and in every action. If following one's essence leads to sin, against one's desire to do good, then this sin is also a part of God's plan and will be turned into merits in the future. Rabbi Shagar lets a person accept themselves, their personal turns, their strong emotions, struggles, and individuality, because of God's creation of individual difference; yet, there is also a centrality of freedom in our lives in that we create our own fates and we determine the meaning of what happens in our lives. In his 21st century version of this idea, Rabbi Shagar cites French psychoanalyst Jacques Lacan who states that, "A letter always finds its address and arrives at its destination," in that there is no actual destination, but the destination imagined in the consciousness of the receiver; hence, it always arrives where the person envisions it to be going. In other words, we always arrive where God wants us to arrive, since we are fulfilling who we are.[26]

Drawing on his ideas on repentance and other themes in his early thought, Rabbi Shagar asserts that we should not judge others. I can change myself, but I do not know the situation of other people; they possibly cannot do otherwise. Compassion (*raḥamim*) is a special basic emotion that reveals the distinctive connection between people.

It is important to note that in the many discussions of repentance and self-acceptance, Rabbi Shagar views the self as the individual as he experiences himself in his daily life and his personality.[27] This contrasts with the self as discussed by thinkers like Rav Kook or in Hasidism, who conceive of selfhood as the inner, true version of a person, discoverable only after he peels away the more superficial layers of his personality.

FAITH – SELF ACCEPTANCE AND SELF-CREATION

Rabbi Shagar pondered the meaning of faith throughout his career. He thought that "the transition from a 'religion of truth' to a 'religion of faith' is the most profound point of post-modernism," moving from a Rav Kook vision of certainty to a Rabbi Nahman vision of uncertainty.

---

26. Ibid. On repentance in the thought of Rabbi Zadok, see Alan Brill, *Thinking God: The Mysticism of Rabbi Zadok of Lublin* (Hoboken: Ktav-YU Press, 2002).
27. See chapters "The Matter Depends Upon Me Alone," p. 6, and "The Candle and the Sacrifice," pp. 80–81.

Rabbi Shagar wanted to avoid any appeals to metaphysical or eternal truths in one's faith commitment to Torah. In Rabbi Shagar's presentation, our faith in Torah becomes the basis of who we are, and our freedom to express ourselves becomes our freedom to live according to the Torah. As Rabbi Shagar states: "A Jew finds his Jewish identity in the Torah, and through that his connection to God."[28]

Levi Morrow, the translator of this volume, has devoted a study to Rabbi Shagar's concept of faith. Faith, as defined by Rabbi Shagar, is consciously submitting to the Torah and mitzvot, an act around which you organize your entire life. Acceptance of the yoke of heaven is explicitly understood here as self-acceptance of who you are, as opposed to the classical approach which focuses on the acceptance of an external, heteronomous element. Faith in this sense of self-acceptance means accepting your life as the will of God, thereby recognizing that how you are is exactly how God wants you to be and you therefore could not, and should not, be otherwise.[29]

A person needs to bind himself tightly and strongly to Torah and mitzvot for an unquestionable sense of identity. "Accepting the yoke" is a covenant; it is the creation of an identity that establishes a person's nature, and only after that is freedom possible. Morrow lays out the dialectical process of faith in Rabbi Shagar's thought as positioned between self-acceptance and self-construction. Before committing, the individual is confronted by an inability to decide who or what he wants to be. Before he can commit to the Torah, he has to recognize that this is what he wants to do. This requires one to be in touch with oneself to a degree that can only be achieved by way of self-acceptance. The secret to maintaining a commitment, Rabbi Shagar argues, is to see the decision as inevitable. What at first may seem like a choice among a variety of options is now recognized as the unavoidable embrace of a singular path, an awareness that you could not have acted otherwise or made choices other than those that you made, and you have the ability to accept that

---

28. See below, "Face to Face," p. 281.
29. For a full discussion, see Levi Morrow, "Between Weimar and the West Bank: Franz Rosenzweig's Afterlife in the Writings of Rav Shagar" (MA thesis, Tel Aviv University, 2019).

fact. In the contemporary condition of contradiction and plurality, faith is a great religious opportunity for recognizing the potential diversity in each manifestation of the divine truth.

Rabbi Shagar's later writings contain a turn to the psychoanalytic language of Jacques Lacan, in which self-acceptance becomes acceptance not of the existence of the individual as he or she is, but of the symbolic order, the linguistic manifestation where the unconscious speaks as symptoms through the ego. Practically, the Lacanian sense of self possesses an intrinsic alienation, an unattainable wholeness. For Rabbi Shagar, the self-construction of faith through the study hall enables a liberating process of identifying with the norms of the community.

Even though Rabbi Shagar emphasizes self-creation, he also speaks of the sense of compulsion in the revelation of Torah. For Rabbi Shagar, even if the source of revelation is man's innerness, it is still experienced as transcending him. Even in an age of autonomy, and more so an age of non-foundationalism, religion is experienced as an outside revelation that overpowers the believer, even if it comes from within. More importantly, because of this sense of transcendence, a believer lives a scrupulous religious life.[30]

THE PROBLEM OF LANGUAGE

Rabbi Shagar at many points stresses that in our current non-foundational world, Torah is a language game in which our life of Torah is the rubric for our commitment, community, and faith. In these ideas, Rabbi Shagar is deeply indebted to Jean-François Lyotard's *The Postmodern Condition*, in which he claims that we have now lost the ability to believe in meta-narratives or to achieve a solid grounding in our ideologies. Micro-narratives, for Lyotard, are Wittgenstein's "language-games," limited contexts in which there are clear, if not clearly defined, rules for understanding language and behavior. We recognize that there are many language games, and it will not satisfy us to legitimate one over the other.[31] Torah today is a non-foundational language game creating

---

30. See below, "Face to Face," pp. 284–286.
31. Lyotard only loosely relied on the philosophy of Wittgenstein. Wittgenstein used the term "language-game" to designate forms of language simpler than the entirety of

the narrative world in which we live. Rabbi Shagar associates the reality where we only have the truth of social constructions as a form of a contraction, a *tzimtzum*, of the former meta-narratives leaving a void and nothingness (*ayin*).[32]

In other places, Rabbi Shagar pursues an approach that focuses on multiple private languages, following Walter Benjamin's concept of private languages. Rabbi Shagar applies this to Rabbi Nahman's concept of holy speech, which can create space for itself in "the secret of the contraction (*tzimtzum*)." This language is wholehearted, because it does not point to an object that is separate from it; rather it itself is the world. This language is not a signifier or primarily for communication; rather, it exists for itself in a world without duality. Rabbi Shagar himself notes the difference between the opinions of Walter Benjamin and Rabbi Nahman in that Benjamin thinks translation reverses Babel and brings us back to the Garden of Eden, while for Rabbi Nahman, the Tree of Knowledge in the Garden propels us forward into creating new languages.[33]

Rabbi Shagar also mentions, as part of his thoughts on language, the semiotician Jean Baudrillard, who states that reality is simulated through cultural assumptions and that all language and cultural rituals are "signs" or symbols of values; there is nothing outside of the linguistic system. Rabbi Shagar thinks language does not point to or describe a virtual reality, but rather, that language is one of holiness as understood through the confines of culture, the "signs" and symbols of the study hall of Torah.

---

a language, such as his example of the "builder's language" meant to serve for communication between a builder A and an assistant B. Lyotard used it in an entirely different sense.

32. Miriam Feldmann Kaye, *Jewish Theology for a Postmodern Age* (London: Liverpool University Press in association with Littman Library of Jewish Civilization, 2019), 180–181.

33. See below, "On Translation and Living in Multiple Worlds," p. 117, footnote 35. For references to Walter Benjamin see p. 125 footnote 51.

THE MULTIPLICITY OF IDEAS AND SECULAR STUDIES

In our current age, according to Rabbi Shagar, we live in a world of multiple cultures, in which multiplicity is inevitable; therefore, we should not resist it, but rather accept the multiplicity.

Rabbi Shagar felt that the encountering of a diversity of contradictory positions would not weaken the believer's faith, but actually strengthen it, ideally, making a person more sensitive, moral, and modest. In contrast, resisting, fighting, or blocking out the wider world of knowledge "would be self-denial, leading to deep, radical injury to our religious faith itself." Rabbi Shagar applies Rav Kook's bold statement about spirituality to living in multiple worlds: "Anyone who does not suffer from spiritual descents has no chance of religious ascent."[34] There is danger in this descent, "but only this descent-endangerment can lead to ascent." For example, he seeks a descent into secular studies for the sake of religious ascent.[35]

In his approach to secular studies, Rabbi Shagar is firmly against the bifurcation of religion and secularism into compartmentalized identities, like that advocated by Professor Yeshayahu Leibowitz, who opened "an unbridgeable gap between them, one that he would never bring together." Leibowitz, Rabbi Shagar writes, "lived with a contradiction." Instead, Rabbi Shagar wants every person to reach "his subjectivity or personal identity," even as it creates multiple worlds. In contrast to compartmentalization, Rabbi Shagar sees that the Religious Zionist soul lives "not in one world but in many worlds, which it likely cannot integrate. It does not compartmentalize them – Torah versus labor, faith versus science, religion versus secularism – but rather manages a confusing and often even schizophrenic set of relationships between them."[36]

> Nowadays, a new type of religiosity has developed, one that cannot be defined by its location on any graph, but rather is scattered across many different, you could even call them "strange," centers. This religiosity does not define itself with the

---

34. See below, "On Translation and Living in Multiple Worlds," p. 121.
35. Ibid.
36. Ibid., 122.

regular religious definitions, but enables a weaving of unusual identities, integrating multiple worlds – a pathless path. This new approach presents a deep personal faith that, in my opinion, carries the potential for religious redemption.

Where does this capacity for integrations and combinations come from? Answer: that very same deep personal faith. This faith is not faith in something, but rather an act of *self-acceptance*. It recognizes a deep core of covenantal eros, which enables the freedom to translate and to make integrations, combinations, and connections that our fathers never dreamed of making.[37]

A person accepts their given situation of life by embracing it fully to make new integrations and connections, however strange or disjoined they seem. It is not located by any one rubric – an approach that is rather similar to Gilles Deleuze's idea of rhizome or chaosmos in that it avoids categorization.

Ecstatic and multivalent figures are sprouting up before our eyes. They cannot be located at any one place in society, for their faith comes from a much deeper place, from times gone by. This faith is a remainder, a psycho-theological symptom manifesting as inexplicable stubbornness. It is a willingness to be on the losing side of the world simply because "this is who I am and this is who I want to be," without conscious justification.... [It is] harmony of an individual with who and what he is, without locking himself into a specific identity. He can be who he is, whoever that may be.[38]

Rabbi Shagar wants "a religious reality overflowing with eros" which can be in excess of the multiplicity of ideas in the world, incorporating and sanctifying them. An eros described in hasidic texts that exists "beyond and in excess of its meaning," which "cannot be named, nor alluded to by any extraneous detail of the conventions of language at all."[39]

---

37. Ibid.
38. Ibid., 123.
39. Ibid., 124.

In a more conventional turn to secular studies, Rabbi Shagar argues that Rav Kook permits the usage of Greek cultural tools, which is ultimately Western culture writ large: "These vessels are, for example, the tools of the academy – reflecting the philological and historical research, as well as the philosophical, literary, and linguistic richness that Rav Kook was not afraid to employ in writing his inspirations."[40]

Rabbi Shagar also notes that Rav Kook thought that sometimes universal ideas needed to be translated and embedded in Torah. In Rav Kook's case, he thought the ideas of freedom, nationalism, and universal morality needed to be translated into Torah. For Rabbi Shagar, there are elements within existentialism, psychoanalysis, and post-modernism that have to be translated into Torah. Rav Kook did not write academic essays about Hegel and Schopenhauer or worry if he was reading them correctly. Similarly, Rabbi Shagar was not concerned with the academic fields of philosophy or psychoanalysis. The goal is for the religious seeker to be exposed to new experiences that are not part of the current religious world. Rabbi Shagar's approach does not fit the usual categories of a theology of synthesis nor of a humanistic model. For Rabbi Shagar, worldly knowledge expands lived life.

Unlike American Modern Orthodoxy, Rabbi Shagar's followers can, and do, study the Yoga Sutras, Derrida, Spinoza, and Talmud criticism in the *beit midrash* as a part of the yeshiva seder or they can study film-making or biblical criticism in the university. They have changed the study hall and religious life and have gone places that Modern Orthodoxy never went. They go headlong into the big questions and they do not worry about answers or resolving contradictions.

FRANZ ROSENZWEIG AND JACQUES LACAN

In the last years of his life, Rabbi Shagar read Eric Santner's *On the Psychotheology of Everyday Life*,[41] a book which puts Franz Rosenzweig in

---

40. Ibid., 108–109.
41. Eric L. Santner, *On the Psychotheology of Everyday Life: Reflections on Freud and Rosenzweig* (University of Chicago Press, 2001). Hebrew translation, Tel Aviv: Resling, 2005.

dialogue with Sigmund Freud and Jacques Lacan and combines existentialism with our psychic life of living out inner drives.

Already in the 1920s, Franz Rosenzweig thought that we now live in an era when those who have faith do so without any proof or certainty of fixed categories. At this stage in Rabbi Shagar's thought, Rosenzweig's existential faith without proof served Rabbi Shagar's theology better than post-modern versions. Rosenzweig's programmatic vision of the human religious condition moving from death into love dovetailed with Rabbi Shagar's own vision. This turn to Rosenzweig by Rabbi Shagar caused Rosenzweig's *The Star of Redemption* to become an addition to the canon at those yeshivas influenced by him.[42]

Rosenzweig's existentialism allowed Rabbi Shagar to find a Jewish language for the quest for God based on love, not law, that integrates the human condition. Loosely based on Franz Rosenzweig's idea that our subjectivity comes to be in our encounter with God, Rabbi Shagar teaches that human existence means that the true existence of the subject is in confronting our human condition directly, whereby we respond to our finite existence and its horizons. Rabbi Shagar, during this era, speaks of meeting God "face to face," and in an "I-Thou moment" with God. Franz Rosenzweig's description of the lover's call, "Love me," becomes God's turn toward man in order for man to receive in love God's kingship as a personal address, thereby establishing man's existence.[43] Divine moments occur in the present moment of revelation, and therefore they cannot be held onto or posited as fixed law.

For Rosenzweig, the meeting of God is empty of determinate content; its content is the meeting in love itself. Revelation is greater than content – it is a renewal of the self beyond scholarship or rationality; however, from that existential moment, Rabbi Shagar returns us to Torah and the knowledge of Torah gained through the meeting in the moment. A believer grounds the love of God as part of his self-creation through creativity in Torah. For Rabbi Shagar, Rosenzweig's "speech

---

42. For an example of this new reception of Franz Rosenzweig within Israel Religious Zionist yeshivas, see Ehud Neeman, *Utterance and Fire: Pathways to the Thought and Life of Franz Rosenzweig* (Herzog College Press, 2016) (Heb.).
43. See below, "Law and Love," pp. 238–239.

thinking" (where the power of spoken words is used in process of dialogue) replaces Lyotard's concept of language games as the life of the
study hall.[44] At some points, he identifies this Rosenzweig-influenced
understanding of revelation with Alain Badiou's concept of the event
as a radically contingent personal rupture of normality, which opens a
space to rethink reality.[45]

From this Rosenzweigian base, Rabbi Shagar again turns to
Jacques Lacan. Lacan believes that we use pieces of language and culture
as a signifier, in which absence is its fundamental feature. Lacan thinks
we recognize a signifier by reference to its place among other signifiers.
For example, if we take a signifying system such as in a library, I know
that a book should be at a certain place on a shelf even if that place is
empty and the book is not there. Rabbi Shagar treats our commitment
to Torah study and the life of the study hall as creating such a place in
which those who made it their home feel the language of the *beit midrash*
as a signifying system. In addition, from Žižek , Rabbi Shagar uses the
Lacanian concept of the remnant. The remnant is what is left over after
the signifiers – it is a residue or remnant of the symbolization process.
For example, when looking at an old photograph, we are touched by the
remnant of the self. According to Rabbi Shagar, faith exists in a modality
of "what remains"– a "remnant of faith." This psychological moment is, for
him, the opposite of the modernist approach of immediacy of presence.[46]

Lacan, however, maintained that religion serves as a cover up
of our psychic wounds and holes using the "imaginary" and the "symbolic." Rabbi Shagar responds to the implicit relativism by claiming
that the symbolic realm of mitzvot is God's need, His signification, but
since we cannot psychoanalyze God, the mitzvot have no reasons that
we can explicate. In turn, Rabbi Shagar identifies the hasidic sense of
finding God in the depth and root of the soul with the Lacanian Real,
collapsing self, God and divine immanence.[47] A further application of

---

44. See below, "Face to Face," pp. 278–279.
45. See below, "The Name of the Father," pp. 170–172.
46. See below, "On Translation and Living in Multiple Worlds," p. 124. Ohad Zecharia,
    Nothingness in Ha-Rav Shagar's Thought (MA thesis, Bar-Ilan University, 2015), shows
    the importance of Lacan for Rabbi Shagar's thought.
47. See below, "A Screen for the Spirit," pp. 92–94.

this notion is that halakha is a closed system, without external referents to human notions of meaning.

POST-RAV KOOK'S ZIONISM

Zionism, for Rabbi Shagar, was unquestionably a revolutionary, even rebellious, movement. Its revolution was not just political, but also spiritual and cultural. Yet Rabbi Shagar is forced to ask: What do we do when we realize that the absolute messianic claims of Merkaz Harav and Religious Zionism cannot be affirmed in a post-modern age? For Rabbi Shagar, we no longer have a clear and absolute sense of how God is controlling history. We now live in an age of the eclipse of God, as described by Martin Buber, and we have no grand history or theodicy after Auschwitz. For Rabbi Shagar, Rav Kook had a God of history, but now, after our turn to Rabbi Nahman, we have a hidden God. Rav Kook wanted to renew the nation, but Rabbi Shagar wants the focus of our redemption to be a renewed Torah as a form of personal redemption.[48]

Rabbi Shagar sees his own views as the next step in the process of Zionism. Rav Kook was the era of the Messiah of Joseph; however, we presently live in an era of the Messiah of David, where we transition from state building to personal growth and universalism. Rabbi Shagar considers Religious Zionism as a renewed attachment to the Land of Israel, but now grounded in nature and a return to a biblical sense of the land. The new era of Zionism will be the development of Israeli democracy, and will include a multiculturalism and multi-national democracy as the next stage in the redemptive process that reflects the hasidic consciousness of containing plurality and divisions.

Rabbi Shagar considers the loss of the social justice ideas which were originally in Rav Kook's writings to be our misfortune, but we will restore them in our new era.[49] He envisions messianism as a utopian stage of universal morals, an elevated humanity, and a revelation of God in our human contingency. A true Messianic Zionism will be a philosophic life and love of God as the inheritance of all the world. We have a universalist

---

48. Rabbi Shagar, *On That Day: Homilies for the Iyar Holidays* (Alon Shevut: Mekhon Kitvei Harav Shagar, 2012), 150–161 (Heb.).
49. See below, "On That Day," pp. 230–231.

Maimonides meeting Franz Rosenzweig and then becoming Walter Benjamin's revolutionary utopianism. For Rabbi Shagar, it remains a desire, an ideal, a vision. Messianism is a wondrous vision against the realism of history, and our banal corrupt world.[50]

Rabbi Shagar was very close friends with Rabbi Menachem Froman (1945–2013), rabbi of Tekoa (a settlement in the West Bank), and a peacemaker. Rabbi Froman and Rabbi Shagar frequently held public panels together and shared a common group of followers. Rabbi Froman possessed an extroverted personality that complemented Rabbi Shagar's introverted demeanor. Rabbi Shagar's conceptual ideas should be understood as related to, but not identical with, Rabbi Froman's explicit political discussions of peace, religious dialogue, and coexistence with Palestinian neighbors. Rabbi Froman believed that religion and love of the land could be unifying forces between Israelis and Palestinians instead of dividing ones.[51]

Rabbi Shagar, despite his moving beyond the Merkaz position on theology, still considered the State of Israel redemptive and messianic, and exceptional compared to other countries in its reception of a special providence and divine causality. Rabbi Shagar envisioned Religious Zionism as spiritually transformative, a renewal of prophecy, messianism, and love of the land.[52] For Rabbi Shagar, the settlement project was the height of showing an immense true love of the land. However, the disengagement from Gaza in 2005 was a setback to this Zionist love of the land. Does this violence signify the end of the settler dream? No, Rabbi Shagar believed. We have to continue to display a love of the state through obedience, even if the Israeli government is not what we wanted or expected, as an "unmediated relationship" of love. Compliance with

---

50. Rabbi Shagar, *My Covenant of Peace: Right and Left, War and Peace* (Rishon Lezion: Yediot Aharonot, 2020), 122–155, 406–433.
51. On Rabbi Menachem Froman, see Yair Ettinger, "Memorializing Rabbi Froman – Not with a Funeral, But a Cultural-Spiritual Happening," *Haaretz*, March 5, 2013; and see Kobi Nahshoni, Itamar Fleishman, and Moran Azulay, "Right, Left Mourn Rabbi Froman's Death," *Ynet News*, March 5, 2013.
52. See below, "Law and Love," pp. 241–246.

the messianic vision of the State is a rejection of the violence inherent in the modern state.[53]

In addition, Rabbi Shagar continued to consider the Jewish nation as exceptional compared to other nations. Rabbi Shagar strangely accepts Slavoj Žižek's claim that Jewish nationalism is a world unto itself, without a "place in the order of nations," which Shagar interprets as a "remnant" that eludes structuring.[54] To explain Haman's antisemitic hatred of Mordekhai, Rabbi Shagar views the Jewish people as a group with a deep exceptionalism, as an "other" outside the natural order, as disrupting the normal core of politics; hence, the impetus for others to hate the Jews, as the "other" that Haman was compelled to destroy.

CONCLUSION

English readers should not take Rabbi Shagar's ideas out of their context. Rabbi Shagar wanted to provide a specific corrective for the ideological narrowness of the Israeli Religious Zionist world. Given that Diaspora Orthodoxy integrated Western culture decades before Rabbi Shagar, readers may look for innovations in places he never intended. For example, viewing Rabbi Shagar as a relativist post-modern philosopher is no more justified than equating Rabbi Soloveitchik's use of existentialism with atheistic French Existentialism. In addition, Rabbi Shagar's passionate personal quest and deep piety may not shine through the translations of his teachings.

In reading the essays in this volume, think of Rabbi Shagar as a tormented master; read him in the same manner as you would read Rabbi Nahman of Breslov. Rabbi Benny Kalmanson calls him "a consuming fire," his obsessive search for personal authenticity taking a heavy toll on those around him.[55] Looking at his students, we can see the immense influence he exerted on their lives. His older students first

---

53. Ibid., 249–251.

54. Rabbi Shagar, *BeTzel HaEmuna* (Alon Shevut: Mekhon Kitvei Harav Shagar), 126; Eric Santner, *On the Psychotheology of Everyday Life*, 114; Slavoj Žižek, *The Puppet and the Dwarf: The Perverse Core of Christianity* (MIT Press, 2003), 131.

55. For a glimpse into his personal effect on his students, see the 2012 made-for-TV movie by Rabbi Mordechai Vardi entitled "To Chase After the Shadow," which deals with the human figure of Rabbi Shagar.

studied in other yeshivot before they came to study with him and found his approach as a way of moving beyond their former teachers, while his younger students were educated exclusively by his methods, knowing their Torah directly through him.

In his life's work, Rabbi Shagar should be remembered for his creativity in the opening of the study hall to new questions, using Hasidism and contemporary philosophy. He gave his students and readers new ways of grappling with contemporary issues of faith, self-acceptance, and the multiplicity of our present lives. Rabbi Shagar's willingness to embrace absurdity, absence, and sacrifice are tempered with his welcoming eros, commitment, and love. He has served as the inspiration for many new yeshivas. These yeshivas, and his students, reflect his legacy and the application of his thought; however, his thought is especially reflected in the people who buy his books and read his works in bus stations and coffee shops, those finding inspiration in his words in both Tel Aviv and the West Bank settlements, and exciting those who are religious, non-religious, and formally religious; all of whom are seeking a new language for faith.

High Holy Days

The Matter Depends Upon Me Alone

They said about R. Elazar ben Durdayya that he did not leave aside one prostitute in the world with whom he did not engage in sexual intercourse. Once, he heard that there was one prostitute in one of the cities overseas who would take a purse of dinars as her payment. He took a purse of dinars and went and crossed seven rivers to reach her. During the act, she passed wind and said: Just as this passed wind will not return to its place, so too Elazar ben Durdayya will not be accepted in repentance.

He went and sat between two mountains and hills and said: Mountains and hills, pray for mercy [on my behalf]. They said to him: Before we pray for mercy on your behalf, we must pray for mercy on our own behalf, as it is stated: "For the mountains may depart, and the hills be removed" (Is. 54:10). He said: Heaven and earth, pray for mercy on my behalf. They said to him: Before we pray for mercy on your behalf, we must pray for mercy on our own behalf, as it is stated: "For the heavens shall vanish away like smoke, and the earth shall wax old like a

Based on a sermon delivered in 5744 (1984), edited by Odeya Tzurieli and published in *Commemorating the First Day: High Holiday Sermons* (Efrata: Institute for the Advancement of Rav Shagar's Writings, 2007), 15–25 (Heb.).

garment" (Is. 51:6). He said: Sun and moon, pray for mercy on my behalf. They said to him: Before we pray for mercy on your behalf, we must pray for mercy on our own behalf, as it is stated: "Then the moon shall be confounded, and the sun ashamed" (Is. 24:23). He said: Stars and constellations, pray for mercy on my behalf. They said to him: Before we pray for mercy on your behalf, we must pray for mercy on our own behalf, as it is stated: "And all the hosts of heaven shall molder away" (Is. 34:4).

He said: The matter depends on me alone! He placed his head between his knees and cried loudly until his soul departed. A Divine Voice emerged and said: R. Elazar ben Durdayya is destined for life in the World-to-Come.

Rabbi [Yehuda HaNasi] wept [when he heard this story] and said: There is one who acquires his share [in the World-to-Come only] after many years [of toil], and there is one who acquires his share [in the World-to-Come] in one moment.[1]

Why did R. Elazar ben Durdayya cry? Did he cry about his sins? If so, why didn't he cry earlier when he first recognized his sins and decided to repent? He cried only once he discovered that the matter depended on him alone. There are two different reasons for this.

First, he cried then because until that moment he thought that he had no control over his fate, and he discovered that he had wasted his time trying to find help from some external source. The wasted time upset him even more than the sins themselves. A person sins, stumbles, fails, but the time he wastes searching for external help, for some person or book that could help him, is the biggest disappointment of all. It is impossible to actively sin all the time, but it is very easy to sit around, wasting time by forever looking for something to motivate you – and that is the greatest sin of all.

Second, he cried then because of the discovery itself that the matter depended upon him alone. This is an awesome and terrifying discovery. It all depends on you! You are the one who sinned, and you

---

1. Avoda Zara 17a. Translation from The Noé Edition Koren Talmud Bavli, with emendations.

are the one who repents. You are the one who wasted your life, and you are the one who can redirect it upwards.

Before this point, R. Elazar ben Durdayya knew that he had sinned, but he was not able to cry over the sin. He had not yet internalized the fact that it all depended on him. In truth, though, he needed nothing but himself, not long conversations or *musar* pep-talks, not people or ideas or books, but only his sincerity, his deep will, his self. As long as a person makes himself subservient, dependent on something outside himself, looking for acceptance or excuses, he cannot really truly cry, the kind of weeping so intense that it can cause the soul to depart.

YOU CANNOT GO BACK

This teaches us the secret of repentance. The origin and starting point of repentance is freedom of choice – the idea that "the matter depends upon me alone."

The brazen sinner lives with the illusion that he can always make do – there is neither king nor judgment. Reality is never decided. Nothing is ever so absolute and final that he cannot come back from it. When R. Elazar ben Durdayya stood before absolute reality, he fell to his knees in fear, as the illusion of his freedom shattered. He started asking for mercy because he never had any real courage, brazenly relying on the idea that he could always escape, that he would always have a way back.

The sinner does not want to accept the yoke of sovereignty upon himself. All sin is about throwing off the yoke – being flippant and frivolous.[2] The sinner thinks that nothing is decisive, no process is irreversible, and that nothing absolute exists. The first step of repentance is confronting the absoluteness of reality: "Just as this passed wind will not return to its place, so too Elazar ben Durdayya will not be accepted in repentance." There is no way back – there is only you.

Next comes the step of searching and asking for mercy. R. Elazar ben Durdayya was not yet strong enough to face reality, to judge himself and feel regret. He could not even really cry because he was not truly sorry. Looking outside himself for help, he turned to the heavens, the

---

2. "Reish Lakish says: A man commits a transgression only if a spirit of folly enters him" (Sota 3a).

earth, people, conversations, proofs, persuasions, inspirations, feelings, ideologies. He was looking for something that would motivate him to act, for someone who would tell him the truths that would push him to change, confer feelings that would give him the power to repent.

At this point, he was no longer a brazen sinner. He was a searcher, one of those people looking to repent but stuck in the search, never to leave it. He discovered that there is nothing that exists that is eternal or absolute – heaven and earth, the land and the seas, are all temporary. Nothing is eternal. Nothing in the entire cosmos can provide an anchor to hold on to when a person needs to change.

Confronting judgment filled R. Elazar ben Durdayya with fear, but he was still unwilling to face it head on. He still lived in an illusion, the illusion of sin itself! He thought that there was someone who would have mercy on him, that the passed wind might ultimately return to its place anyway. He thought that he, as opposed to everyone else, would never die. If he could not stand on his own merit, as he once thought, he would stand on the merit of big things or wise people. Certainly, R. Elazar thought, there must be someone or something that possesses the secret of eternity and who could have mercy on him.

Suddenly, in a flash of inspiration, he discovered the simple fact that there was no one to have mercy on him. In the entirety of creation, there was simply no one and nothing that could save R. Elazar ben Durdayya. He reached the most fundamental conclusion of all: the matter depends on me alone.

A person says, I can't, it's too difficult, I want someone to help me, I'm afraid, I, I, I. But what is this "I"? Is it a thought? An abstraction? No – it is you, exactly as you are! The matter depends on you alone. If you truly want it, then you want it, and you do not need anyone else. R. Elazar discovered the secret of freedom. Repentance, as the kabbalists write, belongs to the *Olam HaḤerut*, the "World of Freedom." Only then did R. Elazar cry his great cry.

Many people waste their whole lives in this stage. They are no longer sinners, but they have not repented. They are waiting for someone to have mercy on them, to teach them, to do something to them, internally or externally. Confused and sad, they are stuck in an unending search for the ostensible truth. The very search itself, however, is falsehood. It is illusory, sinful, because everything is temporary. Nothing in reality, either physical or spiritual, can help. Only God is eternal, and He exists beyond physical reality, and even beyond spiritual reality.

THE CRY

So, R. Elazar cried for the years he wasted searching. He had looked for something in a place where he could not possibly find it. A person only truly feels sorry at the moment he consciously recognizes that he is the one who is guilty and he is the one who needs to repent.[3]

As long as R. Elazar was searching for someone else, even just to help him, he could not really be sorry. Only through taking responsibility – discovering that ultimately it is all up to him – was he able to cry and be sorry. The sinner, who does not understand that judgment truly exists, lives with the *illusion* of freedom. He deludes himself in feeling free, but when he eventually has a confrontation with concrete reality, and recognizes that reality cannot simply be changed back – the illusion of choice disappears. At that moment, he can see how conditioned, enslaved, and wretched he really was.

R. Elazar recognized his sin and ran quickly to find someone who could help him. After years of searching, he discovered that there wasn't anyone who could help him, nor could there be. Only then did he finally accept the yoke of the sovereignty of heaven, when the illusion of choice disappeared. He then stood and accepted judgment, thereby receiving repentance and freedom. The matter depends on me alone. He cried, deeply and painfully, regretting what he had wasted. I cry and regret that I, I, sinned. However, this cry is also happy. He felt genuine joy in the realization that he was no longer enslaved, that the matter depends on him alone.

At the end of the story, R. Yehuda HaNasi also cried, because, "There is one who acquires his share in the World-to-Come only after many years of toil, and there is one who acquires his share in the World-

---

3. [Translator's note: In *Return, My Soul: Freedom or Grace* (Efrat: Yeshivat Siach Yitzhak, 2003), 92n24 (Heb.), Rabbi Shagar traces a similar idea to a line from Rabbi Yisrael Salanter's *Iggeret Hamusar*, "A single individual is he – the sinner and the punished."]

to-Come in a single moment." Some people toil their whole lives on the Torah and the commandments. Yet they still never acquire their eternal life, because reaching the decisive, wholehearted – *unified* – mindset of "the matter depends on me alone" is a function of divine grace. A person could toil for many years and never achieve this change, this revolution, the type of repentance the kabbalistic texts call *teshuva ila'a*, "Higher Repentance."

SHOFAR OF SOVEREIGNTY, SHOFAR OF FREEDOM

The shofar of Rosh HaShana is about sovereignty: "And recite before Me on Rosh HaShana [verses that mention] Kingships, Remembrances, and *Shofarot*: Kingships so that you will crown Me as King over you; Remembrances so that your remembrance will rise before Me for good; and with what? It will rise with the shofar."[4] We are commanded to accept the yoke of heaven twice daily with the recitation of the *Shema*, and it constitutes a fundamental element of the service of God. At the beginning of the New Year, we are also commanded to do so through sounding the shofar.

However, this shofar is also a shofar of freedom: "Sound the great shofar for our freedom."[5] The Jubilee shofar is the shofar of freedom. The rabbis connect the two shofars linguistically:

> The Sages taught: From where [do we know] that [the soundings of Rosh HaShana] are with a shofar? The verse states: "Then you shall make proclamation with the blast of the shofar [on the tenth day of the seventh month; on the Day of Atonement you shall make proclamation with the shofar throughout all your land]" (Lev. 25:9). I only have the Jubilee Year, what of Rosh HaShana? The verse states: "Of the seventh month." Since there is no need for the verse to state: "Of the seventh month," what is [the meaning] when the verse states: "Of the seventh month"? This comes

---

4. Rosh HaShana 16a.
5. The daily *Amida* prayer.

to teach that all the soundings of the seventh month must be similar to one another.[6]

Maimonides writes similarly:

> It is a positive commandment to sound the shofar on the tenth of Tishrei in the Jubilee year. This mitzva is entrusted to the Court first, as is stated: "You shall sound a shofar blast" (Lev. 25:9). Every individual is obligated to sound the shofar, as it states [in continuation of the verse]: "And you shall sound the shofar." We sound nine shofar blasts in the same way as we sound them on Rosh HaShana.... [The requirements] of shofar used for the Jubilee and Rosh HaShana are the same in all matters. Both on Rosh HaShana and in the Jubilee the *tekiyot* [shofar blows] are sounded.... From Rosh HaShana until Yom Kippur, servants would not be released to their homes, nor would they be subjugated to their masters, nor would the fields return to their [original] owners. Instead, the servants would eat, drink, and rejoice, with crowns on their heads. When Yom Kippur arrives and the shofar is sounded in the court, the servants are released to their homes and the fields are returned to their owners.[7]

The freedom and liberation of the Jubilee shofar begin with accepting the yoke of heaven with the shofar of sovereignty on Rosh HaShana.

Similarly, the Talmud famously says:

> The Holy One, blessed be He, said: This ear heard My voice on Mount Sinai when I said: "For to Me the children of Israel are slaves" (Lev. 25:55) – and not slaves to slaves. And yet this man went and acquired a master for himself. [Therefore,] let [this ear] be pierced.[8]

---

6. Rosh HaShana 33b.
7. Maimonides, *Mishneh Torah, Hilkhot Shemitta VeYovel* 10:10–14. From Eliyahu Touger's translation on Chabad.org with slight emendations.
8. Kiddushin 22b.

The servant is the one who did not accept his servitude to heaven.

The Mishna depicts a debate about the relationship between the Rosh HaShana shofar and the Jubilee shofar:

> The shofar for Rosh HaShana is the straight horn of the ibex. ...
> On fast days, it was the curved horn of rams. ... The Jubilee year
> is the same as Rosh HaShana with regard to [the laws of] blow-
> ing and the benedictions. Rabbi Yehuda [disagrees and] says: On
> Rosh HaShana we blow the [curved horn of] rams, whereas in
> Jubilee years, it is [the straight horn of] the ibex.[9]

The Talmud explains the logic behind the debate:

> What is [the basis] for their disagreement? One Sage [R. Yehuda]
> holds that on Rosh HaShana the more a person bends his mind
> [in submission], the better, but on Yom Kippur, the more a per-
> son straightens his mind, the better. The other Sage holds that
> on Rosh HaShana, the more a person straightens his mind, the
> better. On fasts, the more a person bends his mind, the better.[10]

According to R. Yehuda – and the halakha follows his opinion – submission is the trait associated with Rosh HaShana. The shofar of Rosh
HaShana is a shofar of accepting the yoke: "The more he bends his mind,
the better!" The shofar of Yom Kippur represents the trait of straightfor-
wardness and simplicity. On Yom Kippur, the servant returns to his origins, his birthplace and his family. Furthermore, as Rashi comments, the
servant also regains his original dignity when he is freed, a return to the
dignity of his fathers.[11] This shofar is the shofar of freedom, wherein simplicity reigns. Simplicity, as the Maharal explains in many places, is the
trait of selfhood, elementary, essential behavior, rather than submission.

A famous passage expresses the connection between accepting
the yoke of heaven and freedom: "One who accepts upon himself the

9. Mishna Rosh HaShana 3:3–5.
10. Rosh HaShana 26b.
11. Rashi on Leviticus 25:41.

yoke of Torah is exempted from the yoke of government duties and the yoke of worldly cares."[12] Accepting a yoke would seem to limit a person, binding and oppressing him, but this is not the case. "All the shofar blasts of the seventh month should be of the same character," because when a person sincerely accepts the yoke of heaven, with devotion to God and recognition of truth, he is first and foremost liberated from servitude to himself. Only someone who acts according to the supreme principle, the lofty divine principle of the commandments – acting for the sake of heaven rather than for personal profit – gains freedom. He returns to his original self, like a servant returning to the ancestral land of his fathers and his family.

Someone who throws off a yoke thinks he is free. However, this very arbitrariness, the thought that there is no sovereign in the world, brings with it enslavement and lack of freedom.

Let us look again at Maimonides. In the middle of his Laws of Repentance, Maimonides cuts short his discussion of repentance and starts discussing the topic of free will.[13] How are free will and repentance connected? Maimonides explains: "Since free choice is granted to all men as explained, a person should always strive to repent and to confess verbally for his sins, striving to cleanse his hands from sin in order that he may die as a repentant man and merit the life of the World-to-Come."[14] For Maimonides, repentance does not mean merely fixing the past, regretting the past, but changing the future.[15] The essence of repentance is choice and freedom. The individual repents out of a recognition of truth. Recognizing his responsibility for his actions moves him to repent. He is not motivated by moral intuition, regret, or fear of punishment, but by freedom, responsibility, and the understanding that the matter depends upon me alone. I alone am responsible and have obligations. This recognition – the recognition of choice and responsibility – is itself repentance.

---

12. *Pirkei Avot* 3:5.
13. Maimonides, *Mishneh Torah, Hilkhot Teshuva*, ch. 5.
14. Ibid., 7:1.
15. Ibid., 2:1–2.

Just as accepting the yoke of heaven leads to choice, freedom, and repentance, so too the reverse. Freedom leads to accepting the yoke of heaven completely: "Who has reached complete repentance? A person who confronts the same situation in which he sinned when he has the potential to commit [the sin again], and, nevertheless, abstains and does not commit it because of his repentance alone and not because of fear or a lack of strength."[16] The individual who abstains from sin for any reason other than his free choice has not truly repented. The sovereignty of God depends on free choice.[17]

We will conclude with Malbim's words in his commentary on Psalms: "For to the Lord is kingship (*hamelukha*) and He rules (*umoshel*) the nations."[18] Malbim comments, "There is a difference between a king (*melekh*) and a ruler (*moshel*). The king is accepted and chosen by the nation insofar as he is fit for the role, while the ruler must use force." God wants to be king, wants us to enthrone Him willingly, accepting the yoke of His kingship upon us. "And they willingly accepted His kingship upon themselves."[19]

---

16. Ibid.
17. Ibid., 5:4.
18. Psalms 22:29.
19. Siddur, Maariv, Blessings after the *Shema*.

Sin, Guilt, and Covenant

For the leader. A psalm of David,
when Nathan the prophet came to him
after he had come to Bathsheba.
Have mercy upon me, O God,
as befits Your faithfulness;
in keeping with Your abundant compassion,
blot out my transgressions.
Wash me thoroughly of my iniquity,
and purify me of my sin;
for I recognize my transgressions,
and my sin is before me always.
Against You alone have I sinned,
and done what is evil in Your sight;
In order so that You are just in Your sentence,
and right in Your judgment.
Indeed, I was born with iniquity;
with sin my mother conceived me…

(PS. 51:1–7)

Based on a sermon delivered in 5750 (1989), edited by Odeya Tzurieli and published in *Commemorating the First Day*, 35–44.

A year has passed, and again we come to gain forgiveness and purify ourselves before the year to come. This time last year, our hearts were full of hope for a better year. Now, the year 5750 is coming to an end. We must ask: Did the autumn arrive and the summer end without us being saved?

We cannot deny the good we have received. This has unquestionably been a year of miracles. Our brothers immigrating to Israel from Russia is a great miracle. The wicked empire has crumbled, disappearing like smoke before our stunned eyes, and this too is a miracle. The rise of a new world order inspires our eager anticipation of the arrival of "the breath of our life, God's Messiah" (Lam. 4:20), for whom all humanity hopes.

This is not everything, however. The great rabbis – the *gedolim* – have taught us that redemption is not just collective, national, political, or economic. Our redemption will also be spiritual, which first and foremost means personal and interpersonal. Even if a new and just world order rises, the jealousy, bitterness, and lack of love (what we call a lack of communication) between people will remain. The *Shekhina* will not return to its place and the goodness of God will still not descend upon us.

RENEWING THE COVENANT THROUGH GUILT

"A psalm of David when Nathan the prophet came to him after he had come to Bathsheba.... Against You alone have I sinned and done what is evil in Your sight" (Ps. 51:1–4). What is meant by the phrase "against You alone have I sinned"? Was David's sin with Bathsheba purely a sin between man and God, with no one else affected? What about the poor man, Uriah the Hittite, and the stolen sheep, Bathsheba? The continuation is even more astounding: "In order so that You are just in Your sentence, and right in Your judgment" (v. 6). Is this to say that David sinned in order to make God's word just and His judgment righteous? We must examine the ideas of sin and punishment carefully and seriously to avoid falling into the trap of "they deceived Him with their speech, lied to Him with their words."[1]

---

1. Psalms 78:36.

In the act of repentance, we must review our personal history in order to ascertain where we made mistakes, where we transgressed, etc., and resolve to be better. Should we stop reviewing at that point? Is this the extent of our sin and our repentance? Could this be the repentant person about whom Maimonides wrote:

> Repentance brings near those who are far removed. Yesterday, this person was hated by God, disgusting, far removed, and abominable. Today, he is beloved and desirable, close, and dear.... Yesterday, he was separated from God, the Lord of Israel, as it states: "Your sins separate between you and your God" (Is. 59:2). He would call out [to God], but would not be answered.... He would fulfill mitzvot, only to have them torn before him.... Today, he is clinging to the *Shekhina*... He fulfills mitzvot and they are accepted with pleasure and joy as it states, "God has already accepted your works" (Eccl. 9:7).[2]

Can we apply this description to ourselves?

We feel insincere and shallow during the Days of Repentance, and therein lies the problem. Do we really believe we can change? Do we even know what we are looking for? Unfortunately, we often do not feel like something significant happens to us during the High Holy Days because we do not really think of ourselves as sinners. Moreover, we really are not sinners at all! To sin, to truly and deliberately sin, we must first live a life that acknowledges there is such a thing as a sin to begin with. In this sense, our greatest sin is that we do not live that sort of life. This is what we say in the confession of *Al Het*, "for the sin we have sinned of throwing off the yoke." At some point, consciously or not, we threw off our yoke, discarding our awareness of a connection and covenant with God that makes us feel a sense of sin and transgression when we break that covenant.

In the absence of this awareness, we live generic, banal lives. Sin and transgression require meaning, an acknowledgement of existence. As Maimonides wrote, God hides His face from the sinner rather than

---

2. Maimonides, *Mishneh Torah, Hilkhot Teshuva* 7:6–7.

punishing him. Much like Kafka's protagonist, who cannot receive judgment,[3] the sinner lives with happenstance and frivolity. For God to punish a person, that person must live with faith. A person who lives without meaning lives without "the life that is in the light of the king's countenance" (Psalms 16:15), which is not really living at all.

As Rabbi Kook explains in *Orot HaTeshuva*,[4] when we confess, we do not recount the sin so much as we acknowledge that it really was a sin and that we are guilty. Only when we acknowledge our guilt do we admit to sin; we recognize that there is a thing called "sin" and that there is a person ("I") who is a sinner. This "I" is revealed in the process of accepting guilt, laid bare by the sinner saying, "I am guilty."

"*Ashamnu*" – "we are guilty." This statement admits to the guilt we feel. "*Bagadnu*" – "we have betrayed." What is betrayal? Betrayal means breaking the covenant and abusing trust, repaying good with evil and distorting truth. In admitting betrayal, a person recognizes the idea of betrayal, and thereby acknowledges the existence of covenant and faithfulness.

Indeed, "Against You alone have I sinned." Sin, even against another person, is always a sin against God. To sin is to betray a covenant, including a covenant between people where the divine manifests in the human. When I admit guilt, I am therefore admitting my guilt to God. When a person confesses his sin and admits that "I am guilty, and I betrayed," he begins to improve himself through this recognition. This is how a person finds his or her self,[5] by asking, "Did I really do this? What happened to me? Was I so far gone?"

We do not perform sins – we are guilty of sins. The idea of sin depends not on an act but rather on the guilt connected to it. Guilt can never be imposed on me from the outside. I must take it upon myself personally by acknowledging "I really did sin." This guilt thereby leads to a shame wherein I am reborn – I exist as a sinner, a betrayer, a vessel full of

---

3. See p. 28 below.
4. *Orot HaTeshuva* 16:2.
5. Regarding sin as creating the "new man," and repentance as elevating the individual to the "I," see Hermann Cohen, *Religion of Reason from the Sources of Judaism*, 11:§13, 17, 28–31, 50; N. Rotenstreich, *Jewish Thought in the Modern Era* (Tel Aviv: Am Oved, 1987), 24 (Heb.).

shame and embarrassment. Nonetheless, I exist, and I exist before God! Even betraying the other is not betraying a generic, faceless person, but betraying a friend, for we were commanded, "Love your fellow as yourself, for I am God" (Lev. 19:18). Friendship exists in the "life that is in the light of the king's countenance," which represents the space of faith. When that friendship, our social fabric, is disconnected from God, there can be neither sin nor guilt; hence the verse, "Against You alone have I sinned."

SIN AND FORGIVENESS:
REVEALING THE HUMAN AND DIVINE ESSENCE

"In order so that You are just in Your sentence, and right in Your judgment." According to the plain reading, this line connects to the preceding verse, rather than the beginning of this one. It therefore reads, "Against You alone have I sinned. My sin is before me always, so that You are just in Your sentence…" In this sense, the admission and publicizing of the sin is in order to inform people of God's justice in punishing him. However, the rabbis understood it differently:

> Rav Yehuda says that Rav says: A person should never bring himself to undergo an ordeal, as David, king of Israel, brought himself to undergo an ordeal and failed. [David] said before [God]: Master of the Universe, for what reason does one say [in prayer]: God of Abraham, God of Isaac, and God of Jacob, and one does not say: God of David?
>
> [God] said to [David]: They have undergone ordeals before Me, and you have not undergone an ordeal before Me. [David] said before Him: Examine me and subject me to an ordeal, as it is stated: "Examine me, Lord, and subject me to an ordeal" (Ps. 26:2). [God] said to [him]: I will subject you to an ordeal, and I will perform a matter for you; as for [the patriarchs], I did not inform them of the nature of the ordeal, while I am informing you that I will subject you to an ordeal involving a matter of forbidden relations. …
>
> Rava taught: What is [the meaning of] that which is written: "Against You alone have I sinned, and done what is evil in Your sight, in order so that You are just in Your sentence, and

right in Your judgment" (Ps. 51:6)? David said before the Holy One, Blessed be He: It is revealed and known before You that if I sought to suppress my [evil] inclination, I would have suppressed it; but I said: I will sin, so that they will not say a servant overcame his master [and withstood the ordeal even though God said that he would not].[6]

Just as the Patriarchs were tested and passed, David also wanted to undergo difficult trials so that God would be attached to his name as well. The test required him to overcome his humanity, but can the human itself overcome his own humanity? God told David that this was impossible, but David persisted. In the end, he was tested and he failed, despite his best efforts.[7] Attempting to transcend his humanity is exactly what revealed David's humanity and weakness in its crassest form. His weakness is itself his humanity.

Rava then continues Rav's homily. After failing, David claimed that he did not really fail and that he intentionally chose the flawed, human position. He was trying to show that a person should not be arrogant before God, that a person cannot be divine. Sin emphasizes the lowliness of man before his Master, and in doing so, it reveals man's absolute dependence upon Him. Sin therefore plays an integral role in David's piety.[8]

Elsewhere, the rabbis express the same idea in a slightly different form:

---

6. Sanhedrin 107a. Translation from The Noé Edition Koren Talmud Bavli, with emendations.

7. See further in the Talmud there.

8. The Zohar (II:107a) says that David did not really mean that he could overcome his evil inclination. Rather, he meant that since he was constantly joking around anyway, here too he was performing comedy for God, despite his desperate situation. David is "the king's clown," "the court jester," and cannot escape this role. Understanding the Sage's idea as David joking around sharpens the above idea even more: Man is a sinner. There's nothing he can do but joke. The joke reveals the lightness of his existence, so relative and transient before God. This is also David's primary contribution to the Jewish people, according to the Sages: the ability to stand, human and transient, before God, with weakness and sins, and hope for divine forgiveness and rectification.

R. Yoḥanan says in the name of R. Shimon ben Yoḥai: David was not fit in that incident [of Bathsheba], and the Jewish people were not fit in that incident [of the Golden Calf].... Rather, why did they perform [these sins]?

To tell you that if an individual has sinned, one says to him: Go to that individual [who sinned, King David, and learn from him that one can repent]. And if the community sinned, one says to them: Go to the community [that sinned, i.e., the Jewish people at the time of the Golden Calf]....

And this is similar to that which R. Shmuel bar Nahmani says that R. Yonatan says: What [is the meaning] of that which is written: "The saying of David, son of Yishai, and the saying of the man raised on high (*al*)" (II Sam. 23:1)? It is the saying of David, son of Yishai, who raised the yoke (*ullah*) of repentance.[9]

The Maharal explains this passage in the following way.[10] God had decreed that repentance should exist in the world. Sin itself is essentially incidental, however, and has true existence only in that it exists for the sake of repentance. Sin's purpose is therefore repentance. If so, sin is "in order so that You are just in Your sentence, and right in Your judgment." Indeed, "the Holy God proved holy by justice."[11] Sin enables the revelation of divine mercy, revealing a world of repentance and forgiveness. It is interesting to note that the Thirteen Attributes of Mercy, the loftiest attributes of God, appear only after the Sin of the Golden Calf. God is a merciful father. Just as a person reveals his humanity by recognizing his guilt, so too God reveals His mercy, compassion, and forgiveness in caring for the person.

"I was born with iniquity." Sin is inherent to humanity. In a certain sense, it is what makes us human. As Rabbenu Bahya ibn Pakuda writes: "A righteous man once said to his disciples, 'If you had no sins, I would fear for you on account of something worse than sin.' 'What could be

9. Avoda Zara 4b–5a.
10. Rabbi Yehuda Loew of Prague, *Tiferet Yisrael*, 147–148.
11. Isaiah 5:16, cited in the High Holy Day liturgy.

worse than sin?' they asked. 'Pride and pretension,' he replied."[12] Recognizing sin reveals a person's humanity, while forgiveness and mercy reveal divinity.

Forgiveness is embodied in reconciliation, harmony, and peace, which only appear after sin. By way of analogy, imagine a couple who have been living together for some time. Suddenly, they start fighting. It seems like a crisis in their relationship. In reality, this fight leads to regret, with each person discovering his or her partner and each feeling bad for hurting the other. Each partner then becomes conscious of their spouse: "He is suffering because of me, because I hurt him." This process leads to a renewed spirit of purity, conciliation, and forgiveness between the couple, something that was not present before the fight.

At this time of year, we hope for spirit, inspiration, and renewal. We hope for a new heart and a spirit of grace and benevolence, purity and reconciliation with our friends, our Creator, and ourselves. May our hearts not oppose the divine.

> *Fashion a pure heart for me, O God;*
> *create in me a steadfast spirit.*
> *Do not cast me out of Your presence,*
> *or take Your holy spirit away from me.*
> *Let me again rejoice in Your help;*
> *let a vigorous spirit sustain me.* (Ps. 51:12–14)

---

12. Rabbenu Bahya ibn Pakuda, *Duties of the Heart*, trans. Daniel Haberman (Jerusalem and New York: Feldheim Publishers, 1996), vol. 1, 643; Gate of Repentance, ch. 8. See the more in-depth discussion of this passage in the next sermon in this volume, "Renewing Intimacy."

Renewing Intimacy

Here we are again at year's end, on the eve of *Seliḥot*. The year 5758 is about to depart and, as with all endings, we begin to remember "a person's actions and his command, the stories of the footsteps of a man."[1] We return to the fundamental questions: life and death, good and evil, past and future, sin and forgiveness.

The path we are about to embark upon by reciting *Seliḥot* does not lead to Rosh HaShana. We do not say *Seliḥot* on Rosh HaShana, nor do we even mention the Thirteen Attributes of Mercy. Instead, we are busy with coronation rituals and with remembering: "And recite before Me on Rosh HaShana [verses that mention] Kingships, Remembrances, and *Shofarot*: Kingships so that you will crown Me as King over you; Remembrances so that your remembrance will rise before Me for good; and with what? It will rise with the shofar."[2] With the confession rite and the Thirteen Attributes of Mercy at its center, reciting *Seliḥot* actually reaches its peak on the night of "*Kol Nidrei*" on Yom Kippur, and at the great end of that day toward which we are heading: *Ne'ila*. *Ne'ila* is

---

Based on a sermon delivered in 5758 (1997), edited by Odeya Tzurieli and published in *Commemorating the First Day*, 75–80.

1. From the *Zikhronot* prayer of Rosh HaShana.
2. Rosh HaShana 16a.

the time of forgiveness and renewing the covenant. Tonight, we begin that journey.

CONFESSION AND GUILT

Confession stands at the center of *Seliḥot*. Because confession is part of the commandment of repentance, we are used to connecting the two. According to Maimonides, confession is the verbal expression of repentance, which essentially takes place in the heart: "He must verbally confess and state these matters which he resolved in his heart."[3]

Confession is also connected to and actually is a condition for atonement: "Those who bring sin offerings or guilt offerings … their sacrifices will not atone for their sins until they repent and make a verbal confession as it states: 'He shall confess the sin he has committed upon it' (Lev. 5:5). Similarly, those obligated to be executed or lashed by the court do not attain atonement through their death or lashing unless they repent and confess."[4] But why does atonement depend on confession? The sinners were punished! They got what they deserved!

To answer this, we must distinguish between punishment and atonement. A judge can set a punishment, but he cannot make a person guilty – a person must take guilt upon themselves. Guilt is in my readiness to experience myself as guilty, and no other person can do this for me. In this sense, guilt reaches the deep, personal intimacy of a person, that which no one else can reach. In many books, such as those of the Maharal, confession is explained as admitting guilt.[5]

"*Ashamnu, bagadnu* – we are guilty, we have betrayed." "Indeed, we are guilty."[6] Guilt reveals the *yeḥida*, the highest aspect of the soul. When a person takes guilt upon himself, particularly the guilt of betrayal, he reveals his deepest humanity. What did I betray? My parents, my friends, other people, God. The traitor betrayed the basic faithfulness of his life. He betrayed; only he can make himself a traitor. He declares, "I

3. Maimonides, *Mishneh Torah, Hilkhot Teshuva* 2:2.
4. Ibid., 1:2.
5. Rabbi Yehuda Loew of Prague, *Netivot Olam*, "The Path of Repentance," ch. 5.
6. Genesis 42:21. For further discussion of this verse and the deep connection between guilt and the individual self, see the next chapter.

did indeed betray." I betrayed the most fundamental aspects of my life: I was impatient and rough toward the other. I ignored him, I did not care about him, and so on. Admitting guilt – expressing it in verbal confession – constitutes a necessary condition of atonement. Punishment can atone only for someone who has confessed, who has said, "I deserve it."

When a person says "I am guilty" and admits his guilt, he gives meaning to what he did. Though he turns his actions into harsh guilt, this actually elevates them, and he henceforth rereads the story of his life as guilt. Admitting what I am, acknowledging that, "This is me, I'm guilty," is a necessary condition for divine grace and forgiveness. However, the pain does not disappear. In fact, it is quite the reverse: the pain appears as a deep revelation of life. It is only after this revelation that the person really lives, elevating his life and his sins.

In confessing, you admit (*hoda'a*) guilt, but you also give thanks (*toda*). Paradoxically, a person who confesses feels very thankful that he can take guilt upon himself and experience purification through taking responsibility.

Rabbenu Bahya explains in *Duties of the Heart* that guilt is an inherent part of human consciousness. Without guilt, a person could lose his humanity: "A righteous man once said to his disciples, 'If you had no sins, I would fear for you on account of something worse than sin.' 'What could be worse than sin?' they asked. 'Pride and pretension,' he replied."[7] Arrogance means one's heart is hardened and detached. But someone who really feels guilty is incapable of accusing others. His heart is open – "God, You will not despise a contrite and crushed heart."[8]

This sin, guilt, and subsequent confession, are indeed the path to reconciliation and to revealing the attributes of mercy – mercy for the divine spark shrouded in exile. Gentleness and mercy come with the revelation of the *yeḥida* in the soul, which reveals itself as mercy. Only then can two people reconcile.

---

7. Rabbenu Bahya ibn Pakuda, *Duties of the Heart*, trans. Daniel Haberman, vol. 1, 643; Gate of Repentance, ch. 8.
8. Psalms 51:19.

MEMORY

As the year ends, memory stirs. Rosh HaShana – also called "*Yom HaZi-karon*," "the Day of Memory" – is when we say the *Zikhronot* prayer during Musaf.

Memory is what makes life meaningful. Our most basic sins, the sins of modern man, come from inattentiveness and forgetfulness. Tension, irritation, restlessness, and living meaninglessly are all part of forgetful living. Memory gives our actions direction and continuity. It turns them from fragments of incidental events into a full and intentional story.

For our relationship with our friends, spouse, parents, or children, forgetting means forgetting the existence of the other. We forget the people around us when we are inattentive and unfocused. We may be speaking with the other, but we speak only externally, from our lips and outward, not actually caring about or paying attention to what is going on between them and us.

We also forget God. For example, though we stand before God in prayer, we often forget His presence, and that is assuming we even have focus when we pray at all. Living forgetfully means living without meaning – we forget our existence. As in the famous hasidic parable about the king's son who forgets his identity, we forget our existence as sons of the king.

A year has passed, and though the same old weighty questions return, we no longer ask them with any seriousness. In the past, I never truly asked them seriously, but I was not aware of it. I preferred to delude myself, but now I know: I lived a life together with the people around me. We spent our years. The years have passed, and the die is cast. What is done cannot be undone.

When I look back, no radical changes have taken place. I still do not notice the other – the other does not interest me. My lack of focus comes from a deep, inner lack of care. Care derives from recognizing the pleasure and delight in a person's existence, or intimacy laid bare.[9] I lose the intimacy of the other, meaning, his delight. I do not care about

---

9. Hasidic texts, primarily those of the Maggid of Mezritch and Chabad, consider delight to be the deepest and most primordial force in the soul. It is a being's interest in

him, his fate, his hopes, and his troubles. He does not interest me and I do not consider his world important.

To renew the care between us, I must recognize the other's humanity. Only then will I see what he himself cares about and thereby touch upon his delight. In this recognition, I remember the other, pay attention to him, and encounter him anew.

---

its own essence. In regard to God, it is described as "the King's delight in Himself." I find it in intimacy, which is a person's recognition and consciousness of his own existence.

On Admission, Guilt, and Atonement

> *"With no one to advocate for us against the*
> *accuser of sin, speak words of law and of justice to*
> *Jacob, and absolve us in the judgment, O King of*
> *Judgment."*[1]

TO THE COURTHOUSE

The High Holy Days that extend from Rosh HaShana to Yom Kippur are days of judgment, when the unfathomable sentence is decreed – of "who will live and who will die, who by water and who by fire"[2] – and the divine sovereignty is elevated in judgment – "The Lord of Hosts is exalted in judgment" (Is. 5:16). This is why, in the *Amida* prayer, we conclude the blessing on judgment with the phrase "the King of Judgment."

In light of this, it is quite surprising that an atmosphere of joy and celebration is an essential element of the judgment that surrounds these

---

Based on a sermon delivered in 5759 (1998), edited by Yishai Mevorach and published in *The Remainder of Faith: Post-modern Sermons on Jewish Holidays* (Tel Aviv: Resling Publishing, 2014), 181–192 (Heb.).

1. From the liturgy of Rosh HaShana and Yom Kippur in Ashkenazi communities. English from the Koren Sacks Yom Kippur Maḥzor.
2. From *U'Netaneh Tokef*, sung as part of the High Holy Day liturgy within Ashkenazi communities.

days – "My fear flows from my happiness, my happiness flows from my fear."[3] Why is Rosh HaShana called a *"yom tov,"* a "holiday,"[4] when it is a day that one mishna describes as follows: "At four times [of the year] the world is judged.… On Rosh HaShana, all creatures pass before God like sheep"?[5] Though Maimonides often describes Rosh HaShana as a holiday,[6] in one passage, he emphasizes that Rosh HaShana is a day of fear, not happiness: "However, on Rosh HaShana and Yom Kippur we do not say Hallel, because they are days of repentance, fear, and reverence, not days of excessive happiness."[7]

We can answer this question with the aid of Franz Kafka. For Kafka's literary protagonists, such as Joseph K. and the "man from the country," who are searching constantly for an entrance into the courthouse, their hope is found in the place of law and judgment itself.[8] Why? What is so attractive about the possibility of being judged? The answer is that judgment validates a person. Being judged means a person is not a madman or a child, unfit for judgment. No, he is fit to be judged, and so he seeks out the celebration and happiness of existing. Indeed, this subtle, refined type of celebration disappears from our world as our society distances itself from the fundamental idea of judgment. A person today cannot find the doorway to the courthouse – he cannot find hope. Lack of judgment is the Kafkaesque state that characterizes the

---

3. *Tanna DeBei Eliyahu Rabba*, ch. 3.
4. See, for example, Mishna Rosh HaShana 4:1.
5. Mishna Rosh HaShana 1:2.
6. See, for example, *Mishneh Torah, Hilkhot Shofar* 2:6.
7. Maimonides, *Mishneh Torah, Hilkhot Ḥanukka* 3:6. Indeed, Maimonides uses the phrase "excessive happiness" in this law, homing in on how Rosh HaShana and Yom Kippur, while fundamentally holidays, or *yomim tovim* (literally, "good days"), must have a happiness that is not "excessive happiness." Maimonides thus seems to be alluding to the connection between the "excessive happiness" of the holiday of Sukkot (see *Mishneh Torah, Hilkhot Lulav* 8:12) and the lack of "excessive happiness" on Rosh HaShana and Yom Kippur.
8. Franz Kafka, *The Trial*, trans. Mike Mitchell (Oxford University Press, 2009); idem., "Before the Law," in *Collected Stories*, ed. Gabriel Josipovici (London, New York, & Toronto: Alfred A. Knopf, 1993). It's worth noting that the story about the man from the country is brought to the attention of Joseph K. in the novel, *The Trial*. See also the story "The New Advocate," ibid., in which Bucephalus despairs of searching for the lost gate to India, and therefore invests himself in reading ancient laws.

individual in our modern society. No one judges us, which means that no one considers us either. We just exist, with no idea of sin or transgression for which we could be judged. Our life is happenstance and frivolity.

The gate through which Kafka's protagonist fails to pass is the gate for which we pray on Yom Kippur: "Open the gate for us, at the time of the closing of the gate, when the day is ending."[9] We do not want to get stuck outside, in the happenstance, at the end of the day, with the gate locked in front of us. Only in the courthouse, passing with all the sheep beneath the evaluating staff – "like a shepherd pasturing his flock" – can a person have the celebratory experience of being counted by God. When the person is there, he is valuable and he is counted, and as such becomes part of "the soul of all the living":

> Let us now tell the power of this day's holiness, for it is awesome and frightening…. You alone are the One Who judges, proves, knows, and bears witness…. Behold, it is the Day of Judgment, to muster the heavenly host for judgment…. All mankind will pass before You like a flock of sheep. Like a shepherd pasturing his flock, making sheep pass under his staff, so shall You cause to pass, count, calculate, and consider the soul of all the living…. On Rosh HaShana will be inscribed and on Yom Kippur will be sealed.[10]

Finally, the moment arrives when we are judged. We are well-dressed, feeling celebratory, and heading to the courthouse. We do not know the results yet, but we hope for good things. The results do not actually matter, however, because simply standing in judgment is already a good outcome. All judgment carries within it the celebratory excitement of the revelation of divine sovereignty. In this sense, judgment is a revelation of holiness wherein existence receives its value and exits the realm of the mundane.

Observe that various aggadic passages depict the angels opposing the creation of the world and man. They do not oppose the act of creation itself – rather, their opposition is based on the words of the psalmist,

---

9. From the *Ne'ila* prayer recited in Ashkenazi communities on Yom Kippur.
10. From *U'Netaneh Tokef*.

"What is man that you should remember him, the son of man, that you should count him?" (Ps. 8:5).[11] Rather than challenging the act of creation itself, they oppose the divine counting and remembering that complete the creation and give it value. They oppose the judgment – the counting and remembering – wherein everything is halted, examined, and remembered, thereby receiving real existence.

UNCONDITIONAL ADMISSION OF GUILT

In Kafka's *The Trial*, Joseph K. is told repeatedly that all he must do to cross the threshold and enter the hall is admit his guilt.[12] Admitting guilt is self-judgment. Through admitting guilt, a person can enact the lost judgment and escape the Kafkaesque fate that closes in around him: "The day will fade away, the sun will set and be gone, let us come to your gates."[13] Indeed, Kafka writes in his notebooks that admitting guilt opens the hidden gate: "Admission, unconditional admission of guilt, the open gate, appears within the abode of the world that is in its corrupt reflection, hanging behind the walls."[14] As Martin Buber writes, this recognition or illumination is expressed at the end of the story, "Before the Law," when the gate closes and the guard says to the man from the country before his death that each person has their own gate – "admission of guilt is the open gate."[15]

The admission that Kafka was talking about rests deep in the foundation of the High Holy Days – it "opens the gate for those who

---

11. According to the Talmud, these words were spoken by the ministering angels who opposed the creation of man: "Rav Yehuda says that Rav says: At the time that the Holy One, Blessed be He, sought to create a person, He created one group of ministering angels. He said to them: If you agree, let us fashion a person in our image. [The angels] said before Him: Master of the Universe, what will be his actions? [God] said to them: His actions will be such and such. The angels said before him: Master of the Universe, What is man that You are mindful of him? And the son of man that You think of him?" (Sanhedrin 38b).
12. See, for example, Kafka, *The Trial*, 104.
13. From the *Ne'ila* prayer recited in Ashkenazi communities on Yom Kippur.
14. Quoted in Martin Buber, *The Face of Man: Aspects of a Philosophical Anthropology*, trans. Hanokh Kelai (Jerusalem: Bialik Institute, 1989), 212 (Heb.).
15. Ibid.

knock repentant."[16] One of the central rituals of Yom Kippur, the ritual confession – which we repeat numerous times starting with the afternoon prayer before Yom Kippur through the *Ne'ila* prayer at its end – expresses exactly this admission. This is what Maimonides writes about the commandment to confess: "What is repentance? It is when the sinner abandons his sin, removing it from his thoughts, and concludes never to do it again.... He needs to *confess verbally* and speak aloud the things that he *concluded mentally*."[17] According to Maimonides, confession gives repentance its credibility and seriousness. It turns repentance from intention and mental readiness into speech and action externalized toward the world. The admission-confession is not a meaningless abstraction, but a real, present fullness.[18] It means admitting not just the facts, but also their meaning and the price they carry. I do not just say, "I did such and such," but rather, "I am guilty." Guilt means much more than just the facts themselves.

We must distinguish between two concepts: "conscience" and "admission." We experience the conscience as an involuntary illumination that essentially comes and overpowers a person as if from the outside, drowning him in a piercing sense of intuitive morality and deep feelings of shame. The conscience comes to a person as an illumination, shining a light on his shame – laying him bare. This is what causes the feelings of deep embarrassment that overwhelm him.

In contrast to the conscience, admission is an act performed by the person himself, a process of human decision-making. This is where guilt comes from – as opposed to shame, it is not something imposed on me from the outside. The other can accuse me, but to be guilty I

---

16. Based on a line from *Vekhol Ma'aminim*, sung in the High Holy Day prayers: "The one who opens the gate for those who knock repentant."

17. Maimonides, *Mishneh Torah, Hilkhot Teshuva* 5:2.

18. Confession is connected to atonement as well as repentance. It is not enough to repent from sin, and even punishment alone is not enough. There is an additional requirement to confess and cleanse oneself of the stain that the sin left in the soul, as Maimonides codified: "Anyone sentenced to death at the hands of the court... cannot receive atonement by execution or corporal punishment until they have repented and confessed" (*Mishneh Torah, Hilkhot Teshuva* 1:1). In other words, confession is not just part of stepping back from sin, it is also part of the effort to cleanse oneself and heal the wounds that sin leaves in the soul. See more below.

must first take the guilt upon myself. Guilt, according to Jaspers,[19] is only made possible thanks to freedom, because a person only becomes guilty when he freely recognizes his guilt and admits to it. For this reason, the text of the confession in the liturgy reads, "We are not so brazen or stubborn as to say before you, the Lord our God and the God of our fathers, that we are righteous and that we have not sinned. Indeed, we and our fathers have sinned."

Something similar can be seen in Joseph's brothers' confession regarding the sin of selling him: "They said to one another, 'Aval, we are being punished on account of our brother, because we looked on at his anguish'" (Gen. 42:21).[20] Rabbi Joseph B. Soloveitchik asserts that the language of "*aval*" should not be understood as "but" or "however"; it should be translated as "indeed," "in truth," "certainly," or "indeed it is so."[21] In the context of confession, this expression conveys a mental state wherein a person could refuse, wherein he is free to deny the guilt and not take it upon himself, and despite this he admits the truth and says, "Indeed, I am guilty." Yes, I could escape, but I am indeed guilty. The word "indeed" includes the possibility of avoidance that is critical for admission.

If so, true guilt contains within itself the admission and judgment imposed on the freedom of the subject – "Indeed I am guilty." However, guilt not only judges but also takes part in the implementation process, insofar as guilt contains a readiness to take the yoke of guilt upon oneself – a readiness to be guilty and a readiness to bear the consequences. This is the judgment of Yom Kippur, but it is also a source of compassion and empathy. Readiness to stand in judgment, to admit sin and bear the punishment, inspires solidarity in the judge. The individual goes from being accused to being guilty and, as such, merits kindness and mercy.

This enables us to understand why atonement depends on confession but not on punishment. As Maimonides writes, "He has not atoned

19. Karl Jaspers, *The Question of German Guilt*, trans. E. B. Ashton (New York: Fordham University Press, 2000), 25–39.
20. This verse is sung in the song *Otekha Edrosh* in the prayer of Yom Kippur night among Ashkenazi communities.
21. Rabbi Joseph B. Soloveitchik, *On Repentance*, ed. Pinhas Peli (Jerusalem: Maggid, 2017), 86–88.

until he confesses and avoids doing similarly forever."[22] The nature of
the punishment changes with the confession because for a person who
has not confessed, the punishment remains in the judicial-social realm,
like a blow that lands on a person from the outside. Accepting the judgment and justifying it changes the nature of the sentence-punishment
from punishment to a medium for atonement. Though people typically
flee from punishment, accepting it takes away its harshness and changes it
from *punishment* into *atonement*. Desiring punishment nullifies it because
that which a person agrees to – and even wants – simply ceases to be a
punishment. The pain does not disappear, but the individual no longer
experiences it as suffering or discomfort, as suffering derives not from
the pain itself, but rather from how the individual relates to the pain.
The primary discomfort of punishment is the feelings of happenstance
and arbitrariness that come along with it, the feeling that "they set me
up" and "I don't deserve this." The readiness to accept the punishment
sweetens the pain.[23]

CONFESSION, FORGIVENESS, AND UNITY: INDIVIDUAL AND COMMUNITY

Consequently, guilt reveals intimacy. When a person takes guilt upon
himself, he reveals his deepest humanity. Psychologists' attempts to heal
a person of his guilt often prevent the possibility of him really coming
into true, substantive recognition of – and contact with – the reality of
his life and thereby meriting atonement.

Nonetheless, understanding confession from the point of view of
the individual alone does not fit with the communal dimension that the
High Holy Day liturgy gives it. Understanding this dimension requires
an additional perspective on the meaning of the confession as well as
on the meanings of forgiveness and faith.

Three important foundations shape the High Holy Days from
Rosh HaShana through the end of Yom Kippur: the confession-repen-
tance, the one who atones, and the divine unity. The surprising thing is

---

22. Maimonides, *Mishneh Torah, Hilkhot Teshuva* 1:1.
23. Ḥasidut calls this "sweetening the judgments," and teaches that the divine infinite
    dwells even within judgment, and knowing this sweetens suffering.

that these three, which seemingly should need to emerge from within the existence of the individual – who confesses, seeks atonement, and is one with his faith – appear most intensely specifically in the communal framework of the congregation. As people who live in a reality of faith based on an individualistic conception, this seems perplexing – surely the sin is the sin of the individual and therefore the confession, admission, and repentance are also those of the individual!

What place is there for a confession said publicly and for external forgiveness? How is the community relevant to the incredibly personal testimony of faith? Why is the crescendo of the unification a call to the community – "*Shema Yisrael,*" "Hear, O Israel"?[24] Is not the presence of "the other" disturbing? The other's gaze renders a person incapable of embracing his own individuality and sincerity. "Being for the other" causes a person to see himself as the other sees him. Self-awareness – like gazing on a subject and turning him into an object – leads to the confessor losing his sincerity and the believer losing his inwardness. A person must escape this awareness to preserve his inwardness and sincerity.

Nevertheless, the language of the confession is in the plural: "For the sin that *we* have sinned before You"; "*We* are guilty, *we* have betrayed, *we* have stolen." What is more, the confession is not just in plural language, but it is also sung aloud by the whole community.[25] This is also the case with forgiveness and atonement – the individual is not the one seeking atonement but the congregation as a whole: "*The whole Israelite community* and the stranger residing among them shall be forgiven, for it happened to *the entire people* through error" (Num. 15:26).[26] The liturgy of the day thus strongly emphasizes Jewish solidarity, and "interpersonal transgressions are not atoned for by Yom Kippur until the offended party has been appeased."[27] Rabbi Josiah Pinto[28] interprets the following verse in this vein: "For on this day atonement shall be made for you to cleanse you of all your sins; you shall be clean before the Lord" (Lev.

---

24. The *Ne'ila* prayer on Yom Kippur concludes with the congregation declaring aloud the verse, "Hear, O Israel," which concludes with an emphasis on divine unity.
25. The custom in Ashkenazi communities is to sing the confession together.
26. This verse is recited as an opening to Yom Kippur during the *Kol Nidrei* prayer.
27. Yoma 85b.
28. Rabbi Josiah Pinto, 16th century exegete of rabbinic homilies.

16:30) – "on the condition that you, human beings, cleanse yourselves of transgressions between one another."[29] The atonement of the day, including atonement for sins between a person and God, depends on appeasement between man and his fellow. Only via human "togetherness" can the individual person stand and be purified before his God.

Even the divine unification of the *Shema* works like this. Seemingly, unification is a private act of the individual – the faith of the "lonely man of faith,"[30] whose clear inner sincerity brings him to recognition and revelation of the divine unity, resulting in personal commitment. However, the verse that concludes the *Ne'ila* prayer – "Hear, O Israel, the Lord is our God, the Lord is one" – teaches otherwise. The greatest revelation is the appearance of the faith of "the other," a unification that is not just "my faith in my faith," but rather the revelation of "my faith in your faith." This revelation creates the togetherness of the congregation.

The Maharal teaches: "Though the recitation of the *Shema* is said by the individual…it is impossible for it to only be thus. [When one recites] 'Hear, O Israel, the Lord is our God, the Lord is one,' it is as if the individual, who is reciting the *Shema*, is speaking with Israel, testifying that the Lord, blessed be He, is our God, and the Lord is one."[31] The individual utters the *Shema* – the unification of the divine – as an address to the Jewish people, to the community, and to society as a whole, and as an act of self-inclusion within these groups. This address is the condition for true unity.

We therefore search not just for harmony with ourselves, for faith in our own faith, but also for harmony with the other and for faith in the faith of the other. In the prescribed confession we say, "For *we* and our fathers have sinned." What is the condition for saying "we"? Faith

---

29. Commentary of Rabbi Pinto in *Ein Yaakov Im Kol ha-Perushim* (Vilna, 1857), Yoma, 240, s.v. "*averot she-bein adam le- ḥavero.*"

30. See Rabbi Joseph B. Soloveitchik, *The Lonely Man of Faith* (New York: Doubleday, 1992), 40.

31. Rabbi Yehuda Loew of Prague, *Netivot Olam*, "The Path of Worship," ch. 7. Paraphrasing Wittgenstein's claim that there can be no "private language," so too there can be no "private faith." Faith is a function of the collective and not of individuals. In context of the Maharal's words, the addressee of faith is not the individual Jew but the nation of Israel.

in the other. Saying "we" becomes possible through deep partnership, a partnership that does not result from identical interests, collective ego, superficial patriotism, or pride. Instead, it comes from recognizing our ability to be aware of and believe in the sincerity and freedom of the other. Saying "we" when reading *"Shema Yisrael"* serves as the forgiving of "all of the congregation of Israel." All of these indicate that the crescendo of divine unification, the crescendo of the confession, and the crescendo of atonement, take place not within the perception of the isolated individual but in the individual's discovery that he is not the only person who unifies the Divine.

It could be said – to paraphrase a statement of disbelief according to which "not only do I not believe, but I also do not believe that you believe"[32] – that the essence of faith is "not only do I believe, but I also believe that you believe!" The deep discovery is that the other is a partner in my belief and I am a partner in his. This recognition creates a powerful sense of partnership, unity, and solidarity. This is not just some sensation, but rather a very real unity of souls.

Confession in the *maḥzor* is a song – the speech of a choir, which is a third type of speech that is neither monologue nor dialogue. According to Franz Rosenzweig, singing together establishes "the community of the chant, and that not as accomplished fact, not as indicative, but only as a fact just now established."[33] In a choir, individuals mingle by way of consenting choice, and this grants it its power. It is so pleasurable because of the literal and figurative harmony it creates between individuals. There is nothing better for creating the togetherness of a congregation: "Communal singing does not take place for the sake of a particular content; rather one looks for a common content for the sake of singing communally."[34]

---

32. See the words of Sartre: "To believe is to know that you believe, and to know that you believe is not to believe"; "Every faith is a flawed faith: a person never believes entirely in what he believes." Jean Paul Sartre, "Self-Deception," *Selected Writings*, trans. and ed. Menahem Brinker (Tel Aviv: Sifriyat Poalim, 1972), vol. 1, 92–93 (Heb.).
33. Franz Rosenzweig, *The Star of Redemption*, trans. William Hallo (New York: Holt, Rinehart and Winston, 1971), 232.
34. Ibid., 231.

The communal prayer of the High Holy Days reveals the "shared I," in which a person understands the other as sincere, just as he understands himself. The other is a sincere partner in the person's faith and hopes, and this sincerity enables him to trust in the other's freedom – in the divine within him. The other, too, will act freely for the sake of this faith, not necessarily for my specific goals, but his goals are not any worse than mine. The individual thus grants the other inner freedom, enabling the other to be understood as a partner in a shared reality. Bound up in this prayer is the subtle truth that trusting in the sincerity and freedom of the other is itself a divine revelation leading to the kingship and unity of God.

This is the meaning of the reconciliation of Yom Kippur: "By way of the inclusion of the souls of Israel in each other...through this they engender a wondrous matter above, which is the foundation and purpose of the whole Torah, namely, the unity of God."[35] The unity of the individual and the other leads to an ontologically different reality, one of divine unity. The divine unity depends on and is part of the unity of Israel: "'And founded his bundle on earth' (Amos 9:6) – until they all become one bundle."[36] The fundamental idea is that the divine unity is partnership, solidarity, and unity of souls. In a world where this unity is revealed, forgiveness, compassion, and reconciliation appear. This is a world – a world of revelation – where social interaction changes, where object-ness disappears and other-ness no longer necessitates separateness, fear, and lack of faith.

On its deepest level, the ability to pray alongside the other represents the deepest indwelling of the *Shekhina* – a fullness. The *Shekhina* is the spirit that dwells between and within people. This fact has deep implications: the confession in prayer does not stay confined to the realm of private individual transgressions. As the confession of a congregation, it includes injustices deeper than those of any single individual. The sins of guilt and betrayal mentioned in the confession are not necessarily concrete, individual guilts, but are realities connected to the metaphysi-

---

35. Rabbi Menahem Mendel Schneerson (the author of *Tsemaḥ Tsedek*), *Derekh Mitz-votayikh: Ta'amei Mitzvot*, 29a.
36. Menaḥot 27a. The Talmud's discussion pivots around the verse quoted here.

cal guilt and betrayal that lie deep in the foundations of our existence. Betrayal of the other is inherent in the essence of the human situation. I will always care for my children more than I will care for your children: "*Homo homini lupus*," "A man is a wolf to another man." This law is not psychological but ontological – it is the meaning of betrayal.

We must also understand the phrase, "we have stolen, we have spoken falsely" from the confession, in this manner. "We have stolen" confesses to the essence of theft, to taking something that really does not belong to the person, even if he technically paid for it. "We have spoken falsely" confesses to the essence of distorting speech, on it being what Rabbi Isaac Luria called "exiled speech." More than this, throughout the entirety of the confession, we do not mention sins between man and God at all, and this fact gets to the core of the confession. The guilt that the confession deals with is the ethical-existential guilt of betraying the essence of existence, which manifests in societal injustices, not in the religious realm between a person and his God. The social realm is the location of the kingdom of God – in it and through it the divine unification is realized. "Hear, O Israel, the Lord is our God, the Lord is one."

Sukkot

I Praised Happiness:
Two Approaches
to Holiday Joy

Sukkot is the holiday of *simha*, happiness. The special holiday liturgy calls it *"zeman simhatenu,"* "the time of our happiness." The Torah mentions the commandment to be happy on Sukkot three times,[1] in comparison with the single reference to it on Shavuot and none at all regarding Pesah. The rabbis already pointed out this difference, saying: "You find happiness written three times about Sukkot…but about Pesah you don't find happiness written even once. Why? Because on Pesah the produce is judged, and a person does not know if he will make it or not that year, therefore happiness is not written about Pesah."[2] In contrast to Pesah, Sukkot is the harvest festival, taking place when the produce is already gathered from the fields and you can enjoy it.

Based on a draft written in 5763 (2002), edited by Yishai Mevorach and published in *In the Shadow of Faith* (Alon Shevut: Mekhon Kitvei Harav Shagar, 2011), 135–154.

1. Leviticus 23:40; Deuteronomy 16:14, 15.
2. *Pesikta Derav Kahana*, Appendix B, *Parsha Aheret, s.v. "ve-samahta be-hagekha."*

THE TORAH'S IDEA OF HAPPINESS

The Torah and the Prophets contain a conception of happiness that is in opposition to the Dionysian holiday celebrations of the pagans.[3] The happiness of a pagan holiday is essentially about designating a set period of time to loosen the restraints of culture and ethics. The goal of this time period is to bring the pagan worshiper to a state of unity with his gods and with all nature. This unity is achieved through breaching normative frameworks, particularly those of the family, through sexual licentiousness, dancing, and jest, in the same way the Israelites celebrated during the sin of the Golden Calf: "Early next day, the people offered up burnt offerings and brought sacrifices of well-being; they sat down to eat and drink, and then rose to dance" (Ex. 32:6). The prophet does not hide God's disgust with this promiscuous outburst:

> You who trample the heads of the poor into the dust of the ground, and make the humble walk a twisted course! Father and son go to the same girl, and thereby profane My holy name. They recline by every altar on garments taken in pledge, and drink in the house of their God wine bought with fines they imposed. (Amos 2:7–8)

> I loathe, I spurn your festivals, I am not appeased by your solemn assemblies. If you offer Me burnt offerings – or your meal offerings – I will not accept them; I will pay no heed to your gifts of fatlings. Spare Me the sound of your hymns, and let Me not hear the music of your lutes. But let justice well up like water, righteousness like an unfailing stream. (Amos 5:21–24)

In contrast, the Torah focuses the happiness of the holiday on strengthening the social bonds of family and community: "You shall rejoice in your festival, with your son and daughter, your male and female slave, the Levite, the stranger, the fatherless, and the widow in your

---

3. For more on the relationship between the biblical idea of holiday and the pagan idea of holiday, see Rabbi Shagar, *A Time of Freedom* (Alon Shevut: Institute for the Advancement of Rav Shagar's Writings, 2010), 19–28.

communities. You shall hold a festival for the Lord your God seven days, in the place that the Lord will choose; for the Lord your God will bless all your crops and all your undertakings" (Deut. 16:14–15). The Israelite rejoices in the produce and abundance of blessing that providence has brought him, and celebrates together with the members of his family and with the oppressed poor who live at the margins of society. This is a happiness of grace (*simḥat ḥesed*) that leads to harmony with existence rather than promiscuous outbursts and breaches.

This grace creates a deep point of contact with that which is human in the other, leading to a real connection. Based on this idea, the rabbis taught that someone who appeases a poor person is greater than someone who gives charity.[4] As the verse says: "And you offer your compassion to the hungry, and satisfy the famished creature" (Is. 58:10).

The creative power of this grace and the deep connection to others it brings are explored at length in the books of hidden wisdom. According to this wisdom, the light of grace, *ḥesed*, is the first revelation of the *middot* and the Tetragrammaton, highlighting grace as an activity that flows from self-worth. Only discovering this self-worth enables the revelation of this and the rest of the *middot*. This is what leads to the deep satisfaction and the renewed vitality that a person feels when acting kindly.

If so, grace means giving self-worth to existence. The happiness of the Jewish holiday is a happiness bound up with grace. It is therefore a happiness of harmony and wholeness with existence, involving the uncovering of its self-worth. Underlying this happiness is the desire to preserve the wholeness of existence as well as its limits: the holy sentiment, "You will know that all is well in your tent; when you visit your wife you will never sin" (Job 5:24), is in contrast to the pagan spirit that corrupts grace with a desire to burst the boundaries of concrete reality.

Parenthetically, I will note that one thing that often stops people from acting kindly is a sense of the meaninglessness of reality itself, a sense that it has no value. A person stuck in a state where he feels reality has no meaning or value to him is stuck in a poor, impoverished condition. He cannot give or bestow because, as an impoverished person,

---

4. Bava Batra 9b.

he has nothing. The proper response to this terrible situation is to act kindly, as true kindness and grace can bring a person into contact with the inwardness of reality and existence and with the hidden storehouse of grace buried deep within reality.[5]

Every act of grace contains an aspect of revelation of *sod*. Without the *sod* of mystery, reality really has no meaning. A person who does a kind act creates the inner justification of the value of existence. It leads him to sense the inner meaning of existence that grows out of the very act of grace itself.

THE HAPPINESS OF THE IMPOVERISHED

The Torah's happiness of grace and peace is one possibility of happiness for a person standing before his God, both more generally and on Sukkot specifically. However, as we shall see, the religious personality is not necessarily a happy personality, and therefore the character of the happiness of the holiday can take on a much different meaning.

At times, the religious individual may draw his resources specifically from sadness, melancholy, and tragedy, which bring him into contact with the infinite and the absolute. Rav Soloveitchik put it like this: "Catharsis of religious life consists exactly in the awareness of the long interludes during which man finds himself at an infinite distance from God ... Those long periods of black despair (hester panim) contain the cathartic element which cleanses and redeems religious life."[6]

Rav Soloveitchik describes a religious archetype that we might call "manic-depressive," moving between ecstatic happiness and a self-perception of greatness on the one hand and deep depression and pessimistic inner anguish on the other. However, it would be a mistake to think that this depression suppresses or hinders the happiness and greatness. The happiness and sense of fullness draw their intensity specifically from the melancholy, the nostalgia, and the black bile.

---

5. [Translator's note: Rav Shagar is referencing *Likkutei Moharan* II:78.]
6. Rabbi Joseph B. Soloveitchik, "Catharsis," in *Confrontation and Other Essays (Jerusalem, 2015)*, *60*, and see also 34. See also his testimony, "I certainly have tendency toward elegy, religious melancholy…a wave of paradoxical sadness shot through with silent joy washes over my consciousness, and I feel myself saved and redeemed" (idem., *Divrei Hashkafa* [Jerusalem, 1992], 135–136).

Contrary to popular belief, the world of Hasidism does not exempt itself from what Rav Soloveitchik called "long periods of black despair." Hasidism is famously positive about happiness, and hasidic proverbs praising happiness are well-known and popular. However, these sayings can be misleading about the causes and grounds from which happiness, both hasidic and more generally religious, springs. Chabad, for example, says "worship is through bitterness of the heart."[7] This form of worship can bring a person into contact with the abyssal and the real: "'In their adversity they cried to God' (Ps. 107:6), because adversity (*tzar*) refers to a space that is an instance of constraint (*metzar*) and limitation.... Through his bitterness over the reversal, the love for God will be so greatly increased as to become included within the infinite light, blessed is He, just as light that comes out of darkness is preferable."[8] Hasidic happiness is therefore an ecstatic happiness bursting forth from distress: "The person is in the mystery of greatness and diminution, and through happiness and joking he goes from diminution to greatness, to learn and attach to God, blessed be He."[9] This is not simple, natural happiness, the happiness of the harvest, the blessing and grace of the Torah. It is rather a complex happiness, attained primarily through overcoming the self and making a conscious decision, and thus it contains an element of defiance and rebellion.

A person's efforts to overcome sadness, characterized by his struggle with the elements within him that often drag him into feelings of despair and self-pity, make up the fertile soil of hasidic happiness: "How much must a person have pity on himself, when he remembers how great he is at his root, and he says in his heart, 'Behold I am from the seed of Israel, which transcends all worlds, yet where am I now? And God forbid, God forbid, who knows what will happen in days to come?'"[10] Hasidism's repeated, near-constant calls to be happy and to stay far away from sadness only serve to demonstrate its abiding interest

7. In various passages, the *Tikkunei Zohar* calls this religious archetype "*tzaddik vera lo*," "the righteous man to whom evil occurs." This describes his worship, the root of his soul, and his fate. Cf. *Tikkunei Zohar* 93b, 134a.
8. Rabbi Schneur Zalman of Liadi, *Torah Ohr, Vayeḥi*, 45b.
9. Rabbi Yisrael Baal Shem Tov, *Keter Shem Tov*, vol. 1, 37.
10. Rabbi Nahman of Breslov, *Likkutei Etsot*, Charity, 6.

in the painful abysses of the soul. Many of the most prominent hasidic personae, the clearest example undoubtedly being Rabbi Nahman of Breslov, were characterized by pessimism and depressive tendencies, and their happiness emerged as the product of an inner struggle to overcome these tendencies. A deep pessimism underlies the happiness of which they speak, and the happiness draws its strength from this pessimism, through overcoming it. Happiness is a decision, a bitterly declared, "Even so!" leading to a strengthening of faith and hope. Nothing describes this process like Rabbi Nahman's almost tangible words:

> On the topic of happiness. An analogy: sometimes, when people are happy and dance, they grab someone standing outside [the circle] who is depressed and gloomy. Against his will they bring him into the circle of dancers; against his will they force him to be happy along with them. It is the same with happiness. When a person is happy, gloom [lit. "black bile"] and suffering stand aside. Yet greater still is gathering the courage to actually pursue gloom, and to introduce it into the joy.... A person should transform gloom and all suffering into joy. It is like a person who comes to a celebration. The abundant joy and happiness, then, transforms all his worries, depression and gloom into joy.... For at a time of joy, it is the nature of sadness and sighing to stand aside. Yet one actually has to pursue them, and to catch up with and reach them, in order to specifically introduce them into the joy. This is the meaning of "They will attain gladness and joy. ..." Gladness and joy will catch up with and seize the sadness and sighing.[11]

Rabbi Nahman here describes a form of happiness that is entirely focused on dealing with sadness and sighing, which flee before it. The greater the struggle with sadness, the greater the happiness and joy: "Gladness and joy will catch up with and seize the sadness and sighing as they flee and run from joy, in order to introduce them, against their will, into the joy."[12]

---

11. Rabbi Nahman of Breslov, *Likkutei Moharan* II:23. Translation based on that of the Breslov Research Institute.
12. Ibid.

These ideas connect to the happiness described by Kohelet, who, as we read on Sukkot, reaches the following conclusion, specifically amid the great pessimism of his book: "And I praised happiness" (Eccl. 8:15). This, too, is connected to the commandment to sit in the shade of the sukka.

The midrash on the verse, "As an apple tree among the trees of the wood, so is my beloved among the young men; in its shade I delighted to sit, and its fruit was sweet to my taste" (Song. 2:3), teaches:

> "As an apple tree among the trees of the wood." R. Huna and R. Aha said in the name of R. Yosei b. Zimra: The apple tree is shunned by all people when the sun beats down, because it provides no shade. So too all the nations refused to sit in the shade of the Holy One, blessed be He, on the day of the Giving of the Law. Do you think that Israel was the same? No, for it says, "For his shade I longed, and I sat there": I longed for Him and I sat; it is I who longed, not the nations.[13]

Spending time in God's shade is not motivated by any obvious good or protection that might come from it. Quite the contrary, God "has no shade." It is the suffering and lack of security, *bitahon*, from which everyone flees during the heat of the day, that present a person with the *possibility* of committing to his love of God. Suffering and insecurity enable a person to attain the happiness that comes from self-overcoming, as discussed by the great hasidic leaders. The shade of God's lack-of-revelation itself inspires an ecstatic happiness.[14] As the midrash says, the phrase "I delight to sit in his shade" refers to the commandment of the sukka, while "And his fruit is sweet to my mouth" refers to the commandment of the etrog.[15] The happiness of Sukkot that emerges from this understanding

---

13. Song of Songs Rabba 2:3, based on the Soncino translation.
14. This is the position of Rabbi Akiva, who laughed when everyone else was crying over the destruction of the Temple. His faith didn't rely on anything, and his approach was paradoxical: suffering didn't disprove his faith, it proved it (Makkot 24b).
15. As cited in Rabbi Yechiel Michel Epstein, *Arukh HaShulhan, Orah Hayim* 725:5.

does not rely on any good contained in external reality. It is an inner decision, an overcoming of the external reality that is so full of suffering.

THE MYSTERY OF THE LULAV

Rabbi Isaac Luria's contemplative meditations for the holiday of Sukkot describe, in context of the question of security and happiness, a deep idea about the function of the lulav and the sukka. We draw the encompassing lights of the sukka into the heart by means of the lulav, the Hebrew word for which could be read as *lo lev*, "he has a heart":

> For the sukka is the mystery of encompassing light of *Nukva* that is the aspect of graces, and we are sons of kings, sons of the upper feminine, Rachel, and we act corresponding to her, and sit under the sukka, to receive that encompassing light, and this encompassing light remains and covers us, encompassing us on all sides.[16]
>
> Indeed, the mystery of lowering this illumination to *Nukva*, is achieved when you shake and move the lulav back-and-forth, as is known, and you contemplate drawing the end of the lulav, the willow, the myrtle, and the etrog to your chest...and he shakes and raises them to *daat*, so that they receive illumination from there.[17]

These contemplative meditations are explained at length in Rabbi Nahman's teaching:

> Now, there are two types of days: good days and bad days. As is written (Eccl. 7:14), "So on a good day enjoy the good; and on a bad day, look." That is, a person has to look there very well. He will certainly find good days – i.e., Torah – there.... And the letters of the Torah are what give life to each and every thing. However, the lower the level, the more the letters of the Torah there are contracted from what they were on the higher level...so as not to provide it with more light and life-force than is fitting. We see,

16. Rabbi Isaac Luria, *Pri Etz Ḥayim*, Sukkot, 3.
17. Ibid., Lulav, 2.

therefore, that even in the realm of the evil forces (*kelipot*), in the bad days, which are the bad attributes and the languages of the nations – there, too, it is possible to find the Torah letters. But, because of the increased garments (*levushim*) and the increased contraction (*tzimtzum*), the Torah letters – i.e., the good days – do not show through…. But when someone subdues his evil inclination… the letters are more prominent and show through more brightly…the evil is eliminated and the Torah letters are all that remain; they receive abundant light from Above….

Thus, every person, each commensurate with his aspect, is capable of having a taste of the light of the love that is in *daat* even now, within the days. This is when he binds his heart to his *daat*. For each and every Jew knows in a general sense that there is a God…and the attributes and days are encompassed in the heart…. We see, therefore, that when a person binds his heart to his *daat*, he knows in a general sense that there is a God whose "Glory fills the whole world"…. Thus, when he subjugates his heart to this *daat* which he has – i.e., he has control of his heart – then the attributes in his heart are encompassed in his *daat* and so the attributes receive the light of the love that is in *daat*. He thus sees and grasps the hidden light commensurate with his aspect….

I heard in his name[18] that he said this lesson encompasses the *kavanot* -meditations of lulav. I did not, however, merit hearing an explanation of the matter. Yet I delved into it and found a bit. The essence of the meditations of lulav is to draw all the benevolences to the chest, to shine them into *Malkhut*. Thus, we shake [the lulav] in the different directions in order to draw the light from the root of the benevolences in *daat* to the benevolences that are spread out in the body, to amplify them with a great light from their root in *daat*.[19]

---

18. [Editor's note: This paragraph is a comment by Rabbi Natan of Nemirov, Rabbi Nahman's disciple and transcriber, who wrote down many of the teachings contained within *Likkutei Moharan*.]

19. Rabbi Nahman of Breslov, *Likkutei Moharan* 33.

The experience of dwelling in the sukka is an instance of faith as "encompassing lights,"[20] meaning that a person knows about divine providence
but cannot make it into a real, driving force in his life in this world: "They
do not shine like they do on the higher level above."[21] He runs into suffering and distress encompassed by the arcane idea that God can indeed
be found within them. There exists a real divine revelation that happens
through shade, an encounter with the divine that is "found even in the
realm of the *kelipot,* in the bad days, which are the bad attributes and
the languages of the nations."[22] Such ideas are not something a person
has the tools for grasping, justifying, and internalizing in his life in this
world, wherein he is both emotionally and intellectually limited. These
are encompassing lights.

Rabbi Nahman explains shaking the lulav as bringing it to the
heart, turning the encompassing light of the sukka into something internal: "'Know therefore this day and bring into your heart' (Deut. 4:39),
for you must draw *daat* into the heart, and through this it is rectified."[23]
This is achieved by deciding that the unclear truth of the encompassing light is actually reality. Just like hasidic happiness, Rabbi Nahman
says that faith in goodness and providence, both central factors in the
happiness of the believer, come from self-overcoming and from making
an intentional decision, not from contemplating reality and coming to
conclusions. The lulav symbolizes the human ability to draw down and
internalize this encompassing faith.

As opposed to the sukka, into which a person enters and
nullifies himself (similar to entering a *mikve*), the lulav represents a
self-overcoming that the person can himself put into action: "Every
person is able to taste the light of love that is in *daat.*" He has the power
to determine reality, and to believe, and to be happy about it. This is
why R. Avin in the Midrash compares the lulav to a weapon of war,
symbolizing Jewish victory:

---

20. On this term see also pp. 53, 60 below.
21. *Likkutei Moharan* 33.
22. Ibid.
23. Rabbi Nahman of Breslov, *Likkutei Moharan* II:1, 5.

A parable about two that went into a judge and we do not know who was victorious. Rather we know that the one who [comes out] carrying a palm branch is the winner. So [too] Israel and the nations of the world ... when we see that Israel is coming out from in front of the Holy One, blessed be He, with their lulavs and citrons in their hands, we know that Israel are the winners.[24]

Rabbi Nahman further teaches that drawing in the external lights is achieved through "conquering the evil inclination," which in this context means self-overcoming in knowing and epistemology. This is not an act of contemplation or of questioning an idea, but a decision about the space of knowing which acts on reality itself.[25] A person who stands facing a painful, despair-inducing reality is presented with his ability to decide, totally independent of that reality, and see in reality what is not there. However, he can thus transcend even beyond the effort of overcoming and deciding; his conquering decision actually becomes reality! Conquest becomes the capacity for absolute freedom, escaping categories and bursting through reality, leading to an ecstasy of happiness. Make no mistake, this is not a state of liberation with total security. The overcoming is itself the recognition that security is unnecessary. Ultimately, a person can decide for themselves and see all of reality as "the light of love in *daat*, and see and attain the hidden light, each commensurate with his aspect." This enables one to be happy constantly:

It is a great mitzva to always be happy, and to make every effort to determinedly keep depression and gloom at bay. All the illnesses that afflict people are due only to flawed joy.... Eminent physicians, too, have spoken at length about this – that all illness is the product of gloom and depression, and joy is a great healer.... The rule is that a person has to be very determined and put all

24. Leviticus Rabba 30:2.
25. Rabbi Shneur Zalman of Liadi, the Baal HaTanya, teaches that happiness comes from *Bina*, whose roots are from the *Gevurot* of *Atik*; happiness belongs to the *Gevurot Hanimtakot*, the sweetened severities, that are revealed in *Bina*, from where judgment is aroused. Cf. *Likkutei Torah*, Shemini Atzeret, 89a.

his strength into being nothing but happy at all times. For human nature is to draw itself to gloom and depression on account of life's vicissitudes and misfortunes. And every human being is filled with suffering. Therefore, a person has to exercise great effort in forcing himself to be happy at all times, and to bring himself to joy in any way he can – even with silliness. And though contrition, too, is very good, nevertheless, that is only for a brief period.... But the entire of the day one needs to be happy.[26]

* * *

As we saw at the beginning, the Torah of the Israelites dealt with the pagan idea of happiness, which is a Dionysian happiness that wants to achieve unity with God through breaking and suspending law. The Torah's response is a happiness of grace and peace, a happiness of harmonious connection and generosity from within the limits of humanity. The hasidic idea of happiness is different from this conception in that, perhaps like the pagan Dionysian attitude, it encourages the breaking apart. A sharp expression of this is found in the famous hasidic saying, "Man comes from dust and ends in dust, but meanwhile – a drink in hand!" Make no mistake, this may indeed be a happiness of breaking apart which leads to ecstasy, but it is not a happiness of throwing off the yoke. It focuses not on disrupting order but setting aside our perception of this world as the only possibility. It thereby opens up the wondrous ability to defeat and overcome this world. This is the mystery of the contemplative meditations for the lulav on Sukkot: self-overcoming conquers reality.

---

26. *Likkutei Moharan* II:24.

A Space for Faith

THE COMMUNITY OF FAITH

The holy Zohar teaches that the sukka is "the shade of faith." Those who enter it receive a supernal blessing for themselves and their children: "Anyone who sits in the shade of faith inherits for himself and his children eternal freedom and receives the supernal blessing. One who removes himself from the shade of faith inherits exile for himself and his descendants."[1] The sukka is the shelter that creates not only faith – the supernal blessing – but also the community of faith – the blessing inherited for his descendants eternally. The role of the shade of the sukka is social in that it unites individuals into a community of faith, socializing the individual into a life of faith. Thus, the sukka is the house of faith, the place where we enter "into the mystery of faith,"[2] as well as becoming "the holy trunk and root of Israel."[3]

We can explain the words of the Zohar based on the distinction kabbalistic and hasidic works make between *"or penimi,"* "inner light," and *"or makif,"* "encompassing light." Inner light is the light that exists within us, and encompassing light is the light within which we exist. In

---

Based on drafts written in 5764–5765 (2003–2004), edited by Yishai Mevorach and published in *The Remainder of Faith*, 51–68.
1. Zohar III:103a.
2. Ibid., 103b.
3. Ibid., 103a.

our context, the sukka of faith surrounds a person rather than existing within him. This means that faith is not something within a person, an inner light found in feeling, experience, thought, or any other inner element within a person. Rather, a person exists within faith – it encompasses him, even though he may not always be aware of it. The sukka expresses space, the environment in which a person lives. This environment creates the person and makes him what he is.

The rabbis teach that the space of the sukka belongs to the collective, to the public. For example, the Talmud establishes a critical distinction between the commandment to take the four species (represented by the lulav) and the commandment to dwell in the sukka: "Although they said that a person does not fulfill his obligation … with the lulav of another, he does fulfill his obligation with the sukka of another, as it states, 'All the homeborn in Israel shall reside in sukkot' (Lev. 23:42). This teaches that all of the Jewish people are fit to sit in one sukka."[4]

Everyone is fit to sit in one sukka. Indeed, in order to create the space of the sukka, a person needs a companion. Without a companion, faith would remain a private matter, an inner light relevant only to the person himself.[5] The person discovers that he and those around him share the same faith, living and acting within the same space, and this discovery leads to solidarity among the faithful. Many homiletical works and hasidic discourses therefore teach that the sukka unites the Jewish people, creating the solidarity of the community of the faith.[6]

A THIRD PARTY TO INTIMACY

Rabbi Joseph B. Soloveitchik's essay, *The Lonely Man of Faith*, provides another perspective on faith. Rabbi Soloveitchik distinguishes between two types of communities, the "natural community" and the "community of faith." The social ties of the first community are essentially functional. The members collaborate in work and creativity, relating to each other

---

4. Sukka 27b.
5. For example, the Maharal explains the reason for giving the Torah to the Jews as a community, and not to the forefathers as individuals, in a similar manner. See Rabbi Yehuda Loew, *Tiferet Yisrael*, ch. 17.
6. For example, see Rabbi Natan of Nemirov (student of Rabbi Nahman of Breslov), *Likkutei Halakhot, Hilkhot Netilat Yadayim* 6:99.

only technically and instrumentally. In contrast, the partnership of the second sort of community is not limited to work alone, but expands to include partnership in "being":

> "To be" is a unique in-depth experience of which only Adam the second is aware and it is unrelated to any function or performance. "To be" means to be the only one, singular and different, and consequently lonely. For what causes man to be lonely and feel insecure if not the awareness of his uniqueness and exclusiveness? The "I" is lonely… because there is no one who exists like the "I" and because the *modus existentiae* of the "I" cannot be repeated, imitated, or experienced by others.[7]

Rabbi Soloveitchik further teaches that only "existential companionship" can redeem the "man of faith" from the torment of his existential loneliness. In this sort of companionship, not only laboring hands join together, but also hearts and experiences.[8] This "companionship" creates a shared faith, a covenant between God and man. Standing together before God leads to "existential companionship." Partnership redeems the "lonely man of faith," removing him from the existential loneliness that shuts him in and isolates him within himself, "offering him the opportunity to communicate, indeed to commune with, and to enjoy genuine friendship."[9]

Slavoj Žižek's statement about spousal relationships – as a paradigm of relationships in general – clarifies the potential that Rav Soloveitchik saw in faith:[10]

> When we try to preserve the authentic intimate sphere of privacy… it is privacy itself that changes into a totally objectivized "commodified" sphere. Withdrawal into privacy today means

---

7. Rabbi Joseph B. Soloveitchik, *The Lonely Man of Faith*, 40–41.
8. Ibid., 41.
9. Ibid., 53.
10. See Rabbi Shagar, "Love, Romance, and Covenant," in *Faith Shattered and Restored* (Jerusalem: Maggid Books, 2017).

adopting formulas of private authenticity propagated by the modern culture industry.... The way – the *only* way – to have an intense and fulfilling personal (sexual) relationship is not for the couple to look into each other's eyes, forgetting about the world around them. Rather, while holding hands, to look together outside, at a third point (the Cause for which both are fighting, to which both are committed).[11]

In our era, we no longer stand "face to face." Due to the culture industry manufacturing modern romance, we have lost the ability for a man and woman to truly see each other. In striving to reveal the "self" and to attain private intimacy with one's partner, Western romance prevents us from looking each other in the eye. You could say that this romance longs to grab hold of the other, but this longing actually ends up hindering romance and preventing the desired intimacy. Striving to grasp the thing itself, to reveal the essence in its entirety, obstructs intimacy, since the "self" cannot be grasped. It is not a "thing" that you can hold on to. At best, it appears and then disappears like sudden lightning. This process also contains an additional pitfall: this private intimacy, so nurtured by the media, becomes an imitation. We see ourselves through the media, so we cannot free ourselves from this duality. At this point, "one can only repeat what has already been said and ... one can only act as an actor in an anonymous and stereotypical play."[12]

Žižek proposes a way out of this entanglement. The solution lies in realizing that intimacy is a by-product, not a goal – it results from focusing on a "third point," a shared purpose to which the couple commits. Selfhood awakens only when a couple lose focus on each other and turn their gazes outward to their mutual covenantal obligations.[13]

---

11. Slavoj Žižek, *The Puppet and the Dwarf: The Perverse Core of Christianity* (Cambridge: MIT Press, 2003), 38. Despite the similarity between the statements of Rav Soloveitchik and Žižek, there are substantive differences in their approaches. See Rabbi Shagar, "Love, Romance, and Covenant."
12. Eva Illouz, *Consuming the Romantic Utopia: Love and the Cultural Contradictions of Capitalism* (Berkeley: University of California Press, 1997), 179.
13. This discussion raises some interesting questions: Does a child in a Jewish family filled with other children necessarily feel neglected? Does the relationship of a

Furthermore, we should see this outward-looking gaze as full of modesty and shame. The couple does not look each other in the eye. They avoid the direct gaze encouraged by the media, which lacks modesty and shame.

Shame is not just the result of sin – before which "the two of them were naked, the man and his wife, and yet they felt no shame" (Gen. 2:25) – nor is it simply a punishment for sin; it is also sin's rectification. Averting your gaze constitutes revelation and discovery just as much as it does hiding and concealing.[14] "Gazing toward a third party" creates modesty and incorporates intimacy without risking externalization. In our world, the direct gaze at the other always passes via the gaze of the media. This gaze, which seems so intimate and individual, causes a foreign entity – the media in all its forms – to penetrate the relationship. The media thus separates between the individual and the other, creating externalization. The solution is not to look directly into the eyes of one's partner, but instead to look at a third party, at the other. Intimacy takes form incidentally, when two people stand side-by-side facing a third point. This is a path of modesty and shame, which carries within it the longed-for intimacy.

This seems to be the case regarding the community of the faithful as well. Members of the community do not create deep solidarity by gazing directly at one another, but by recognizing their shared fate and destiny – "the third point." Recognizing shared faith leads to the solidarity of "being together." The *Kedusha* prayer that the community sings together in the synagogue on the High Holy Days embodies this principle: "A crown is given to You, Lord our God, by the multitudes of angels above, and by Your people Israel assembled below. Together, all proclaim Your three-fold holiness."[15]

---

couple in such a family lack all intimacy? Do spirit and inspiration not fill the home even though the Shabbat table is full with the family's guests? I find something very Jewish in Žižek's words – in their wake, we champion, with some success, the idea of family as the symbol of Jewishness. I do not intend to create a cheap idealization of the situation, and I am aware of its deficiencies as well. More on that below.

14. For more on shame as the remedy for sin, see Rabbi Shagar, "Modesty and Shame," in *We Will Walk in Fervor*, 261–270.

15. From the *Kedusha* in the Musaf prayer of the High Holy Days. Translation from

Though the people stand together during the *Amida* prayer, this does not require conscription or local patriotism. The people praying together can encounter each other, thus engendering in them a deep fondness for the entire community. This is an encounter with the collective "we," rather than with the private, individualistic "you." The praying community turns toward this "we," but this "we" can be sufficiently gentle not to suppress the "you," but rather to clothe it and hide it from cheap voyeurism.[16]

THE BROKEN BARRIER

Is faith in God unique among commitments in its potential to create a covenant and a deep partnership, an "existential" partnership that can redeem a person from his loneliness?

The problem of loneliness seems to be one of duality. The difference between inside and outside creates a wound, and a person cannot overcome this gap in order to bring his inside to the outside.

A true encounter requires inner connection. On the one hand, the person standing before me does not limit me. On the other hand, his eyes do not repel me. Our eyes lock. This sort of encounter is impossible in the material world. Two physical entities cannot occupy the same space – one body must push aside the other. Only the revelation of the divine infinitude in faith can actualize this impossible possibility, which is part of the divine omnipotence. "Inasmuch as a king's command is authoritative, and none can say to him: What are you doing?" (Eccl. 8:4). Furthermore, faith essentially functions as the indwelling of the Divine Presence, the *Shekhina*, in the world. The divine permeates the world, enabling the passage from inside to outside.

In my opinion, the Jewish experience of God is not the experience of the "Other" and "Otherness" that Emmanuel Levinas discusses,

---

http://www.templeinstitute.org/103-Kedushah.pdf.

16. The sukka in which we shelter is not a house – it has no roof, and its walls are not strong. Its temporary nature makes it susceptible to the turbulent "outside," and this exposure is part of the effect of the sukka. These elements create a feeling of a group gathered together on deck of a boat tossing in the heart of the ocean. "Togetherness" of this sort connects people to one another.

where the divine reveals itself in total and quintessential Otherness.[17] Nor is it Jacques Derrida's description of the experience of difference, the absolute negation.[18] All these merely sustain the powerlessness of the gaze, stopped short by the face of the other, unable to embrace or meet the other because of the gap between them.

In contrast, Judaism's Divine Presence bridges the gap and breaks the barrier that separates people. Doing God's will leads to the reality described in the *Amida* prayer of Rosh HaShana: "They will all form one group to do Your will wholeheartedly, as we know God Almighty that the scepter is before You." The rabbis described the covenant at Sinai similarly: "'They traveled from Refidim and came to Sinai Desert, and camped in the desert, and Israel camped there facing the mountain' (Ex. 19:2) – wherever it says 'they traveled and they camped,' they went in discord. However, here, they were all of one heart, and so it said, 'And Israel camped there facing the mountain.'"[19]

The Jewish approach to intimacy is the opposite of the modern individual-based approach, focusing on the collective that shelters in the shade of the sukka of faith and revealing every individual within it. I am aware of the dangers of this approach. Modesty can turn into alienation and community can become oppressive totalitarianism, erasing individuality and any possibility of achieving intimacy. These dangers – into which the world of faith often falls – are the underlying cause for the resistance that we sometimes feel toward Judaism's characteristic focus on the collective. We identify a focus on the community with a lack of individualism and privacy, as well as with a heartless, oppressive, and alienated idealism. Yet this approach at its best is an example of what Hasidism and Kabbala call the "unification" which is realized "through the mysterious and hidden."[20] Self-transcendence, total commitment to

---

17. See Ze'ev Levi, *The Other and Responsibility: Studies in the Philosophy of Emmanuel Levinas* (Jerusalem: Magnes, 1997), 62 and on (Heb.).
18. See Gideon Ofrat, *The Jewish Derrida: Judaism as a Wound and the Thought of Jacques Derrida* (Jerusalem: The Academy), 93 and on (Heb.).
19. *Yalkut Shimoni* I:275.
20. As part of the kabbalistic declaration preceding any commandment's fulfillment, one says, "In the name of unification of the Holy One, blessed be He, and His *Shekhina* through the mysterious and hidden."

"the mysterious and hidden," can create the "companionship" of faith and the intimacy of a couple.

THE LANGUAGE OF THE SUKA

Rabbi Nahman of Breslov provides an in-depth treatment of the idea of the sukka as the space of faith, as an encompassing light that rests on the community of believers. Rabbi Nahman identifies the sukka with the *sefira* of *Bina*, which, according to kabbalistic symbolism, is the mother's womb, which creates and protects the fetus. Rabbi Nahman further identifies the sukka with divine speech – the words which created the world – which he also identifies with "prayer speech." Prayer is the divine language, which is the womb, and, in our context, the very place where we shelter in the shade of the sukka's embrace:

> *Bina* is where the fetus is formed ... and this is the concept of sukka, as it says, "You fashioned me in my mother's womb" (Ps. 139:13). This is an instance of the power of prayer when a person prays powerfully, "All my bones shall say" (Ps. 35:10), which is an instance of sukka, as it is written, "And wove me of bones and sinews" (Job 10:11). For the power that a person puts into his words (of prayer) are the twenty-eight letters of the work of Creation[21] through which the world was created ... and the statements that one says with power are themselves the statements of the Holy One.[22]

According to Rabbi Nahman, the sukka, which is the womb, is divine language. What does this mean? A language, in creating social connections, brings with it a burden or charge shared by its speakers. This charge includes forms of thought, possibilities for expressing feelings, associative connotations, memories, and so on. A language creates a partnership and understanding between people, even if they are unaware of its

---

21. [Hebrew Editor's note: In the first verse of the Torah "In the beginning ... " there are twenty-eight letters. Twenty-eight is the *gematria* of the word "*koah*," "power," and so these letters describe the power of the act of Creation.]

22. *Likkutei Moharan* I:28.

underlying assumptions. As people, we are born into a language. We speak a language that we did not create, and this language contains what its speakers have in common. In this respect, language corresponds to the idea of the "encompassing light" mentioned above. Indeed, Rabbi Nahman himself continues on to say that "this is the concept of the 'encompassing lights,' the concept of sukka."

However, the language-sukka Rabbi Nahman speaks of is not just any language, but that of "*tefilla bekoah*," "powerful prayer." This is a central term in Rabbi Nahman's teachings,[23] but for our purposes, it will suffice to define it as prayer that is full of vitality, where we open up to the inner truth of statements spoken from the core of the praying person's personality: "All my bones shall speak" (Ps. 35:10). Power flows from the person praying into his prayers, or into him via the words of the prayer. These statements have the power to invent and create. The person praying reaches a space of creativity where the gap between speech and reality narrows.[24]

The language of powerful prayer carries a charge of vitality and meaning. Rabbi Nahman further teaches that it is a language of kindness and embrace, as it contains faith with its implicit positive assumptions. In the continuation of the teaching, Rabbi Nahman teaches that along with this language there are other languages, other sukkas and embraces:

> However, statements that are not holy statements arouse the sukka of the Christians, the sukka of idolaters, as it says: "Whose mouths speak lies and whose oaths are false" (Ps. 144:8), which refers to the embrace of the Other Side (*sitra ahra*). This is the meaning of "You shelter them in your sukka from contentious tongues" (Ps. 31:21). When the tongues of the idolaters gain power, God forbid, the *shekhina* contends with the Holy One.

---

23. See ibid., I:1, II:84.

24. See ibid., "For the power that a person puts into the words are the twenty-eight letters of the act of Creation through which the world was created. And the ten statements that created the world receive the power of these twenty-eight letters."

The sukkas of the idolaters, the languages of idolatry and the *sitra aḥra*'s embrace, dwell alongside the language of prayer. In Rabbi Nahman's teachings, "contention" and "falsehood" inhere in the very grammar of these languages. Rabbi Nahman teaches that fallen, corrupted language[25] creates conflict on both interpersonal and ontological levels: "When the tongues of the idolaters gain power, God forbid, the *shekhina* contends with the Holy One." This language is the language of conflict, which thrusts a person who speaks it in a state of unavoidable conflict, wherein "a man is a wolf to another man."

In light of all this, we must ask: Is the language of faith the language of our present reality? Rabbi Nahman teaches that the language of faith is the language of "the future yet to come," which at present is realized only in prayer. Powerful prayer, the language of the sukka, means suspending yourself in the ideal, the World to Come, rather than our present reality. Jews are tasked to not live in this world, but rather in a sukka that suspends itself from this world. Of course, one can also identify this language of faith with the Torah. The Torah is a Jew's encompassing light, the realm in which he lives. The laws of the Torah are not the laws of nature, which impose a weak-spirited language of technical facts, but rather they are laws of justice. By fulfilling the Torah, a Jew who speaks the language of faith alienates himself from the world and from the realm of the language of nature, the language of the nations, wherein man is a wolf to man.[26]

Yet, one should not see using the Torah's language of justice as willful escapism from a world that carries on in misdeeds and conflict. We are not satisfied with personally conducting ourselves justly – we want justice and ethics to reign in the world. We pray for this on Rosh HaShana. In praying for the Kingdom of God, we pray for the reign of justice to break the grip of evil and to annihilate wickedness. The Kingdom of God is the kingdom of justice and ethics – we enthrone God

---

25. [Translator's note: For Rav Shagar, the critical distinction is between languages that maintain a posture of humility, vulnerable sincerity, and good-faith engagement, on the one hand, and languages that are instrumental and deceptive, always attempting to get the better of the other.]

26. See further in the sermon "Seventy Bullocks and One Sukka," in Rabbi Shagar, *Faith Shattered and Restored* p, 173–192.

on Rosh HaShana specifically for the sake of this ethical vision: "And all wickedness shall be wholly consumed like smoke, when You make the dominion of arrogance pass away from the earth."[27] This kingdom focuses on rectifying social injustice. We express the hope that the grip of the wicked will be shattered and that the just and upright will celebrate: "Then shall the just also see and be glad, and the upright shall exult."[28]

Why aren't the just and upright glad right now? The suffering of the just is not a function of poverty and material conditions, but rather the result of injustice, of the embarrassment and lack of justice in those material conditions. They therefore pray for the creation of a new solidarity, of Jews and of all of humanity, "that they may all form a single bundle to do your will with a perfect heart."[29] Herein lies the "good hope for those who seek you,"[30] and their happiness and joy – "And the Lord of Hosts is exalted in judgment, and the Holy God in justice" (Is. 5:16).[31]

HE MAKES HIS SUKKA PERMANENT:
THE LETTER AND ITS DESTINATION

I began my talk with the words of the Zohar about the sukka of faith – the partnership of fate that ties believers to each other when they gaze at a third party. Then I spoke about the language of the sukka, the language of justice and righteousness that forms boundaries separating its speaker from – suspending him outside of – the world of injustice and corruption. To conclude, I want to consider the moment of entry into "the shade of faith," the constitutive act that enables someone outside the sukka to begin to speak its language, wrapping himself in the encompassing light which creates "the space of faith."

The sukka reflects the paradox of faith – we leave our permanent, safe, and secure residence and enter the "fallen sukka of David" (Amos 9:11), so that it will shelter us until we come to live there permanently. The Talmud explains the verse, "You shall dwell in the sukka seven

---

27. From the *Amida* prayer of Rosh HaShana.
28. Ibid.
29. Ibid.
30. Ibid.
31. This verse appears in the *Amida* prayer of Rosh HaShana.

days" (Lev. 23:42), in a similar manner: "'Dwell' in the same way as you would reside. Based on this they said that one should make the sukka his permanent residence, and his house transient. How so? If he has nice utensils – bring them into the sukka, pleasant bedding – bring them into the sukka; eat and drink and walk within the sukka."[32] The sukka of faith provides security only after a person enters it. Beforehand, it was nothing but a transient residence prone to collapse. Giving up on security, as manifest in entering the sukka, is what ultimately brings security. The rabbis expressed this paradox in numerous homilies. One of the most famous compares sitting in the sukka's shade to sitting in the shade of a tree that has no shade:

> "As an apple tree among the trees of the wood." R. Huna and R. Aha in the name of R. Yosei b. Zimra said: The apple tree is shunned by all people when the sun beats down, because it provides no shade. So too all the nations refused to sit in the shade of the Holy One, blessed be He, on the day of the Giving of the Law. Do you think that Israel was the same? No, for it says, "For his shadow I longed, and I sat there": I longed for Him and I sat; it is I who longed, not the nations.[33]

Faith, as shade that does not provide any shade, justifies itself only if you already believe – just like the sukka which protects you only after you have entered it. Faith, in Freudian terms, means suspending the reality principle. It is therefore impossible to prove it, but also impossible to disprove it. You can always explain what happens according to faith. Does this empty it of its meaning? To my mind, absolutely not! Faith permits the believer to relate to reality without being bound to reality.

I will attempt to examine the significance of providence and faith with the aid of a provocative metaphor of Jacques Lacan: "The letter always reaches its destination." How do you explain this utter faith,

---

32. Sukka 28b.
33. Song of Songs Rabba 2:3. Based on the Soncino translation.

which shocked even Derrida?[34] The answer is that the letter reaches its destination, not because it has a fixed address, as in the traditional-teleological approach to providence, but because the destination reached is always its true destination. The letter reaches its destination when the person "opens his eyes and realizes that the real letter is not the message we are supposed to carry but our being itself."[35] The person is not the addressee before the letter is sent – he becomes the addressee the moment the letter reaches him, the second the person confronts the transpiring event (i.e., the letter). So too regarding the meaning of the letter. If the letter was not intended for him from the beginning, what message could it convey to him? Its meaning does not exist outside its destination, but the place it arrives at is what gives it its interpretation, which is its meaning – the hermeneutic circle closes upon itself. This creates a different type of mindset, one that does not see concrete reality as a projection of a pre-existent rule. For this mindset, the believer derives the rule from concrete reality.

In a religious context, one can talk about faith in providence, in a divine plan that precedes reality. "A person does not prick his finger below unless it was thus decreed above."[36] This mindset leads to the attempt to lay bare the logic of the providence that precedes reality. This logic signifies the divine plan, and thus gives reality meaning. The realization that there is no duality of the signifier and the signified challenges this. The signifier is itself the signified, and reality itself expresses the divine will. As Slavoj Žižek put it:

> The stain spoiling the picture is not abolished, effaced: what we are forced to grasp is, on the contrary, the fact that the real "message," the real letter awaiting us is the stain itself…. Is not the letter itself ultimately such a stain – not a signifier but rather an object resisting symbolization?[37]

---

34. See Slavoj Žižek, *Enjoy Your Symptom! Jacques Lacan in Hollywood and Out* (New York: Routledge Press, 1992), 15.
35. Ibid., 8.
36. Ḥullin 7b.
37. Žižek, *Enjoy Your Symptom!*, 9.

Events in our lives do not signify something that precedes them, some latent hidden meaning, but are, rather, the message (i.e., the stain) itself. A person's life is not something separate from him – there is no duality of events and their meaning. A person's fate is the person in his entirety – you are what you are, and what you are determines the meaning of what happens to you.

For example, I knew a man who had been a yeshiva student, but the challenges of life, worries about making a living and so on, led him to find gainful employment. I ran into him recently and he enthusiastically told me that due to an illness he had retired early and now spent half of his time learning Torah.

What does this chain of events – falling ill, retiring, and returning to learning – mean? Is the story about how he suffered misfortune, forcing him to cut short a thriving career at its inception? Perhaps he only retired when he did to avoid losing a good retirement plan? Perhaps he only told me about his studies to make himself seem like someone who is still "worth something" from the perspective of spirituality and Torah? The illness that struck could have been an immanent manifestation of the feelings of emptiness and depression he felt after abandoning his calling as a Torah student. Or perhaps the enthusiasm with which he told me about his studies is the stain on the picture attesting that that letter had reached its destination? If so, then the unfortunate illness was really fate, the yeshiva student went back to being a yeshiva student, and his professional career had been nothing but an attempt to evade himself! The true interpretation is in the hands of the addressee. The meaning of his life is given to him and him alone – he determines the contents of the letter.

This does not mean that there was some pre-existent edict that was finally revealed, for it is history that determines that which was pre-existent – the interpretation determines the initial point. However, it is critical to note: the persuasiveness – the interpretation turning into a fact – derives from illumination, from a sense of self-evidence that ties things together. The letter reaches its destination in a moment of illumination wherein everything comes together – when the story is born. This is similar to Pharaoh's dream in Genesis when Joseph's interpretation was the only one able to calm Pharaoh's mind: "The plan pleased

Pharaoh and all his courtiers. And Pharaoh said to his courtiers, 'Could we find another like him, a man in whom is the spirit of God?'" (Gen. 41:37–38). It calmed him because "dreams follow the mouth":

> R. Bizna b. Zavda said that R. Akiva said that R. Panda said that R. Nahum said that R. Birayim said in the name of one elder, namely, R. Bena'a: There were twenty-four interpreters of dreams in Jerusalem. One time, I dreamed a dream and went to each of them. What one interpreted for me the other did not interpret for me, and all of the interpretations were realized in me, to fulfill that which is stated: All dreams follow the mouth [of the interpreter].... This is in accordance with the opinion of R. Elazar, as R. Elazar said: From where is it derived that all dreams follow the mouth of the interpreter? As it is stated, "And it came to pass, as he interpreted to us, so it was" (Gen. 41:13).[38]

An additional Lacanian formulation brings the present investigation to a slightly different resolution: one could speak of faith as an occurrence of "the Real," of "the domain of whatever subsists outside symbolization."[39] The Real is the formless chaos that precedes all symbolization, labeling, and speech, much like an infant's world prior to all examination and differentiation. In the language of faith, the divine existence reveals itself as an event, for it precedes all of these things. "He alone is He just as He was before the world's creation, absolutely was He alone.... He is absolutely without any change, as it says: 'For I am the Lord, I do not change' (Mal. 3:6)."[40]

In the Real, duality does not yet exist – whatever happens happens, without it signifying or symbolizing anything. Here is "the life substance in its mucous palpitation,"[41] before any symbolization and interpretation. Peeling all interpretation away from reality – "when the

---

38. Berakhot 55b.
39. Dylan Evans, *An Introductory Dictionary of Lacanian Psychoanalysis* (London and New York: Routledge, 1996), 162.
40. Rabbi Shneur Zalman of Liadi, *Tanya*, 1:20.
41. Žižek, *Enjoy Your Symptom!*, 23.

words suddenly stay out"[42] and all that is left is oneself – makes it possible to encounter this reality. Taking a stance like this leads a person to astonishment and wonder in encountering existence, in the fact that existence exists – the revelation of concrete reality in its concreteness. This leads the believer to feel gratitude for the happenstance of existence, for everything that happens to him. Providence is found within this happenstance, since the divine is found wherever the "Real" is! Thus, the letter inevitably reaches its destination, not because of the interpretative work of the addressee (which is what makes him into the addressee), but because he does not need to give a theological account of the phenomenon – it is enough that the letter reaches his hand….

* * *

"As an apple tree among the trees of the wood, so is my beloved among the young men. In its shade I delighted to sit, and its fruit was sweet to my taste…. Let his left hand be under my head, and his right hand embrace me" (Song. 2:3, 6). The embracing right hand of the sukka is the shade of the apple tree, whose fruit tastes sweet only for those willing to sit in its shade.

APPENDIX: THE LETTER THAT ARRIVES AS EVENTS HAPPEN

I would like to share an interpretation of an anecdote: one Ḥol HaMoed Sukkot day, I had a bag containing the Žižek book that I have quoted here. Innocently, I thought I had left the bag in the sukka, while, in reality, I had mixed it together with other bags to be thrown into the communal trash barrels. Suddenly, as I was throwing out the various bags, a light switched on in my head and I realized that I was in the midst of accidentally throwing out the book that I had so enjoyed reading. What was the message?

One could say that this was a typical Freudian slip – a will to free myself from a pleasure that had become a compulsion, leading me to disregard relatives and friends due to such intense reading – a situation that creates feelings of guilt. The warning light switched on, so I was not

---

42. Ibid., 24.

completely unaware. In some small corner of my consciousness I knew that I was about to throw away the book.

The classic Freudian interpretation would say that "I did it," I plotted the hidden process in my subconscious. In other words, the repressed unconscious – the hidden hand that pulls the strings and carries the process to fruition, from beginning to end – is precisely myself. However, there is another way to look at it. The anecdote demonstrates the idea that "the letter reaches its destination," which I read above in Žižek's own words: "There is no repression previous to the return of the repressed; the repressed content does not precede its return in symptoms."[43] Both the warning light that flashed in my head and the special significance I felt because it was specifically Žižek's book that was being thrown away are the type of illuminations that occur while events are happening, rather than expressing something that preceded the event. "The true meaning of the subject's words or deeds – their reason – is disclosed by their actual consequences."[44] (Freudian) providence does not precede reality and our existence; rather, reality and existence precede providence. This is the paradox of faith of the sukka. The letter, as we have said, reaches its addressee in the moment of illumination, when all the different threads of existence come together – the moment when the story is born.

---

43. Ibid., 15.
44. Ibid., 14. See further there: "The letter arrives at its destination when the subject is finally forced to assume the true consequences of his activity.... Lacan defines 'hero' as the subject who... fully assumes the consequences of his act, that is to say, who does not step aside when the arrow that he shot makes its full circle and flies back at him."

ADDENDA: IMMERSIVE PRAYER*

Rabbi Nahman identifies faith with prayer. Prayer provides an opportunity for a person to rehabilitate his faith. Prayer enables a person – even someone who does not normally live in the realm of faith – to rise to a higher level and to experience faith through the words of prayer. This works just like reading a book, which enables the reader to become immersed in its content, transported from his own world to the world of the book. The reader really exists with the characters and directly experiences the events that it describes. Prayer depends on being totally present in it, so what a person experiences while praying can be much more emotionally intense than what he experiences while reading.

The ability to be present in prayer depends on the degree to which a person is capable of giving up, for even just a second, on his reflectivity. A person should not examine himself in every possible moment, thinking about where he is and whether or not he believes, but he is simply there, in the words of prayer.[45]

On the one hand, the very act of prayer shifts a person from his current state to an existence of faith, and on the other hand – complementing the former – faith leads to prayer. This circular movement creates a person's service of God.

Prayer, as Franz Rosenzweig said, anticipates "the kingdom of heaven":

> Thus the prayer for the advent of the kingdom mediates between
> revelation and redemption or, more correctly, between creation
> and revelation on the one hand, and redemption on the other....

---

* Based on a lecture on *Likkutei Moharan* 7 delivered in 5764 (2004), edited by Netanel Lederberg and published in *Expositions on Likkutei Moharan* (Alon Shevut: Mekhon Kitvei Harav Shagar, 2013), vol. 1, 77–78.

45. While discussing how to deal with intrusive foreign thoughts, Rabbi Israel ben Eliezer, the Baal Shem Tov, described perfect prayer as being absolutely focused: "I heard from my teacher an interpretation of the verse, 'You will make their hearts firm; You will incline Your ear' (Ps. 10:17). This means that if a person manages to prepare his heart and pray before God without any foreign thoughts, or with love and fear according to his personal nature, then it is a sign that his prayer was accepted" (Rabbi Jacob Joseph of Polonne, *Toldot Yaakov Yosef* [Jerusalem: Agudat Beit Wielopole, 1973], 478).

> Prayer is the force which lifts over the "threshold." From out [of]
> the mutely created mystery of the self-growth of life … to the silent
> enlightenment of the completely fulfilling end.[46]

Prayer and redemption are connected because the practical world of daily life is a world where the Divine Presence is in exile; we do not sense the Divine Presence or the spiritual meaning of our lives. Prayer possesses a hidden importance: we do not just perform prayer, we live in it. It signifies the eternal future, bridging between the future and our reality. The very act of praying expresses the decision of faith, overcoming the norms of this world in favor of the desire to bring about the kingdom of heaven through prayer. Rosenzweig expressed this strikingly: "The cultic prayer stakes everything on the one plea for the advent of the kingdom…. It shows love that the eternal is the nighest…thereby it compels the redemptive advent of the eternal into time."[47]

Meaningful prayer only becomes possible when it is preceded by a person's decision to introduce faith into his life and make it real. Prayer is a doorway to hopes of rectification and redemption, touching eternity.

---

46. Franz Rosenzweig, *The Star of Redemption*, 294.
47. Ibid., 293.

PROVIDENCE AS REFLECTED LIGHT*

For Rabbi Nahman, providence is the "reflected light" of the Torah. The Torah represents how God sees the world. When I learn Torah with this in mind, I illuminate the world and make it meaningful – a world with providence. Providence does not refer to a specific plan and we cannot describe in advance how God runs His world. Providence is reflected light, or our reflectivity on reality. As we will see in Walter Benjamin's discussion of redemption,[48] providence depends on our interpretation of what happened, on constructing a narrative that finds God's wisdom in the various events.[49]

Providence is the ability to see the inner sense and logic of all events, how the things that happen to us come together. The individual details create a story, or a work of art. Practically speaking, this is how the Torah is revealed in the world. A person in the rare state of providence merits understanding the meaning of his life, saving him from a sense of happenstance. Sometimes, a person with a providence mindset feels a strong religious intensity, a clarity about what happens to him, in advance of the event itself. Rabbi Nahman calls this *"Torah atika setimah,"* "the Torah of the ancient sealed one"[50] – the Torah of the future yet to come. This state feels like falling in love, when every event feels sharp and clear. Providence is essentially this sharpness.

---

*   Based on a lecture on *Likkutei Moharan* 13 delivered in 5765 (2005), edited by Netanel Lederberg and published in *Expositions on Likkutei Moharan*, vol. 1, 151.

48. Ibid., p. 150.

49. This is similar to Jacques Lacan's statement that "the letter always reaches its destination." See the discussion at the end of the sermon "A Space for Faith," p. 63.

50. See *Likkutei Moharan* 13.

Ḥanukka

The Candle and
the Sacrifice

A Sermon for Shabbat Ḥanukka

LIFE AND DEATH

Nahmanides, in his Torah commentary, equates the Ḥanukka candles with the candles of the Menora in the Temple.[1] Other commentators take the opposite approach, instead contrasting the Menora, which was lit only while the Temple stood, with the Ḥanukka candles, which we light throughout the exile. Based on this dichotomy, I want to explore some of the different meanings of candle lighting and its holiness, the candle of the Menora, the Ḥanukka candle, and the Shabbat candle.

While lighting the Ḥanukka candles we say, "These candles, they are holy." What is holy in a candle? Is it the light, or perhaps specifically the way the candle burns, in consuming itself?

Lighting the candles of the Menora was one of the priestly services in the Temple: "Speak to Aaron, saying: In lighting the candles

Based on a draft written in 5764 (2004), edited by Yishai Mevorach and published in *To Illuminate the Openings* (Alon Shevut: Mekhon Kitvei Harav Shagar, 2014), 40–49.
1. Nahmanides on Numbers 8:2.

toward the face of the Menora, light seven candles" (Num. 8:2). The nature of this service emerges with greater clarity when contrasted with bringing a sacrifice. The sacrifice returns the "thing," the object-animal, to nothingness via its destruction and consumption, as clearly expressed by the *Olah* sacrifice that is burnt up entirely on the altar: "The priest shall offer up and turn the whole into smoke on the altar. It is an entire offering by fire, a pleasing aroma for God" (Lev. 1:13). However, we need to be precise:

> The principle of sacrifice is destruction, but though it sometimes goes so far as to destroy completely (as in a burnt offering), the destruction that sacrifice is intended to bring about is not annihilation. The thing – only the thing – is what sacrifice means to destroy in the victim.[2]

In other words, the sacrificial act returns the object-ness (the thing-object) to the intimacy of existence, to a state where everything merges with everything else, like "water in water."[3] The sacrifice is therefore not elimination and absence but "returning to nothingness" – a return from existence, from the world characterized by functional and instrumental distinctions that tear things from the deep intimacy of the divine world, to where there is no accounting.[4]

On the one hand, the death of the sacrifice represents the idea of limitation. From the perspective of the living, it represents death, the way the end draws near, and the differentiation of the world of things. The idea of limitation grants a thing its self, its existence, because existence requires limitation. On the other hand, death grants existence its unity with itself. Through the disintegration of distinct things, existence becomes liberated from thingness, ascends to nothingness and envelops itself.

2. George Bataille, *Theory of Religion,* trans. Robert Hurley (New York: Zone Books, 1989), 43.
3. Ibid., 19.
4. Ibid., 44–45.

From the perspective of the living thing, the sacrifice ends in defeat, as it leads to dead-ness and annihilation. It is impossible to "destroy the animal as a thing without denying the animal's objective reality.... One cannot at the same time destroy the values that found reality and accept their limits."[5] Now that death manifests, the animal no longer exists from the perspective of life in the world of things. The sacrifice therefore turns into an existence of emptiness.

The absolute annihilation of the sacrifice expresses one of the primordial religious experiences: rejection and nullification of the value of the world. Religiosity inherently bears within it an experience of destruction[6] in that "it destroys or nullifies any existence other than the existence of the Creator, and denies any possibility of understanding the Creator and encountering Him."[7] Hasidic conceptions of nullifying existence, such as the Chabad contemplation of "everything before God is as nothing," ultimately take part in the nullification of the world.[8]

Hasidic teachings grant broad attention to the experience of destruction in descriptions of the all-consuming yearnings of the soul, comparing it to a sacrifice that burns the pleasures and enjoyments of this world. In *Ḥasidut*, the sacrifice represents "the elevation of feminine waters,"[9] a process of love that focuses on the liberation from things and a return to a pantheistic state of simplicity and oneness with existence. Faith grows out of this state. Reality receives its spiritualization from death, which deconstructs the barriers between things. This is expressed in Judaism in various ways, such as statements regarding the loss of the soul in sleep,[10] or the lowering of one's head in prayer.[11] This

---

5. Ibid.
6. See Avi Sagi, *The Challenge of Returning to the Tradition* (Jerusalem-Ramat Gan, 2003), 92 (Heb.).
7. Eliezer Goldman, cited in *The Challenge of Returning to the Tradition,* ibid.
8. This mindset is rooted deep in the role of the religious language, which is ultimately meaningless in context of the divine absolute, the divine intimacy.
9. See, for example, Rabbi Shneur Zalman of Liadi, *Tanya, Iggeret HaKodesh,* 28.
10. "Sleep is one-sixtieth of death" (Berakhot 57b).
11. On the prostration of Moses and Aaron when faced with Korah's rebellion: "'And they fell on their faces and said, O God, God of the spirits of all flesh' (Num. 16:22) – Come and see, Moses and Aaron committed themselves to death.... This is the tree of death, and every mention of prostration refers to this" (Zohar III:176b). Sleep

spiritualization leads to a liberation from the ordered laws of existence, but it is bound up with frustration and inner pain, since our existence does not experience death and the destruction of existence as liberation. That experience belongs to the intimate nothingness, what a person "sees only at the moment of his death."[12]

The sacrifice in the Temple resonates with the requirement of martyrdom, "with all your heart, with all your life, and with all your might" (Deut. 6:5). The Midrash comments: "With all your life – even if He takes your life."[13] "With all your might (*me'odekha*)" also relates to death, as the Midrash states: "In Rabbi Meir's Torah scroll they found it written [instead of], 'Behold it was very (*me'od*) good' (Gen. 1:31), [the words], 'Behold death (*mavet*) was good.'"[14] A person must commit his whole world to death in order to open up to the divine absolute, as only in the consuming of life does there exist the possibility of encounter with the infinite.

In contrast to sacrifice, the character of lighting the Menora candles is different in that it leads to illumination and vitality. Certainly, the candle consumes itself, but this happens in the process of living, as a consuming that is itself part of living, as "the soul that I placed in you is called a candle."[15] The consuming is also present in the oil and the wick, which consume themselves as they burn. However, lighting aims not at eliminating, but at burning, kindling, and illumination that give life. The inanimate oil and the wick transform into energy, movement, and light. Just as a person consumes his stores of energy when integrating the spiritual and physical parts of himself in the process of living, so too in the lighting of the oil and the wick they unite and shine, receiving life. From this perspective, the lit candle reflects the process of life, the

---

and prostration are a form of suicide and return to a state of simplicity and oneness. Therefore, it is no wonder that, in *Likkutei Moharan* 35, Rabbi Nahman asserts that sleep is one of the ways to return existence "to the place from where it was taken."

12. Rav Tzaddok HaKohen Rabinowitz of Lublin, *Tzidkat HaTzaddik*, §127. Based on *Pirkei DeRabbi Eliezer* 31.

13. *Sifrei, Va'ethanan*, 6.

14. Genesis Rabba 9:5.

15. Shabbat 32a.

activity of the soul.[16] Lighting the candle does not express self-sacrifice, but the powerful eros of life.[17]

The role of the high priest in lighting the candles is therefore different from when he sacrifices the offering. With the Menora, his role is to illuminate souls, to ignite them, to give them the passion and the eros of existence.[18] With the sacrifice, his job is to bring a person to self-sacrifice and personal consumption, to give up on the finite nature of his existence by overcoming himself. This is a different kind of eros, wherein "strong as death is love, hard as hell is jealousy, and its darts are darts of fire, a blazing flame" (Song. 8:6).

TWO HOLIES

As a general principle, bringing a sacrifice and lighting the candles present two different types of consciousness regarding the holy: the numinous and the pleasant. This echoes a split found in the Bible, where the holy sometimes appears as the awful and terrifying *mysterium tremendum*, which demands the destruction of sacrifice, and sometimes as the illuminating good, replete and pleasurable.[19]

---

16. The ancient custom mentioned already in the Mishna (Berakhot 8:6) of lighting a memorial candle is the act that best expresses the metaphor of the candle as the soul of man. With the lit candle, it is as if the person resurrects the departed in his memory. Due to its comparison with the soul, the candle becomes the medium for the embodiment of the departed's soul, his soul shining in the candle.

17. [Hebrew Editor's note: The eros of life combines Eros and Thanatos; death takes some part in in it. However, death's presence appears as part of life itself, not as the absolute consumption of the sacrifice. If there is death, it is as part of life and serves as the background – the intensity of light emerging from darkness.]

18. The eros that we find in contemplating the light of the candle is the same eros of the soul of man, a consequence of this duality of light and consumption. This eros leads to the nostalgia that we find in various Ḥanukka songs. The light of the candle is the small and raw existence of the candle-soul, the dim candle that stands outside under threat of the great darkness. The loneliness, the quiet, and the monotony of the lit flame create the illusion of eternity, as if it will continue forever, that the candle and the soul will never go out. From this perspective, the eros of the small candle is greater than that of the mighty, brazen, light of the torch.

19. See Rudolf Otto, *The Idea of the Holy: An Inquiry into the Non-Rational Factor in the Idea of the Divine and its Relation to the Rational* (London: Oxford University Press, 1936).

The holy arouses fear and brings with it the destructive. In the language of Levinas and Derrida, the holy represents the "other" and manifests the "gap" and "difference" that cannot be bridged: "Anyone who touches the mountain shall die. No hand shall touch him; he shall be either stoned or shot; beast or man, he shall not live" (Ex. 19:12–13); "They shall not enter to see the dismantling of the holy, lest they die" (Num. 4:20). However, the holy also appears as good and pleasing, overflowing its bounds: "Go, eat rich foods and drink sweet drinks and send portions to whoever has nothing prepared, for the day is holy to our Lord. Do not be sad, for your rejoicing in the Lord is the source of your strength" (Neh. 8:10). The holy day is sanctified when it is called "a delight, the Lord's day, honored" (Is. 58:13), and the favor of God is sought through eating rich foods and drinking sweet drinks: "Then you can seek the favor of the Lord. I will set you astride the heights of the earth, and let you enjoy the heritage of your father Jacob; for the mouth of the Lord has spoken" (58:14). The symbol of pleasure is oil: "You anoint my head with oil; my drink is abundant. Only goodness and steadfast love shall pursue me all the days of my life" (Ps. 23:5–6). Oil bears an erotic connotation in the Hebrew Bible: "Your ointments yield a sweet fragrance, Your name is like finest oil; therefore do maidens love you" (Song. 1:3). It can also be holy: "Make of this a sacred anointing oil, a compound of ingredients expertly blended, to serve as sacred anointing oil" (Ex. 30:25).

This facet of holiness is manifest on Shabbat – when we light the Shabbat candles – in the Shabbat foods, which are generally rich,[20] as the poet wrote: "To delight in pleasures / swan, quail, and fish";[21] in

---

20. It seems to me that the difference we find in the Hebrew Bible between the holy as the numinous other and the holy as harmony and pleasure is root of the debate that I sometimes have with some of my students about the Friday night meal. Some of them are accustomed to eating a dairy meal in order to avoid eating rich and exhausting foods. Opposing them, I claim that this damages the holiness and pleasure of Shabbat. In response, they say that each person's pleasure is different, which is correct. Despite this, I answer them that the fact that they prefer dairy to meat, the light over the fatty, is a lack in their Judaism.
21. From the song "*Ma Yedidut*," traditionally sung in Ashkenazic communities on Friday night.

Shabbat sleep, which is pleasure; and in the command of marital intimacy for scholars, especially on Shabbat.[22] All of these flow into the candle – the oil and the wick.

The Shabbat candle is like the light of the home, gentle and pure; it does not impose a blinding otherness on a person, nor dread. It is also not part of the thunder and lightning of Mount Sinai, where anyone who touched the mountain would die. The candle lights up its surroundings, the home. The holiness here is familial, the light belongs to the home and is meant for the home, like a good meal, overflowing with good and grace for the participants; the good and grace connect the participants one to another.

It is therefore not surprising that the holiness of Shabbat is inseparable from the hosting of guests, as Rabbi Nahman of Breslov asserted, "Hosting guests is like hosting Shabbat."[23] The pleasure of Shabbat is manifest in the harmony of the body and the soul. The additional soul of Shabbat, which, according to Rashi, is "an additional soul that expands his consciousness for eating and drinking,"[24] leads to reconciliation between contradictory elements, a reconciliation that is parallel to life, connecting body and spirit, oil and wick. The Shabbat candle is a candle of harmony in the home: "What is 'My soul is removed far off from peace' (Lam. 3:17)? R. Abbahu said: That is [lacking the opportunity for] the lighting of the Shabbat candle,"[25] because the candle provides the satisfaction and fullness of the home. This is the origin of hosting guests on Shabbat – a person has a homey dimension, a "being with himself," and it is with this that he hosts guests. This is reconciliation of contradictory elements on a social level, where the walls between a person and "the other" fall down for the sake of unity of souls and fellowship.

---

22. Maimonides, *Mishneh Torah, Hilkhot Shabbat*, 30:14. See Rabbi Shagar, "The Commandment of *Onah*," in *We Will Walk in Fervor*, 17–58.

23. Rabbi Nahman of Breslov, "*Hakhnasat Orḥim*," in *Sefer HaMiddot*, 4. Regarding hosting guests, see Rabbi Shagar, *Your Face, I Seek* (Efrata: Institute for the Advancement of Rav Shagar's Writings, 2005), 53.

24. Taanit 27b.

25. Shabbat 25b.

Can we identify these characteristics in the Ḥanukka candle? This is a candle of "each man and his family,"[26] rooted in at-homeness. However, "we have no permission to use them, only to gaze at them"[27] – this light, the light of the candle, evokes the gap between it and the person who lights it. Since a person does not have permission to use it, he necessarily must keep his distance from it. Moreover, this candle is located "just outside the *doorway* of the house,"[28] and "sin crouches at the *door*" (Gen. 4:7). The candle belongs not only to the home and to the feeling of at-homeness, but also to another space, a dark space outside the known, familiar boundaries – the demonic space. This candle's roots are in war, the war of the Maccabees, not in the harmony of Shabbat. To sum up: the Ḥanukka candle carries within it both facets: the sacrifice and the Menora; consumption of the soul and the eros of life; the outside and the home, otherness and hosting guests.

HOSTING GUESTS

Two different types of hosting guests follow this approach: that of Shabbat, which is when a person opens the doors of his well-lit home, and that of Ḥanukka, connected to the *gevurot*, the harsh aspects of the divine, when a person transcends himself toward "the other" who is outside the door and brings him into his home as an "other."[29] Rabbi Yitzhak Isaac Halevi of Homil, a student of Rabbi Shneur Zalman of Liadi, describes it in the following manner in his Ḥanukka sermons: Shabbat is "specifically a person for himself, in his home, with his household who obey his will. In contrast is Ḥanukka, which is outside the home where there is authority besides him, and his will is not sovereign. This is why you must behave differently there."[30]

---

26. Shabbat 21b.
27. *Masekhet Soferim* 20:6.
28. Shabbat 21b.
29. We can understand the particular Ḥanukka type of hosting guests from Rabbi Nahman's story, "*Ma'aseh Me'oreya*," which takes place at the time of candle-lighting. Rabbi Nahman depicts hosting guests in this story in a manner entirely un-Shabbat-like. In the story, it is full of fear and terror of the otherness of the unknown that the guest brings with him. See Rabbi Shagar, *To Illuminate the Openings*, 125–135.
30. Rabbi Yitzhak Isaac Halevi of Homil, *Hannah Ariel* (Ashdod, 1998), Genesis, 57b.

Hosting guests on Shabbat develops out of a person "being with himself," the solidarity of a person with himself and of his household with each other. The basis for hosting guests is the state suitable to revealing the familiar in a person and between people. He invites the "other" into his home due to the fellowship and closeness that will exist, and perhaps already exists, between him and the household. The "other" is invited to be a member of the household and to take part like a son or daughter in a home lit up by Shabbat candles and angels of peace. Ultimately, this mutual acceptance flows from the commonalities between people and it reveals what they share, the soul, which is a person's good intentions, to which all sons and daughters of the home belong.

Hosting guests on Ḥanukka is something else entirely, because it requires self-sacrifice and inspires fear, rather than the harmony of Shabbat. This hosting of guests requires a person to overcome himself and his "I," as an absolute process, a decision, a revolution that he undergoes in relation to the other, overcoming the otherness of the other.[31] It is a process of consuming through self-overcoming and putting faith in the other despite his otherness. This hosting guests does not deprive the other of his freedom, and therefore does not expect solidarity and interpersonal closeness but simply otherness – often deep chasmal otherness – between guest and host. This lets strangeness invade the home, and therefore, this hosting of guests destroys any feelings of at-homeness as the reality of the home loses its everyday familiarity. The candles are lit and shining – seemingly warm and familiar – but there is no permission to use them, only to gaze at them. Thus, they estrange themselves from the person lighting them.

Hosting guests on Ḥanukka does not occur in the lit home, but just outside the front door. Just as the sacrifice represents the idea of limitation, of the boundary between the existence of things and their annihilation, so too the Ḥanukka candles stand on the border between the home's at-homeness – which has its rules, definitions, and distinctions – and the lack of at-homeness that crouches at the door. On Ḥanukka, hosting guests does not force the guest to accept the house

---

31. See Rabbi Shagar, "Happiness, Solidarity, and Kinship," in *In the Shadow of Faith*, 107–111.

rules, and therefore it requires the host to overcome himself and allow the guest his freedom to be, without knowing what effects this freedom will have and without restraining the other by the light of the candles of the home.

The Ḥanukka candle therefore presents multiple facets. As a candle, its center is the home, but as a sacrifice, it lacks at-homeness. Minimally, it possesses a perturbed at-homeness. The Ḥanukka candle is exilic, the candle of a broken house. Only such a candle enables the wondrous Ḥanukka hosting of guests and opens the door to the abnormal, which can create connections never before possible. Ḥanukka illuminates within us the time when concepts like the home and at-homeness will not require the exclusion of otherness but can and will include it without crumbling.

A Screen for the Spirit, a Garment for the Soul

A Lecture on the Baal HaTanya's
Torah Ohr on Ḥanukka

> *"It is you who light my candle;*
> *the Lord, my God, lights up my darkness."*
>
> (PS. 18:29)
>
> *"For the commandment is a candle,*
> *the Torah is a light."*
>
> (PROV. 6:23)
>
> *"The soul of man is the candle of the Lord."*
>
> (PROV. 20:27)

Based on various lectures delivered between 5747 (1986) and 5764 (2003) and drafts from 5764 (2003) and 5766 (2005), edited by Yishai Mevorach and published in *To Illuminate the Openings*, 53–72.

THE SOUL AND THE COMMANDMENT

Many hasidic rabbis have a custom on Ḥanukka to sit in front of the lit candles and contemplate them, sometimes for hours. The meditation washes over their consciousness, opening them up to a whole host of imaginings, discoveries, thoughts, and emotions – eventually making their way into their sermons. We therefore see persistent use of elements like light and candles in hasidic sermons for Ḥanukka, attesting to the source of the sermon and to the contemplation of a candle's illumination.

For example, in a sermon by Rabbi Shneur Zalman of Liadi, the Baal HaTanya, he distinguishes between two different types of light emanating from the candle: "The idea is that the candle consists of both the oil and the wick, and two types of light: a darkened light immediately around the wick, and the clarified white light."[1] This distinction gave rise to a sermon on two forms of religious consciousness. To a certain extent, we can say that the different colors of light in the candle's flame inspired the Baal HaTanya's sermon. Without those different colors, he never would have thought of the sermon.

The motif of the candle, especially the imaginings it conjures, appears throughout biblical and rabbinic texts: the candle of the commandment, the candle of the soul, and the candle of God. Many hasidic discourses therefore try to clarify the relationship between the soul, the commandments, and God. In studying the Baal HaTanya's sermon, we will primarily encounter the tension between the divine and the commandment, specifically the way the divine infinitude contradicts the limits and restraints of the system of commandments. Prior to doing so, we will dedicate a few words to the tension between the soul and the commandment, to the way the inner life of the believer contradicts the externality of the ritual commandment.

The spread of Hasidism raised a difficult question: must focusing on inner service of God necessarily move a person away from the practical framework of halakha? To put it differently, does the focus of Hasidism on "the candle of the soul" necessarily dim the light of "the candle of the commandment"?

---

1. Rabbi Shneur Zalman of Liadi, *Torah Ohr, Miketz* 33a.

The tension between the two is clear: a person's external obligation to do specific things at specific times clashes with an individual listening to his own inner voice. This is true beyond just the context of Jewish religious life. Empirically speaking, a person following his own personal truth does not behave according to the dictates and accepted norms of society. For example, a person who desires to act authentically may be less polite because he sees "the rules of the game" as external social constructs that dull his inner life. He will also experience halakha as holding him back from his own truth. Moreover, he will sometimes perceive halakha as false. According to halakha, he must pray at specifically ordained times, but deep within him he knows that he cannot pray from his heart and with intent at this moment. If he tried, he would be just praying by rote. Must this individual now pray in response to the external command, or should he follow his inner life and reject his obligation to the halakhic norm?[2]

This question has another dimension that may help clarify things: the chasm between the objective and subjective realms. Should an individual seek out the truth through their own subjective experience, or should they rather find it in the absolute and objective realm of reality? When a person sees truth as a reflection of his own subjective internal experience, the concept of truth loses its absoluteness and becomes relative. Truth becomes dependent on a person's particular perspective, his emotions, feelings, and personal experiences. In this dichotomy, halakha falls on the side of the absolute and the fixed – God commanded us to follow it, and we cannot be relativists about it.[3]

---

2. The controversy around delaying the time of prayer provides a well-known example of this. Throughout the history of Hasidism, many hasidic rabbis (such as the Seer of Lublin, the "Holy Jew," and the Kotzker Rebbe) thought that prayer could be delayed while a person prepared his heart, despite the clear opposition in the *Shulḥan Arukh*'s ruling on the topic.

3. This tension comes into play when we look at the difference between Kabbala and Hasidism. The religious service of the Kabbala is different from hasidic service, despite Hasidism basing itself on Kabbala and understanding itself as an interpretation thereof. Generally (and somewhat simplistically) speaking, Kabbala is primarily concerned with fixing the upper worlds, while the Hasid is primarily concerned with achieving inner attachment. The goal of the Hasid's spiritual service takes shape in light of the hasidic interpretation of Kabbala. Hasidism shifted the kabbalistic

Ideally, an individual's inner truth will match the objective truth.[4] This would mean that his inner life burns strongly while his sense of obligation to this inner life is unassailable. He understands his inner life as absolute, objective reality. Such a person's inner life stops feeling relative and gains the strength of an external command; it obligates him no less than external truth would.

Unfortunately, we live in a situation where our inner lives lack strength and force. Our inner lives and our relation to them are prone to ups and downs. The dullness of our inner lives makes them susceptible to all kinds of outside influences, and therefore they feel inauthentic. This is the reason that the *Shulḥan Arukh*, rather than our inner lives, is the basis of our religious obligations. It anchors our lives absolutely.

Ultimately, divine truth reveals itself via different levels and planes. A person should not think that truth can be obtained in only one place, either in the internal or external life. Complete, ideal reality includes and unifies both the internal and the external. However, in our incomplete, non-ideal reality, both dimensions and perspectives have advantages and disadvantages, and we cannot ignore either of them.

---

concepts and structures to the consciousness and soul of the individual, teaching that human psychology and epistemology express the upper worlds of the *sefirot* and *partzufim* discussed by Kabbala. To clarify, this does not mean psychology in its normal sense, but psychology wherein the soul is "a portion of God from on high," and anything that happens in a person's inner light is mystical. In a certain sense, Hasidism did not just psychologize kabbalistic teachings; it also mystified human psychology.

This fact is incredibly significant. Whereas the kabbalist seeks a world-fixing mystical action in the commandments, the Hasid seeks mystical attachment, locating all the worlds within his inner life and in the mystery of "man is a microcosm of the world" (*Sefer HaTemuna* [Lemberg, 1892], 25). See Rivka Shatz-Oppenheimer, *Hasidism as Mysticism: Quietistic Elements in Eighteenth Century Hasidic Thought* (Jerusalem, 1988), 129–147 (Heb.). The kabbalist understands the focus of his religious service as a cosmic event that corresponds exactly to these actions. The Hasid, in contrast, turns his gaze inward toward attachment to God. He achieves "*tikkun olam*" within his self-awareness in being one with himself and focusing on understanding the grain of the world, writ large, and his inner life. The kabbalist thus commits to the external and the Hasid to the internal.

4. Thus preventing conflicts between a person's inner and practical lives. See Rabbi Shagar, *Expositions on Likkutei Moharan*, vol. 1, 68 and 295–310.

To this end, our rabbis taught us that we must serve God out of both fear and love: "So the rabbis said, serve out of love, serve out of fear."[5]

THE BAAL HATANYA: A GARMENT FOR THE LIGHT

Thus far, we have looked at the tension between the candle of the commandment and the candle of the soul, between the formal halakhic system and the spirituality sought by Hasidism. Hasidic spirituality demands authentic action as one of its central prerequisites, and authenticity contradicts the command for the believer to perform certain actions at narrowly appointed times.

In his sermon for Ḥanukka, the Baal HaTanya deals with yet another tension addressed by Hasidism, especially in the thought of Chabad Hasidism: What is the connection between physical actions – the acts of the mitzvot – and the spiritual effect that they are supposed to engender, such as closeness with God? Furthermore, the commandments, as they are realized in actions, belong to the "*yesh*" – to finite and created human reality. How are they connected with faith in the divine infinitude?

As we shall see, the Baal HaTanya takes a dialectical approach. On the one hand, he presents the commandments as strictly functional, without any independent value. However, on the other hand, this very "lowliness" gives the acts of the commandments their "root" in the divine will itself:

> "A commandment is a candle and the Torah is light." The commandments are called "candle." It is also written: "The candle of God is the soul of man," for the soul is called "candle." The Zohar explains that the commandments are called "garments"... and in order to be fully clothed, the soul must fulfill all six hundred and thirteen commandments.... The soul's garments are explained...

---

5. Commentary of Rabbi Ovadia Bartenura on Mishna Avot 1:3. I will point out, however, that commanding a person to follow an external command is basically impossible. Even external obligation is a matter of personal prerogative, and is therefore a function of personal freedom. A person's inner life itself transitions between many different phases, sometimes appearing as the freedom to be unfree and inauthentic.

as boundless illuminations ... for there are countless understandings of the light and the glow, which is an illumination from the Infinite Light, blessed be He....

The delights that derive from the infinite light, the source of all delights, are limitless. Similarly, we perceive with our senses that even ... physical delights are without measure, for there are infinite ways to experience pleasure.... Because of this, the soul, as a finite thing, is unable to fully apprehend the revelation of this glow, the essence of the divine, except through a garment, a screen, which enables the soul to receive the light and the glow.[6]

The soul requires garments, for without these garments it cannot comprehend anything. I will try to explain what I mean. For example, when we speak about creating a memorial of a person's life, are we talking about transcribing the details of a person's life, like the transcribing of reporter's notes into a computer? Of course not. The events of a person's life are "garments," the medium for the substantial reality that the person experiences through them. This substance is not something specific, nor is it a defined content. Though it itself lacks any specific sense, it is the thing that grants meaning to the content of those experiences.[7] Thus, eternal life is life that retains the meaning of these experiences, something that can never simply be entered into a computer.

The Baal HaTanya refers to the undefinable thing that grants meaning and existential weight to everything as "the glow of the infinite light." It is not simply meaning, but the meaning of all meaning. In the sermon before us, as well as in other sermons, the Baal HaTanya essentially equates this glow with the delight that in our world always appears via a medium or object. Enjoyment never materializes in its pure state: "Delight in the earthly realm always derives from something

---

6. Rabbi Shneur Zalman of Liadi, *Torah Ohr, Miketz*, 32d.
7. We must distinguish between "sense" and "meaning" [translator's note: these terms appear in English in the original]. As we shall soon see, "the glow of the infinite" is what gives "sense" its "meaning." "Sense" is completely attached to the level of content – words, actions, situations. "Meaning" is the internal, animating force behind these, granting these things spiritual "weight."

outside it, like when we take pleasure in some delicious food or in the study of some wisdom."[8]

The commandments are the garments through which our world receives its substance, existence, and meaning. In the language of the Baal HaTanya, the commandments act as a conduit for the delight of the infinite light to penetrate our world. As an entire system of life, the commandments form a space within which a person experiences the eros of meaning.[9] Through them, an individual feels alive and experiences satisfaction, excitement, longing, the joy of commandment, and intimacy. We may include all of these ideas within the words "light" and "holiness," what the Baal HaTanya calls "delight."

We cannot apprehend this light except via the garments, the commandments. The commandments themselves are not the light and delight, nor are they the meaningfulness of existence. They are only garments, which receive their light from a person experiencing holiness and pleasure through them. As the Baal HaTanya explains in the sermon we are studying:

> Behold, the acts of the commandments … the divine infinite light does not infuse them unless it is through … the divine soul itself performing the commandments, thereby drawing into them a revelation of the divine infinite light. As it is written [about the commandments], "the individual shall perform them" (Lev. 18:15). The individual is the one who makes them into commandments, by drawing into them the infinite light.[10]

---

8. Rabbi Shneur Zalman of Liadi, *Likkutei Torah*, addenda to *Parshat Vayikra*, 52a.

9. We can present these things from a different perspective. The commandments are garments for the revelation of the light's glow. As contemporary philosophies show, meaning and sense depend on a person's way of life, which gives words their sense and meaning. We use tables and chairs in certain ways, and this gives them their linguistic sense. In hasidic terms we might say that the act is a garment (an encompassing light) that grants the language its sense (a pervading light). In the religious context of the Baal HaTanya, the commandments are a religious way of life which gives sense and meaning to religious language.

10. Rabbi Shneur Zalman of Liadi, *Torah Ohr, Miketz*, 33c.

THE ROOT OF THE COMMANDMENTS

To be sure, we could say that any way of life or cultural system is a garment for the infinite light in that the system bears within it the substance of existence. An individual experiences the critical existential elements of his life, such as love, longing, lower and higher fears, loyalty, etc., through social constructs and cultural frameworks. They grant his life its weight and significance, something he would not trade for anything. Hasidic thought connects this idea to the fact that the world was created through "ten utterances" in the first chapter of Genesis. The world thus reveals the divine light even without specifically religious language like the Ten Commandments. However, according to the Baal HaTanya, there remains a difference between these systems and the system of the commandments. The commandments may be a human system, but this system is rooted in the essence of the divine infinite.

At this point, the Baal HaTanya ceases to see the commandments as merely a garment or tool alone, but rather they themselves constitute the immediate presence of the divine. This means that the commandments are a symbolic system that signifies the infinite itself.[11] They do not simply express the infinite but signify it as well. How do the commandments signify the infinite? They are a closed system, without determination or meaning, and thus they point to the divine will itself. One might even say that the signifier does not signify something that we are meant to understand, but rather that it signifies incomprehensibility itself, a "black hole."

To understand this, we must make note of the Baal HaTanya's distinction between "the infinite light" and the "essential will of the infinite light":

> It is impossible for the essential will of the infinite light to be revealed to any created being, unless that divine will is embodied in some physical act, which is the performance of the commandments…. The root of the commandments is very lofty, rooted in the uppermost realms of the supernal crown, *Keter*…until

---

11. This may be likened to the Lacanian idea of the Real. For more on this concept see the sermon "A Space for Faith," p. 67.

it devolves into our realm through physical actions and things, tzitzit and sukka. The divine will is specifically revealed in these things, as "the final in action is first in thought." In action, heaven was created first ... but in thought, physicality came first ... for the light is revealed from the aspect of divinity that encompasses all realms....

Thus, the performance of mitzvot, whose roots lie in this encompassing aspect of divinity – the supernal *Keter* – cannot be expressed below as "inner light," but rather must find its expression in exterior, physical actions. It is well known that that which in its essence is loftier and elevated falls to the lower depths.

Therefore, the performance of the commandments creates an encompassing screen, so that through the commandments [the soul] can delight in the delight of the infinite light.... When the soul clothes itself in the garment of the commandments, it delights in the delight of the infinite light.[12]

The Baal HaTanya teaches that the commandments have a dual character. As a garment, they are a vessel that expresses the infinite light, the delight of the soul, holiness, anything that is experienced as the "*tokho shel olam*," "the inwardness of the world." The commandments themselves are not the inner aspect of life but rather a medium for this inwardness.

On the other hand, the Baal HaTanya identifies them with the "encompassing lights," a reality that cannot be truly apprehended or experienced within our categories. As the vessels of reality, the commandments are rooted beyond it, in "the essential will of the infinite light." The Baal HaTanya is here expressing a classic Chabad teaching: "That which in its essence is loftier falls lower." The commandments, which exist as purely instrumental and without essential, inherent meaning, find their root in the very essence of the divine.

The Baal HaTanya claims that the source of the commandments is the divine will itself. The meaning of the commandments is not explained by some system of rules, some ethical or moral ideal, or some

---

12. Rabbi Shneur Zalman of Liadi, *Torah Ohr, Miketz*, 32d–33a.

historical idea which guided their creation.[13] Simply put, God wanted commandments. Through this there developed a system with meanings and connections, what we might call "wisdom." The will of the Creator does not depend on this system, however, nor is this system necessary in any absolute sense.

The Baal HaTanya also asserts that the final action precedes the thought that ostensibly explains and gives meaning to the action. The physical acts of the commandments come directly from the divine will, which wants them exactly as they are for no reason. This is the nature of will, desiring independent of any externally motivating factor. One might say that since they are grounded in will, the commandments signify a degree of arbitrariness and happenstance. The commandments point to the incomprehensible will that wants just because it wants. For this reason, the commandments take the form of actions, not intentions. As actions, the commandments present themselves as opaque objects. They are independent of their meanings and reasons, of the light and the delight that we can grasp through them.

WILL OR WISDOM

Fundamentally, the Baal HaTanya seeks to oppose Maimonides' approach. In the *Tanya*, he claims that Maimonides comprehended up to the *sefira* of *Ḥokhma*, or to the World of *Atzilut*, whereas Hasidism reaches beyond that to the *sefira* of *Keter*, to the infinite itself.[14] While the *sefira* of *Keter* is identified with divine will, the *sefira* of *Ḥokhma*, in line with its name, is identified with the concepts of wisdom and meaning. On what critical basis does God act or God create? According to

---

13. The Baal HaTanya's position here parallels somewhat Yeshayahu Leibowitz's opinion with regard to the commandments. See further Rabbi Shagar, "Faith and Language According to the Baal HaTanya of Chabad," in *We Will Walk in Fervor*, 175–178. For the approach of the Baal HaTanya more generally, see the rest of the essay there.
14. "God and his wisdom are one, as Maimonides wrote (and the kabbalists ceded to him)...but not beyond the level of Emanation...for the blessed infinite is elevated and lofty without end, beyond the essence and aspect of *Ḥokhma, Bina,* and *Daat,* to the point where the essence and aspect of *Ḥokhma, Bina,* and *Daat* is like physical action in comparison" (Rabbi Shneur Zalman of Liadi, "*Sefer HaBenoni,*" in *Tanya,* ch. 2). For more on this debate, see Rabbi Shagar, "Theodicy in Light of the Holocaust," in *On That Day* (Alon Shevut: Mekhon Kitvei Harav Shagar, 2012), 43–51.

Maimonides, God acts according to wisdom, from which the desiring will arises. Will derives from wisdom, as Maimonides makes clear in his language about divine providence: "His wisdom decided so."[15] There is no such thing as an absolute, independent will. Will exists against the background of wisdom's rules. The essences of God and the world are the logical order out of which God acts and creates in the world. Discovering this order leads to ultimate, exhaustive clarity. Wisdom needs no justification for its being; it simply is being. In contrast to Maimonides, the Baal HaTanya proposes that will precedes and gives rise to wisdom. He asks a question that Maimonides would consider illegitimate: What makes this thing specifically wisdom? Why does God act according to this order specifically? His answer, of course, is will. Wisdom does exist, and there is an order which explains reality, but it is secondary rather than primary.[16]

The Baal HaTanya's sermon discusses two depictions of the creation of the world, corresponding to the difference between Maimonides' opinion and his own.[17] The first chapter of Genesis tells of heaven preceding earth: "God began to create heaven and earth" (Gen. 1:1). The second chapter, on the other hand, says that earth preceded heaven: "Such is the story of heaven and earth when they were created, when the Lord God made earth and heaven" (Gen. 2:4). The Baal HaTanya sees the heavens as the spirituality and meaningfulness of existence, as wisdom: "'Heaven' generally refers to spirituality." Earth, in contrast, refers to reality as an

---

15. Maimonides, *Guide for the Perplexed*, II:25.
16. A person who takes Maimonides' approach lives in a world of meanings, ideas, and clarity, what Hasidism calls "vision of Ḥokhma" (see Rabbi Shagar, *In the Shadow of Faith*, 101). Meanwhile, a person who takes the Baal HaTanya's approach lives in a world of freedom on the one hand and total finality on the other. Reality's finitude, grasped against the background of the divine will that wants it as it is, gives existence finality. In other words, the finite itself lacks absoluteness. It is always part of a framework and is defined by finite objects separate from it. This means that it is always only "a possible existent," as Maimonides would say. The finite exists, meaning that it could have been otherwise. Therefore, it is possible and incidental. Only its connection to the highest will gives existence its infinite dimension of finality; it is thus and not otherwise.
17. Rabbi Shneur Zalman of Liadi, *Torah Ohr*, 32–33. All quotations in this paragraph are from this text.

object, for "'earth' refers to the aspect of physicality." According to the first depiction, heaven – wisdom and spirituality – precedes and underlies earth. As the Baal HaTanya puts it, "Spirituality gives life to and creates the aspect of physicality." This position fits with Maimonides'. According to the second depiction, earth – the final, physical object – precedes heaven, which represents spirituality and reason. The final act precedes the thought that explains it: "The aspect of physicality comes first; the final act is first in thought." The Baal HaTanya identifies this approach with will. An act that precedes thought is an act rooted in the highest will that precedes all wisdom. Wisdom itself develops from this will: "Fulfilling His will in truly physical matters…reveals the will." In this context, "truly physical matters" means without spirituality.

If we return to his characterization of the commandments, the Baal HaTanya says that even the physicality of action precedes thought and spirituality: "The root of the commandments is incredibly lofty, for they are rooted in the aspect of the highest crown (*Keter Elyon*) … which ultimately devolves down into physical action…precisely there we find the divine will. The final act is first in thought."[18] By its very nature, the essence of the infinite will cannot be revealed in a garment, or in sense, in the finite. It therefore does not appear as the inner light of reality, as meaning, as clarity, or as the delight of holiness. Though these things cannot be defined, they are comprehended and contained in the "vessels" of existence, through our experience, just as meaning is comprehended through sense. The essence of will appears only as light that surrounds reality, overlapping the opaque act by virtue of it lacking sense. This opaque act defies human existence, which relies on reason, knowledge, comprehensibility, and meaning, wherein every effect has a cause and everything that happens is determined by a thought or experience.

Based on this idea of the Baal HaTanya, we might say that people fail to understand will because it is performative.[19] Its only justification

---

18. Ibid., 32.
19. [Hebrew Editor's note: The linguistic philosopher J. L. Austin created the idea of performative speech. Austin distinguished between two types of speech. Constative speech makes a claim about reality, and we can therefore determine if this claim

is its being. It has no value as a logical assertion, as a statement or claim, and it cannot serve as an argument for anything. The will wants a specific act because it wants it,[20] and this is what makes "the highest will" absolute. Because it is will, it does not need to rely on any external justifications.

WITH ALL YOUR MIGHT

From the Baal HaTanya's perspective, only the act he calls "accepting the yoke" enables the infinite divine will to be present in the finite life of the individual. In the sermon under discussion, he calls this "*itkafiya*," "self-disciplining," or "*bekhol me'odekha*," "with all your might":

> The aspect of "with all your might," the soul's descent into the body, is a descent for the sake of ascent, to convert the animal soul. Through the aspect of self-disciplining and self-transformation (*itkafiya ve-ithafekha*) with all your might (*bekhol me'odekha*), without limit and beyond any intermediary, the highest light shines and is drawn down, but not by way of the order and system of emanation.... Through refining the animal soul "with all your might," a revelation descends from this aspect. This explains the idea that, "In the place where repentant people stand, even the

---

is correct or incorrect. Performative speech, in contrast, does not describe reality but rather engenders something within reality. You can't distinguish between the correctness or incorrectness of the statement, you just have to see if it really does something. "There is something which is at the moment of uttering being done by the person uttering." See John Langshaw Austin, *How to Do Things With Words* (Cambridge, Massachusetts: Harvard University Press, 1975), 60. For example, when a groom says in a Jewish wedding, "You are married to me," and the rabbi leading the wedding says, "She is married," the groom and the rabbi have created the marriage, enacting it through their speech. In this sense, will is performative. It creates a reality wherein something becomes desired/commanded by simple virtue of it appearing as will.]

20. The *musar* masters maintained that the action, as opposed to the intent, is what matters. The act is more than just a test of the reliability of the decision, it is the change itself. Any other change is within the subject and therefore is not within the essence.

completely righteous do not stand" (Berakhot 34b), with great strength, an instance of "with all your might."[21]

The Baal HaTanya is talking about an absolute act that escapes the finitude of human categories. In our context, he means that entering the normative framework of the commandments comes from will, not from "inner vitality." A person does not accept the commandments based on some understanding, but rather because of an intentional decision that constitutes passionate commitment and sacrifice. Meanings and concepts, or inner lights, only develop after a person takes up these specific garments, and even then, they do not serve to explain the existence of the commandments or justify keeping them. A person should not gravitate toward the commandments because of their inner light or because of the reasons for the commandments. He should gravitate toward them because of his encompassing will.[22]

"With all your might" describes the nature of a *baal teshuva*, a penitent person who stands outside the religious framework and relates to it dualistically and self-consciously. Without any compulsion or external justification, he puts himself into this framework. His self-overcoming comes from this duality and self-consciousness, which Chabad thought sees as the source of "the animal soul."[23] This lets a person overcome himself and escape the deterministic order that

---

21. Rabbi Shneur Zalman of Liadi, *Torah Ohr*, ibid., 33b.
22. This means that a person who tries to base his faith on the mitzvot and more generally on any external justification will always feel threatened, for any justification can ultimately be disproven. See Rabbi Shagar, "My Faith: Faith in a Postmodern World," in *Faith Shattered and Restored*.
23. The animal soul derives from the mirror that is a person's reflectivity, which stands before itself. It thus destroys immediacy and creates relations of control between subject and object. A person is not one of the things; he is torn from them and tries to impose himself upon them. In hasidic language, we would call this "*ani emlokh*" – "I will reign." Reflectivity creates what Chabad discourse calls "a sense of self," meaning the "I" that underlies a person's feelings. The animal soul gives a person the possibility of redemption in that reflectivity can detect the other and identify him as another "I," thus overcoming the person's own "I" by overcoming the subjective point of view that claims to be the center of the world. See more in Rabbi Shagar, *In the Shadow of Faith*, 91–112.

encompasses him. This order means two things. First, every effect has a cause. Second, the order of the world seems to deny religious values because it has a rhythm, sense, and meaning all its own. Duality and self-consciousness are in some sense a person's "encompassing lights." They exist beyond and outside of a person, enabling him to change his own nature precisely because they are not bound by the ordered framework, or inner light, of his life.[24]

To clarify, a repentant person who acts based on the aspect of "with all your might" does not overcome himself by using force against an opposing force. He does not "break" the order that encompasses him. Such an act, at the end of the day, would simply leave him in the same order. What I am talking about is the ability to take force itself and redirect it one hundred and eighty degrees. The aspect of "with all your might" is the very essence of the self, the will that posits the law as law, the fact that "I am thus and not otherwise." The order that binds a person is itself a function of will's arbitrariness, of it being thus and not otherwise. A person who passionately commits himself acts based on totally unbound will and enables himself to escape his own order. Moreover, he can even create a new order by taking up the garments of the commandments.

According to the Baal HaTanya, when a repentant person accepts the yoke of the religious world, it can open him up to creation and renewal, even regarding this world itself. He can renew the garments of Divine Presence in the world without simply accepting them as they are. Driven by the encompassing lights of will, he is equally free in relation to both himself and the world that he is accepting upon himself. Only thus can there be a cosmic renewal of divine revelation. Such a person is the opposite of a perfectly observant person, who lives with the same religious garments he has always had. Shut into his religious framework, the perfectly observant person cannot renew this framework, because he cannot imagine any other possible horizon. In contrast, the repentant

---

24. The journey of a repentant person parallels, on the human level, the divine contraction (*tzimtzum*). This too creates duality, when the infinite "withdraws itself." See Rabbi Isaac Luria, *Etz HeHayyim, Heikhal Adam Kadmon*, 1:2, *Derush Iggulim Veyosher*.

person knows that "things could be otherwise." He therefore relates dualistically to this framework and is free to draw down new lights from above his level, "with great strength."

THE SPECULUM: BETWEEN UNITY AND DUALITY

The Baal HaTanya thus distinguishes between two religious states or archetypes. One lives through the religious garments of the commandments in an unmediated form, while the other relates to them dualistically. The first archetype lives with what the Baal HaTanya calls a mindset of a speculum that shines (*aspeklaria hame'ira*), while the second lives with a mindset of a speculum that does not shine (*aspeklaria she'ena me'ira*):

> There are two types of mirrors. A speculum that shines is clear glass, through which you can see great distances, via direct light. It characterizes Moses, as opposed to the rest of the prophets. The Torah says that Moses saw "in a vision and not in riddles" (Num. 12:8), and the word "vision" (*mareh*) is vocalized as a masculine noun, representing a speculum that shines, with which a person can see distant things through direct light. So too the performance of the commandments.... By performing a commandment the soul delights in the glows of the *Shekhina* in the Garden of Eden... drawing down and revealing the light of the infinite.
>
> The rest of the prophets saw via a mirror, a speculum that does not shine, "And spoke parables through the prophets" (Hos. 12:10). The idea of a speculum that does not shine... is that a screen covers the glass. However, the screen is not thick enough to block out the light entirely. It is thin and wispy like a silver coating. Then when you look into this speculum, you see reflected light but you can't see direct light through the lens, so you only see... a mere figure, which can be seen with a speculum that does not shine.
>
> However, a speculum that does not shine surpasses a speculum that shines in one way. With it, you can see yourself, and what is behind you, which is impossible with a speculum

that shines.... The idea of a speculum that does not shine is the aspect of "with all your might."[25]

Someone who lives in a reality of a shining speculum experiences the light, meaning, and reason of the religious world, what the Baal HaTanya calls "light of the infinite," without any intermediary. He compares this to a telescope, through which "you can see great distances, via direct light." Though the telescope lets a person see things clearly and directly, it only shows him what is already visible, not what is hidden. In other words, a speculum that shines enables you to see the delight that the garment of the commandments reveals, but nothing beyond this. A person immersed in the garments of the commandments has great personal delights. However, being unified with the garments like this prevents him from seeing beyond the light of the garment, beyond the sense and meaning of his existing context.

In contrast, someone who lives in a reality of a speculum that does not shine experiences distance or even a certain degree of alienation from the religious world, but he can see beyond his level and thus learn about the thing itself. The Baal HaTanya depicts this via the image of a mirror, which enables a person to see what is hidden behind him. He lacks direct, unified contact with the object he contemplates, only seeing its reflection, but this distanced position is what allows him to see beyond what can be observed with a telescope.

I will try to clarify with an example from a different area, studying a passage of Talmud. A person learning a passage may, by virtue of being familiar with traditional talmudic discourse, understand what he is reading without being conscious of what exactly he understands. He can repeat the detailed back-and-forth of the arguments, asking questions about the passage and creating legalistic distinctions to answer them, arriving at new conclusions. However, with all of his engagement in Talmud study, he is entirely unreflective regarding what he did or did not understand. The student unites completely with the study, flowing with it undisturbed. Even his challenging questions are part of the rhythm and music of the study. The person never asks himself, "What

---

25. Rabbi Shneur Zalman of Liadi, *Torah Ohr*, 33a.

exactly did I not understand? What new idea came from refuting the challenge? Was something meaningful said? Did the answer 'really' answer the question?"

This form of study, wherein the "student, study, and studied material" are totally united,[26] contains meaning and understanding. It provides vitality and contentment to the student. Even for us, who are just listening in, the experience conveys something. However, since the student does not organize the ideas or examine them externally with conscious duality, something is lacking in the depth of the study and its conclusions. We certainly cannot ignore the way self-consciousness and external examination deaden the joy and natural flow of the study, what the Baal HaTanya calls "simḥa shel mitzva," "the joy of commandment." As mentioned in the sermon under discussion, each approach has advantages and disadvantages. The reflective approach seems artificial, but this is exactly what broadens the possibilities of the student, opening new doors of understanding that were once closed before him. In contrast, the spontaneous, flowing approach ultimately leaves a person locked into his preexisting understanding.[27]

Returning to the Baal HaTanya's sermon, a shining speculum finds its root in a life clothed in the garments of the commandments. The commandment is the tool that lets a person see the divine in his life. God reveals Himself in the world in the Shabbat-ness of Shabbat and the joy of the holiday, in the holiness of tefillin and the words of prayer. When a person lives in oneness with these garments, his life flows with faith and holiness.

---

26. [Translator's note: Rabbi Shagar is creatively referencing the unity of the knower, the knowing, and the known, an important idea in Chabad thought, with its background in Maimonides and the Neo-Aristotelian tradition.]

27. Let's say I have a talent for drawing. If I am satisfied with my talent, I am limited. However, if I learn to draw, I expand my abilities. Similarly, while some people rely on their natural talents, human development actually depends on learning. However, this is not without its problems. The same goes with Torah study. Some hasidic rabbis prefer to rely on inspiration when they speak Torah. Others, like Rabbi Nahman for example, prepared their teachings in advance, toiling over them, writing multiple versions of each teaching before presenting them publicly.

However, sometimes a person gains perspective on his world, suddenly becoming aware of the specific revelation of God that he encounters. He then asks, "What does the idea of God mean in the world? How is this idea revealed? Are the commandments the only garments of this revelation? What is the specific way that the commandments shape the revelation of God?" To the degree that a person reflects on the revelation that he experiences, he can see, for example, that the commandments highlight God as a commander and us as obeying His will. This is one of the garments through which religiosity is revealed.

On the one hand, reflectivity dulls the spontaneous and unmediated blaze possessed by someone who sees through a speculum that shines. On the other hand, this reflectivity deepens the religious stance of the person. It clarifies his religious language: how it functions, what it does, and how it colors life and divinity. According to the Baal HaTanya, this frees a person to see what is hidden, to comprehend what cannot be seen or recognized, namely the divine essence. Someone who lives with a shining speculum may identify God totally and absolutely with the light, delight, and the specific world in which he lives. In contrast, someone who looks into a mirror is aware that he is looking at a reflection, which is a possible but not exclusive revelation. The commandments in their essence are a garment without light, a vessel without content, derived from the divine will. He knows God is not an object and therefore cannot be confined to a specific world of meanings and signifiers. He opens his religious world to a broader horizon. In this sense, the Baal HaTanya would say that a person sees God in the act of the commandment: "'I beheld my Lord' (Is. 6:1), meaning with a speculum that does not shine, with which you can see God."[28]

* * *

"For the commandment is a candle, the Torah is a light" (Prov. 6:23). We began by speaking about the tension that exists deep within hasidic existence, the relationship between authentic action and the commandment framework that obligates actions regardless of their authenticity. This tension made hasidic thought bloom. Hasidic rabbis like Rabbi Mordekhai Yosef Leiner of Izbica and his student, Rabbi

---

28. Ibid.

Tzaddok HaKohen of Lublin, enriched the Jewish world with deep, exciting teachings on this topic. The Baal HaTanya's teachings also grow out of this painful tension, though he takes the surprising route of embracing the commandments specifically because of the alienation they bring with them. For him, the essence of God's will reveals itself as this alienation. The candle of the commandment really is the candle of God: "For it is you who light my candle; the Lord, my God, lights up my darkness" (Ps. 18:29).

On Translation and Living in Multiple Worlds

THE EROS OF WISDOM

"Greeks gathered against me / in the days of the Hasmoneans. / They breached the walls of my towers / and defiled all the oils. / But from the remaining jugs / a miracle was made for the lilies. / Wise men, eight days / established for song and rejoicing."[1]

Many commentators have viewed the holiday of Ḥanukka as the holiday which, more than any of the other holidays of the Jewish calendar, expresses the complex tension in the interaction between Torah and other wisdoms and cultures. To them, the war between the Greeks and the Maccabees was not really about independence and control, but rather a culture war over the purity of the "jug of oil," symbolic of the wisdom of Torah. In other words, it was seen as the conceptual battle that the Jewish religion fights against Greek wisdom. I want to present the discussion of this tension in the philosophies of Rabbi Abraham Isaac HaKohen Kook and Rabbi Nahman of Breslov. Through them, we can provide context to the religious phenomenon of new combinations of identities, enabling a broad range of new religious options.

Based on drafts written in 5762–5766 (2001–2005), edited by Yishai Mevorach and published in *The Remainder of Faith*, 87–108.

1. From the traditional Ḥanukka song "*Ma'oz Tzur.*"

Before I begin, I want to make a methodological point. It was once the case that signifiers such as "the wisdom of the Torah" and "the wisdom of Greece," as well as "the holy language" and "Greek language," were clear and distinctive. The Torah is, obviously, the holy canon of the Jewish people, and the holy language is their language, while Greek wisdom and Greek language belonged to the Greeks. Over time, however, these signifiers became broadened to represent two different spiritual realities. They no longer signified specific languages or books, but rather modes of being and thinking. Greek wisdom, therefore, no longer meant the wisdom of the historical Greek people, but a way of relating to reality. It should be noted that this definition of Greek wisdom is something that can exist even within the walls of the traditional Jewish study hall. A person reading homilies using these terms – both ancient rabbinic homilies and more modern ones – must determine how these signifiers are functioning in the homily at hand.

Another term used throughout Jewish history to refer to Greek wisdom is "external wisdom." Calling this wisdom "external" does not mean that it is believed to be evil. It simply belongs to the outside, meaning it lacks the intimacy of "being with itself," and it aims at the objectification of the knowledge. In this vein, the conflict between Torah and Greek wisdom does not have to focus on the context of the wisdom or the language used, but on intimacy and personal identity, the intimacy and identity that are the eros of the wisdom.[2] Out of this emerged the distinction between the wisdom of Greece and the wisdom of the Torah as between "the beauty of Japheth" and "the tents of Shem."[3] Japheth, the biblical father of Greece who symbolizes Hellenism, is the wisdom that is beautiful,[4] effective, but lacks all passion and intimacy; the Torah,

---

2. This is why the family and the struggle over family propriety are integrally connected to the struggle over wisdom, since both are essentially struggles over intimacy and identity.
3. "The tents of Shem" is a symbol in rabbinic discourse for the Jewish/Torah-governed space. See, for example, Genesis Rabba 63:6.
4. For example, the Jerusalem Talmud cites the halakha that a person is permitted to teach his daughter Greek wisdom because "it is like an ornament for her" (Y. Pe'ah 5:1).

however, represented by Shem, is a wisdom overflowing with meaning and intimacy, a revelation of existence and substance.

Japheth and Shem, external wisdom and internal wisdom, do not just oppose and reject each other, but also sustain each other and are imprinted on one another. On the one hand, the rabbis warned that "a person who teaches his son Greek wisdom is cursed,"[5] in a sense aiming to protect "the remaining jugs," the oil stamped with the seal of the high priest. On the other hand, the rabbis also read the verse, "God shall expand (*yaft*) Japheth and he will dwell in the tents of Shem" (Gen. 9:27) as: "The beauty (*yafiyuto*) of Japheth will be in the tents of Shem."[6] Japheth must participate in "the tents of Shem," in the intimate Jewish space.

The commandment of lighting the Ḥanukka candle expresses this tension. We light the candle of wisdom "just outside the entrance to the home."[7] On the threshold of the tent, against the darkness of Greece, stands the candle of wisdom.[8] This begs the question: In light of this complex relationship between Shem and Japheth, what is the real character of the Ḥanukka candle in showing the relation between Shem and Japheth? Is it a candle of strife, accompanied by the sounds of the war songs of the sons of light against the sons of darkness, a candle that drives away the darkness and removes the blackness by way of light and fire? Or, perhaps, is it that the candle relies on the darkness around it to a certain degree, specifically shining from the outside into the inside of the home?

GREEK LANGUAGE ON ITS OWN

At the inauguration of the Mizrahi movement's *beit midrash* for teachers during Ḥanukka of 1932, Rabbi Kook delivered a speech dealing with the topics of the holiday, including the relationship between wisdom and language:

---

5. Sota 49b, Bava Kama 82b, Menaḥot 64b.
6. Megilla 9b.
7. Shabbat 21b.
8. Ibid.

We have to note the additional distinction made by the rabbis: "Greek language on its own and Greek wisdom on its own" (Bava Kama 83a). We see that the main intent was to distinguish between content and style. Hellenism as wisdom, as a worldview – harshly injures holiness, profanes it and defiles it. Greek language, however, the language in terms of its expressive capacity, in terms of how richly it describes things – this is an entirely different matter. In the latter, there is no clash between the contents of frameworks of beliefs and ideas. In this, there is only an external improvement, which in and of itself does not make contact with or impinge upon internal matters.... The content we need not accept other than from our holy Torah.... This is not the case when it comes to style, to the external beautification of things....

After all the wars with Greece and Hellenism, the rabbis found support [i.e., scriptural proof] for importing linguistic aspects into the world of the Jewish people, in a verse, "God shall expand (*yaft*) Japheth and he will dwell in the tents of Shem – the beauty (*yafiyuto*) of Japheth will be in the tents of Shem."[9]

Rabbi Kook is delineating a boundary between the content, the light of the candle, and the medium and the language, the vessel that holds the light: "Greek language on its own and Greek wisdom on its own." This distinction means that pouring the light of Torah into the Greek container will not damage or change the light of Torah, but it is capable of contributing an external improvement which does not interact with or impinge upon the essential, internal matters.

Rabbi Kook is not referring to Greek language specifically, but rather the vessels of Greek culture, symbolizing for him Western culture writ large. These vessels are, for example, the tools of the academy – reflecting philological and historical research, as well as the rich

---

9. Rabbi Kook, cited in Rabbi Moshe Zvi Neriyah, *The Holidays of Rav Kook: Festivals and Seasons in the Life and Thought of Our Teacher Rabbi Abraham Isaac Kook, zt"l* (Jerusalem: Moriah Publishing, 1982), 183 (Heb.). This passage unquestionably reflects a significant facet of Rabbi Kook's thought, but as in other areas, Rabbi Kook's perspective on this includes multiple, often contradictory, voices about the tension at play here.

worlds of philosophy, literature, and linguistics, that Rabbi Kook was
not afraid to employ in writing his inspirations.

Furthermore, elsewhere in his writings, Rabbi Kook made the
following assertion:

> Any idea or thought that comes from academic research, investi-
> gation and criticism – when it is on its own, in its pure freedom,
> it would never result in evil, neither in the general faith shared
> by all people straight of heart and knowledgeable...nor in the
> foundation of eternal Israel and its connection to God who is its
> strength.... Only an evil heart, a straying heart...is what causes
> all the disturbance.[10]

Rabbi Kook had complete faith in the capacity of a thinking and prob-
ing individual to be unbiased and exact, such that he will not injure "the
general faith" or "eternal Israel." He believed that critical examination
of the Torah, even the improvement of its external garb through Greek
language and similar changes, will not overshadow its original holiness,
as long as the researcher and the inquirer do so with hearts clean of the
desires that can darken their conclusions.

Rabbi Kook tried to distinguish between the medium of language,
and the content expressed through it. In Greek language, he found the
possibility of externally improving the light. His thought should be
seen against the background of the Hegelian understanding according
to which the spirit clarifies itself and advances by way of reflection. The
spirit, which is the metaphorical Jewish jug of oil, clarifies itself by way
of Greek language, which examines it from an external perspective, inves-
tigates it, gives it definitions and conceptual characteristics. However,
Greek language does not defile it internally. To Rabbi Kook, the problem of "Hellenism" only appears when we try to import an "idol" into
the Temple of God (meaning the content itself), attempting to integrate
it with the wisdom of Greece: "Not so the Temple – it is dedicated for

---

10. Rabbi Kook, *Eder HaYakar* (Jerusalem: Mossad Harav Kook, 1967), 52.

inwardness, a foreigner may not approach there, the spirit of Shem, the spirit of Israel in its purity, needs to be preserved there."[11]

In contrast to Rabbi Kook, Rabbi Nahman of Breslov does not think that the Greek medium is indifferent to the light. He identifies Greek wisdom as a deep threat, and ferociously attacks attempts to connect the tents of Shem with the beauty of Japheth. Rabbi Nahman, who lived on the threshold of the bursting of the Enlightenment into the Jewish world of Eastern Europe, saw the clouds predicting its arrival, sensing the storm and the deep schism that it could and did create among faithful Jews: "Someone who, God forbid, learns books of scholarly research and philosophy introduces doubts and heresy into his heart…. Therefore, we do not find any person who was made fitting and God-fearing by books of scholarly research."[12] For this reason, he exhorts his devoted followers toward wholehearted naiveté as a way of life: "Fortunate is he who knows not of their books [i.e., of scholarship] and only goes naively."[13] He continues, "It is wisdom and great service to be like an animal,"[14] meaning people of naiveté and simplicity (an instruction, however, that he did not necessarily aim toward himself).

Rabbi Nahman understood that there is a structural opposition between Jewish and Greek discourse, as between a discourse that depends on revelation and a discourse that depends on human understanding, which originates in the individual's rebellion against revelation and the tradition. The foundation of the scientific method is a reliance only on logical and empirical proofs, seeing man as in constant opposition, lacking any readiness to nullify himself.[15] The characteristics of Greek language are not imprinted in the ideas of the culture, but rather in the essence of the discourse and in the nature of how the language functions. Rabbi Nahman therefore concluded decisively, "Though their words contain some ideas about good virtues and the like, even so, it is all nonsense, for they are more trouble than they are worth, for they

11. Rabbi Kook, cited in Neriyah, *The Holidays of Rav Kook*, 159.
12. Rabbi Nahman, *Siḥot HaRan* #5.
13. Ibid.
14. Ibid., #15.
15. For example, see Rabbi Nahman, *Likkutei Moharan* II 4:5–6; Idem., "Maaseh BeḤakham VeTam," in *Sippurei Maasiyot*.

greatly confuse a person's mind."[16] The confusion that concerned Rabbi
Nahman was not a confusion caused by problematic conclusions but,
primarily, a result of the very essence of the method.

Indeed, it is impossible to ignore the fact that Rabbi Kook's
approach is not at all simple. The Sages compared the day when the
Torah was translated into Greek to the day when the Golden Calf was
made![17] This statement rejects the distinction between form and content
that Rabbi Kook traces.[18] For the Sages, it was clear that the form shapes
the content and the medium penetrates into the core of the message.[19]

---

16. *Siḥot HaRan* #5.
17. *Masekhet Soferim* 1:7.
18. Rabbi Kook's words might have made sense in the Modern Era, when knowledge
and education took part in a technological-instrumental culture. In such a culture,
we could still distinguish between expression and essence, language and content.
However, that sort of position finds no purchase when it comes to, for example, Far
Eastern culture, or the cultural reality in which we live, wherein the medium is the
message. Thus, for example, people used to distinguish between social and natural
sciences like psychology and sociology, on the one hand, and the humanities, on
the other. These distinctions no longer exist – in fact, they never really existed at all.
There is no neutral, self-contained science isolated from any social, humanistic, or
spiritual axioms of some form or another. Similarly, all science is structured based on
axioms of just these sorts. The scientific method, as a tool, is not passive in regard to
the content to which it is applied, nor is it neutral about reality. It already inherently
makes certain theoretical assumptions about reality which cannot be avoided and
which inevitably structure the way a person thinks when employing it. The message
is not the ideas themselves, it is the assumptions built into the language.
    Indeed, we can see in our own era how the threat to religion and faith comes from
the entirely opposite direction as it did in the past: It's not the opaque rigidity of
matter that threatens the believer, but the very instability of matter itself. The world
of Jewish monotheism is a world of unity, order, stability, providence, discipline, and
meaning. This world had once been threatened by naturalistic determinism which
screened divine providence out of the world. Today, the world of monotheistic
faith is threatened primarily by the relativism, instability, and lack of an absolute
standpoint emerging out of the many branches of science and philosophy without
necessarily being explicitly connected to religion and theology. These are the things
that lead to damage to the covenant (*pegam habrit*) in its deepest sense. Again, I am
not talking about any specific idea, but about the axioms and assumptions built into
the methods of the different sciences.
19. This influence is bidirectional, in that when we adopt Greek language, it does not
remain the same Greek language as before. Think of it as when a yeshiva student

I would add further that Rabbi Kook's trust in the purity of the thinker and the scholar leads to the conclusion that if there is indeed a contradiction between the two – faith and research, light and vessel – the thinker and the scholar will be accused of lacking sincerity, of harboring a wicked heart. Similarly, the *musar* masters saw lack of faith as the result of deficient character traits. The existential damage caused by such a position might be unbearable. Parenthetically, I would add that even if we accept the *musar* position that deficiency in faith is deficiency of character, this still does not mean that this deficiency is a sin or that it is at all within a person's control, or that the existence of this deficiency is a reason to besmirch the inner integrity of that faithless person.

THE PASSION THAT IS IN SPEECH – THREE LANGUAGES

Of course, Rabbi Nahman instructed his devoted followers to avoid contact with the medium of Western enlightenment. He taught that since the jug of oil that is the Jewish soul must be pure, simple, and wholehearted, therefore, as noted above, the Sages said, "A person who teaches his son Greek wisdom" – and Rabbi Nahman would add, Greek language as well – "is cursed." As the *tzaddik* of the generation, however, Rabbi Nahman himself was destined for a different path: "In truth there is a great prohibition against being a scholarly researcher, God forbid, and against the teaching of books of wisdom, God forbid. Only the very great *tzaddik* can enter into this."[20] Rabbi Nahman saw himself as a *tzaddik*, an inspired person with intense religiosity and humanity. Entering the depths of the negative spirituality of heresy and denial was necessary for him to extract the fallen souls that fell into these traps as a result of the knowledge and skepticism of the Enlightenment.

This is why Rabbi Nahman sought to create "irregular combinations" in his teachings, calling the latter "*pesolet Eretz Yisrael*," "waste

---

learns philosophy or reads secular literature. The context from which he approaches the texts inevitably influences the content and the meaning of the reading and learning. With regard to Rabbi Kook, for example, we can say that Rabbi Kook did not really apprehend the spirit of the West – he read Kant like a yeshiva student. This fact has both positive and negative implications.

20. Rabbi Nahman, *Likkutei Moharan* II 19.

of the Land of Israel."[21] He allowed himself to translate the Torah into Greek, so to speak, even though he was aware of the high cost of translation. On the one hand, the translation "rearranges the combinations" of the original Torah. On the other hand, it enables the *tzaddik* to elevate the souls that are "far from the truth"[22] because of the Enlightenment which misled them. However, it would be a mistake to think that Rabbi Nahman only attempted this translation, which he calls "the Tree of Knowledge of Good and Evil," in order to redeem the fallen. I will attempt to show that in "Greek" language (the parallel in Rabbi Nahman's terminology being "idolaters' language"), Rabbi Nahman found a great option for religious devotion that is lacking in someone who only speaks the wholesome holy language. Translation is therefore necessary in its own right.

Rabbi Nahman's primary discussion of the translation of the Torah is in *Likkutei Moharan*, 23 wherein he teaches about three languages: the holy language, idolaters' language, and the language of translation. Of course, Rabbi Nahman himself switches between the language as a concrete language and the language as a meta-historical archetype, wherein a certain religious substance occurs:

> How great and precious is the value of the holy language, with which the world was created .... This is why it was called the holy language, "for any place where you find separation from inappropriate sexuality you find holiness" (Leviticus Rabba 24:6) .... For through the holy language, the desire for adultery, a bonfire, is bound and imprisoned ... for the holy spirit removes of the spirit of folly. This is an instance of repairing the covenant, which is an instance of the Holy Spirit, an instance of "spirit did not rise again in any man" (Josh. 2:11) ... for repairing the covenant is dependent on the holy language.[24]

21. Rabbi Nahman. *Likkutei Moharan* 81.
22. Ibid.
23. Rabbi Nahman, *Likkutei Moharan* 19.
24. Ibid., 19:3.

The holy language is a language where the one who speaks it is at one with himself. This is the creating language of God where "it says nothing that would make sense beyond the event itself."[25] This is a language without any gap between it and substantive reality; it does not maintain the duality of the signifier.

As we shall see below, this is speech spoken out of a consciousness of "I am who I am." It does not have a rule that precedes speech; the speech imagines and legislates the law for itself. This speech creates space for itself in "the secret of the contraction." This language creates without anything preceding it. This language is whole and perfect, because it does not point to an object that is separate from it; rather, it itself is the world. This language is not a signifier, and its primary function is not communication. It exists for itself in a world without duality.[26]

This language preserves the sexual covenant. Since the person who speaks the language of the covenant is not grasping for something outside himself, he is entirely faithful to what he is. The holy language is not "speaking about." It speaks in a language without any reflectivity whatsoever, and therefore structures a world entirely contained within the language. Rabbi Nahman expresses this by depicting the world as composed of the words and letters of the holy language.[27] A language like this can be experienced through the practice of Breslov or Chabad-style learning, with their various jargons, intuitions, movements, and inflections. This practice reveals that this is not study that refers to reality, but study that itself becomes reality. It does not have an object, but rather exists in itself – existence as a Breslov world or existence as a Chabad world.

---

25. Jacques Derrida, "Des Tours de Babel," in Difference in Translation (Ithaca and London: Cornell University Press, 1985), ed. and trans. Joseph Graham, 204.

26. In contrast to Wittgenstein, who claimed that there is no private language, Walter Benjamin claimed that the original language was exactly a private language. See Walter Benjamin, "The Task of the Translator," in Selected Writings, Volume 1: 1913–1926, ed. Marcus Bullock and Michael W. Jennings (Cambridge, MA, and London: The Belknap Press of Harvard University Press, 1996), 253–263; "On Language as Such and on the Language of Man," ibid., 70–73.

27. "Every individual thing has in it many combinations of letters with which the thing was created. Through the perfection of the holy language...the power of the letters in each thing is aroused and increased" (Rabbi Nahman, Likkutei Moharan 19:6).

The holy language stands in contrast to the idolaters' language of "the seventy nations" that corrupts the covenant. The language of "the all-inclusive evil, in which are contained all the evils of the seventy languages, is the burning bonfire that is the desire for adultery, in which all seventy languages are immersed and contained … for someone who damages the covenant destroys the holy language."[28] The root of adultery is the will to dominate and acquire; in order to acquire something, a person must externally position themselves against the object and dominate it.

According to Rabbi Nahman, the will to conquer and control via the word leads to corrupted sexuality. The connection between the corruption of language and damage to the covenant is the desire to know,[29] but from the outside. This desire causes splitting duality and corrupts both language and sexuality.[30] Language loses its unity with reality and becomes a language of duality and lack of faith, which "speaks about" and takes an objectifying and dominating stance. This distorts the point from which the substantive speech of the holy language is possible, and thus does not allow the language to speak or the event to occur. Instead, it inspires doubt and a desire to prove, hindering itself.

A linguistic situation like this makes the covenant impossible because the language creates gaps between the individual and reality. Speech like this can never accept itself or enable the speaker to be what and how he is. Similarly, in other teachings, Rabbi Nahman states that this language presents itself as beautiful, wise, and refined, but ultimately is insincere speech. This is the language of the "demon Torah scholar," who uses his linguistic aesthetics and rhetoric to place an impression on the other and dominate the other via language:

> Jewish demon Torah scholars receive their Torah from the demons, who possess a fallen Torah…. This is why all of their speech is parable and poetry, and wondrous intonations…. And

---

28. Ibid., 3.
29. [Hebrew Editor's note: It is worth noting that this knowing has a clear erotic context – "The man had known his wife, Eve, and she conceived and gave birth" (Gen. 4:1).]
30. Damage to the covenant is bound up with imagination, in the "woman" which Lacan said does not exist. This is Lilith.

these Torah scholars…exhaust people who come to hear their Torah and sermons, and people think that this will bring them some value, that they will come to know how to serve God. However, these people do not gain anything of value, for the Torah of these scholars lacks the power to guide people in the good path, for the bad can never produce the good.[31]

THE TREE OF KNOWLEDGE –
THE LANGUAGE OF TRANSLATION

Like a Ḥanukka candle standing between the interior of the house and the outside world, Rabbi Naḥman locates the language of translation between the holy language and the language of the idolators, seeing this translation as within the aspect of the Tree of Knowledge of Good and Evil, and of the "*kelipat noga,*"[32] which is between holiness and the impure spiritual entities.

We can identify the evolution of the concept of language in the case of "the language of translation" as well.[33] Originally, this term referred to a concrete language, the Aramaic language that the ancient Sages used to translate holy texts into a language spoken and understood by everyone. In Rabbi Naḥman's teaching, the translation changes from a concrete language to a signifier of reality, specifically the reality of the language of translation that stands at the threshold:

> The Tree of Knowledge of Good and Evil is the language of translation, which is an intermediary between the holy language and the language of the seventy nations…. The language of translation is an instance of "an insightful (*maskalet,* lit. prudent) wife" (Prov. 19:14)…for the language of translation is both good and bad, sometimes it makes you smarter (*maskil*) and sometimes it makes you bereaved (*meshakel*). The foolish wife

31. Rabbi Naḥman, *Likkutei Moharan* 28:1.
32. [Hebrew Editor's note: A kabbalistic term meaning the "grey area" between holiness and impurity (the *kelipot*)].
33. [Translator's note: See the methodological discussion near the beginning of the sermon.]

[i.e., the idolaters' language] seduces the wise wife [i.e., the holy language] by way of the insightful wife... which is the language of translation, Aramaic....

The primary construction and completion of the holy language is only through casting away the evil of the translation and picking out the good from the translation for the holy language, for through this the holy language is completed...for the primary construction of the holy language is through translation. By picking out the good from translation for the holy language and casting away the evil in it, all seventy languages fall, an instance of "language falling on language."[34]

The language of translation is born in the sin of the Tree of Knowledge of Good and Evil,[35] wherein it distinguished itself from the *temimut*, the wholesomeness, of the holy language. Rabbi Nahman teaches that, from this position, it can turn in one of two ways. It can make you smarter or it can make you bereaved – truly a knowledge of good or knowledge of evil.

The language of translation as "knowledge of good" manifests through beautiful speech spoken for the sake of heaven. It is serious speech that attunes itself to the substantiality of the original holy language. While the speaking of the holy language occurs enveloped within itself, translation stands outside it, granting a necessary reflectivity to someone who speaks the holy language and whose world-existence is bounded by it. However, this reflectivity does not try to appropriate the holy in a meager instrumental manner. Rather, the translation

---

34. Ibid. 19:4. [Translator's note: The Hebrew for "language falling upon language," "*lashon nofel al lashon*," is a classical rabbinic idiom for repeated sounds connecting different words or phrases.]

35. I would add that this is the difference between the opinions of Walter Benjamin, in his "On the Task of the Translator," and Rabbi Nahman. Benjamin thinks that translation can fall into the sin of the Tree of Knowledge, while Rabbi Nahman thinks the sin of the Tree of Knowledge is what causes the translation, which is the primary construction and completion of the holy language. [Hebrew Editor's note: This is why Rabbi Nahman once chose not to give his sermon to his followers on the holiday of Shavuot, because "they are not really sinners that I should tell them Torah...for there are many teachings that are made specifically by sins" (Rabbi Natan of Nemirov, "*Nesiyato Veyeshivato Be'uman*," in *Ḥayei Moharan* #18).]

"illuminates the letters of the holy language," aiming to clarify the spoken letters, not conquer them.[36]

This seems similar to Rabbi Kook's Hegelian outlook described above. For his part, Rabbi Nahman calls translation "an insightful wife," because someone who speaks the language of translation can see the language's great spiritual richness precisely out of their distanced position from it. According to Rabbi Nahman, however, the language of translation does more than that. It also transforms the holy language itself, changing its primary sense: "The primary construction and completion of the holy language" requires translation, beyond just a sharper appearance of the contents of the holy.

> Laban the Aramean ... called it "Pillar-Witness" ("*yegar sahaduta*") (Gen. 31:47), Jacob raised the translation to the holy language, and therefore called it "Pillar-Witness" ("*gal'ed*") in the holy language ... because the primary construction of the holy language is through translation.

Rabbi Nahman's words pivot around the biblical event wherein Jacob and Laban the Aramean build a pillar as a memorial and a testimony: "Jacob took a stone and set it up as a pillar. Jacob said to his kin, 'Gather stones.' They took stones, they made a mound, and they ate there by the mound" (Gen. 31:45–46). Laban calls the pillar "*yegar sahaduta*" in Aramaic, and then Jacob calls it "*gal'ed*" in Hebrew. Rabbi Nahman identifies Jacob's action as elevating the language of Laban the Aramean into the holy language. The translation changes the original meaning of the holy language when Jacob assimilates the language of translation, Aramaic, into the holy language, thus creating a change in the concepts of holiness itself – the strange language penetrates the feeling of at-homeness of the holy language, creating a new formulation – "Pillar-Witness," "*gal'ed*."

Practically speaking, we are talking about Rabbi Nahman's creative capacity as the *tzaddik* of Breslov. In particular, we are speaking of

---

36. Like the Ḥanukka candles that "are holy and may not be used, only looked at" (from the prayer "*Hanerot Halalu*," which originates from *Masekhet Soferim* 20:6, and is recited after the lighting of the Ḥanukka candles).

the capacity for religious renewal, radically interpreted as the renewal of Divine Presence in the world, or at least as the renewal of the vessels which enable this presence.

Rabbi Nahman's involvement in telling fantastic stories – what he called "tales from the days of yore" – shows a self-awareness of this approach.[37] The main purpose of Rabbi Nahman's stories is to "translate" – to transport the listener to a magical, mythical world "from the days of yore." This world has kings and princesses, fantastic lands, and wondrous creatures, including giants, spirits, men of the woods, and a prince made entirely of precious stones. Not only do these worlds not belong to holiness or religious discourse, for the most part these stories do not have any Jewish characteristics, nor even particularly religious ones for that matter.

Furthermore, the stories expose the listener to a world of experiences that is entirely disconnected from the religious experience and its normal, accepted forms in the traditional Jewish world. However, because Rabbi Nahman, leader of a hasidic court and grandson of the Baal Shem Tov, is the one telling the story, this throws the religious listener into a fantastic literary world to which he himself does not belong. Rabbi Nahman renews certain religiosity incorporating elements that were initially strange to it. For example, when Rabbi Nahman describes the Messiah as a trapper living in the wilderness or as a hippie playing songs,[38] he is not just signifying him with random and interchangeable characteristics. He intends to color the image of the Messiah anew. In this manner, the language of translation functions to complete the holy language.

Understanding that we must raise translation into the holy language causes us to read the words of the rabbis with which we opened in an original fashion: "The beauty of Japheth will be in the tents of Shem." In the words of Rabbi Kook, we saw the classical understanding of this

---

37. See Rabbi Shagar, "Introduction to *Sippurei Maasiyot*," in *Life of Yearning: New Interpretation to the Tales of Rabbi Nahman of Breslov*, ed. Roee Horen (Jerusalem: Yediot Sefarim, 2010), 11–31.
38. As Rabbi Nahman described him in his "scroll of secrets." See Zvi Mark, *The Scroll of Secrets: The Hidden Messianic Vision of R. Nachman of Breslav* (Boston: Academic Studies Press, 2010), 94–103.

statement: we clothe the tents of Shem, the holy language, in the beauty of Japheth. This is only the first stage of translation, wherein we clothe the Torah in external terminology, clarify the spirit, and make its richness known. However, Rabbi Nahman's approach goes even further. Sometimes, Japheth is clothed in the tents of Shem. This is the important and crucial process by which the world of religious terminology – the holy, fear and love of God, and devotion to God – receives new and unexpected meaning from the elements and formulations assimilated into it.[39]

SPLIT IDENTITIES AND FAITH AS A COVENANT

We should emphasize that Rabbi Nahman repeatedly notes that "the Tree of Knowledge of Good" can easily plummet to become "the Tree of Knowledge of Evil." In such a case, the language of translation serves as a means for the idolaters' language to appropriate the holy language, preventing its creative renewal and thus leading to duality and religious barrenness: "Know that this foolish wife is all the evil of the seventy languages. These languages cannot draw on the wise wife, on the holy language mentioned previously, except by way of the Tree of Knowledge of Good and Evil, with which they seduce her and infect her with pollution."[40] Furthermore, we cannot ignore the fact that Rabbi Nahman believes that only the *tzaddik*, the perfect person, is able to translate. For his followers, of course, he laid out a different path, guiding them toward the innocent naiveté of the holy language.

The catch is that today we have to ask whether, possibly, our situation has changed and has become one of "And Your people are all righteous (*tzaddikim*)" (Is. 60:21), where we have no choice but to exist in the space between inside and outside, between identity and strangeness. Rabbi Nahman's guidance toward innocent naiveté and simplicity does not correspond to our way of life. Of course, I am not invalidating religious

---

39. We find the same process elsewhere in Rabbi Kook's writings, but with the roles reversed. See Rabbi Kook, *Orot* (Jerusalem: Mossad Harav Kook, 1993), 155–156. The dilemma he raises is not whether it is possible to dress Judaism in modern clothing, but whether and how it is possible to dress universal human ideals in Jewish clothing. See Rabbi Shagar, *Tablets and Broken Tablets* (Alon Shevut: Mekhon Kitvei Harav Shagar, 2013), 128–129.
40. Rabbi Nahman, *Likkutei Moharan* 19:3.

naiveté. Heaven forbid, I do not see it as bad faith or self-deception. However, for most of the young men and women whom I know, translation is the only option for sincere and substantive religious lives. Some have said that entering into these negative aspects using the language of translation is too dangerous. They dismiss me, because how could we succeed in what Rabbi Nahman saw as the task of "the very great *tzaddik*"? To them, I quote a passage from Rabbi Kook that says that anyone who does not suffer from spiritual descents has no chance of religious ascent. He supports this with the verse, "The rocks are a cover for hyraxes" (Ps. 104:18).[41] The soul endangers itself by its very descent into the world, but it is only through this descent-endangerment that it can ascend.

For better or worse, we are citizens of multiple cultures. We live in more than one world of values. We cannot deny this situation, nor do we wish to deny it, for denying it would be self-denial, leading to deep, radical injury to our religious faith itself. Rabbi Nahman's approach to translation is therefore not only desirable, but also the only option for elevating the translation that is already happening anyway.

I see great importance in this characterization, because we do not meet the true problem of the encounter between Torah, religious life, and the Greek language – which affects us through the media, academia, literature, and much more – only after years of learning in yeshiva and starting our studies at university. Rather, this problem presents itself at a much earlier stage: in the religious education that we receive, in the foundation of our faith, and in the limited constructs through which we grasp it. We therefore need a meaningful religious-spiritual-Jewish alternative, or we will not be able to avoid the internal contradictions that bear a heavy price. We can see those contradictions in various forms: the formerly religious (called in Israel "*dati'im leshe'avar*," or "*datlash*"), the laissez-faire religious (called "*dati lite*"), Ultra-Orthodox nationalists (called "*haredi leumi*," or "*hardal*"), and so on.[42]

In order to understand the special position of the Religious Zionist and the translation work he must do, we need to distinguish between multiple, split identities, and compartmentalized identities. I

---

41. Rabbi Kook, *Orot HaKodesh* (Jerusalem: Mossad Harav Kook, 1985), vol. 2, 314.
42. [Editor's note: This paragraph was originally a footnote in the Hebrew.]

call the latter concept the "two worlds" mindset, and it is exemplified by Professor Yeshayahu Leibowitz.[43] Leibowitz lived in two worlds: the scientific-secular and the religious. He did this by opening an unbridgeable gap between them, one that he would never bring together. He lived with a contradiction, but it remained external to him without reaching his subjectivity or personal identity.

In contrast, the multiple, split identity model puts together different worlds without recognizing compartmentalized truth-values or different realms of truth. We should describe the Religious Zionist soul as a soul that lives not in one world, but in many worlds which it likely cannot integrate. It does not compartmentalize them – Torah study versus labor, faith versus science, religion versus secularism – but rather manages a confusing and often even schizophrenic set of relationships between them.

Nowadays, a new type of religiosity has developed, one that cannot be defined by its location on any graph, but rather is scattered across many different, what one might even call "strange," centers. This religiosity does not define itself with the regular religious definitions, but enables a weaving of unusual identities, integrating multiple worlds – a pathless path. This new approach presents a deep personal faith that, in my opinion, carries the potential for religious redemption.

Where does this capacity for integrations and combinations come from? Answer: that very same deep personal faith. This faith is not faith in something, but rather an act of self-acceptance. It recognizes a deep core of covenantal eros, which enables the freedom to translate and to make integrations, combinations, and connections that our fathers never dreamed of making.[44] The existence of faith is not dependent on some sort of faithfulness of a given individual; its roots are much deeper than

---

43. See, for example, Yeshayahu Leibowitz, "Religious Praxis: The Meaning of Halakha," in *Judaism, the Jewish People, and the Jewish State* (Jerusalem and Tel Aviv: Schocken Books, 1976) 13–36 (Heb.); Idem., "The Individual in Nature and in History: A Faith Perspective," ibid., 357–359.
44. I am talking about, for example, someone who is careful about minor commandments as much as the major ones, to the point where we would define him as "*mehadrin*" Orthodox, yet, still, he remains "unorthodox-Orthodox." His foundation, his language, his cultural and social contexts, and the connections between these contexts, give rise to an Orthodox existence without any orthodoxy, an existence

the consciousness of its bearers. It is present as a fact, and this gives rise to the covenant. Only thus can a person accept his faith and his way of life, a necessary condition for the novel religious phenomenon we are suggesting.

Let me clarify. Faith is not some essence a person has, some essence that a person discovers within himself after removing all the excess, superficial layers around his true and stable identity. Whether its conscious source is a social construct, linguistic usage, national inheritance, etc., faith as a "form of life" cuts across the various spheres of identity. Faith is a leftover excess that a person cannot remove or digest. This leftover excess destroys the dichotomies and definitions of identity, readying them for encounter and creation. Faith is not grounded at the pole of any fixed image, nor is it part of a "whole." It does not fall under any definition; therefore, it is often manifest as nonconformity. Ecstatic and multivalent figures sprout up before our eyes. They cannot be located at any one place in society, for their faith comes from a much deeper place.

This faith is a remainder, a psycho-theological symptom manifesting as inexplicable stubbornness. It is a willingness to be on the losing side of the world simply because "this is who I am and this is who I want to be," without conscious justification.[45] As per Rabbi Nahman's words we saw earlier, the deep meaning of preserving the covenant is eros – the small jug of oil with the seal of the high priest, the harmony of an individual with who and what he is, without locking himself into a specific societal identity. He can be who he is, whoever that may be.

I will add that self-acceptance opposes attempts by a religious community to enforce observance of yarmulke, prayer, fringes, phylacteries, etc. These attempts make religiosity forced, cowardly, and alienating, all of which are causes of spiritual superficiality in the religious community. A religion that sees itself as at war for its survival is a religion without depth and roots.

---

purged of the unbearable Orthodox weightiness, entirely replaced by a lightness that is unbearable to the true *mehadrin* Orthodox person. This believer's presence undermines the classic distinctions and definitions of orthodoxy and secularity.

45. Based on Eric Santner, *On the Psychotheology of Everyday Life: Reflections on Freud and Rosenzweig* (Chicago and London: University of Chicago Press, 2001), particularly the second and third chapters.

In contrast, a Chabad idiom is useful for conveying an ontology of a religious reality overflowing with eros: "I am who I am, which is the innermost aspect of the highest will,"[46] a dimension that exists "beyond and in excess of its meaning."[47] Chabad discourse says that this dimension "cannot be named, nor alluded to by any extraneous detail of the conventions of language at all,"[48] because this reality promises eternity, the guarantee that "I will be as I will be" (Ex. 3:14).

This characterizes the personality of the ideal believer, for whom preserving the covenant means faithfulness to his eros, to his interest and participation. This faithfulness enables the exciting and impossible encounter between parallel and contradictory worlds.

We read, "A *tzaddik* lives by his faith" (Hab. 2:4). This faith comes from man's acceptance of its presence in his life. It is a readiness to live with what the Creator gave him. At this level, the believer's act comes from the qualities of humility, self-nullification, and not-knowing that open him up to devotion to what he is, to what was given to him, and to achieving oneness and personal identity. This is not the type of identification that compares the concrete manifestation of a person to a picture, symbol, or idea that exists "outside," beyond him. Instead, the revelation of the person as he is, without any "beyond" – this is me.

"A *tzaddik* lives by his faith" – if this is his faith, whatever it may be, by it will he live.

> However, when the *tzaddik* enters into these seven wisdoms, he holds strong and remains steadfast in his faith, an instance of "a *tzaddik* lives by his faith." For "a *tzaddik* falls seven times and gets up" (Prov. 24:16), for the great *tzaddik* takes the path of these seven wisdoms, even though he could slip and fall because of a stumbling block…. However, the *tzaddik* falls seven times, and gets up through faith.[49]

---

46. Rabbi Shneur Zalman of Liadi, *Likkutei Torah*, Pinḥas, 80b. In this context, "the innermost aspect of the highest will" is the eros.
47. Santner, *On the Psychotheology of Everyday Life*, 44.
48. Rabbi Shneur Zalman of Liadi, *Likkutei Torah*, Pinḥas, 80b.
49. Rabbi Nahman, *Likkutei Moharan* II 19. [Editor's note: The seven wisdoms are a refer-

ADDENDUM: TRANSLATION AND LANGUAGE[*]

Should we see the project of translation as an ideal, or as something meant only for those who have fallen low? This question is irrelevant for us – we have no other option. If we want to turn the Torah we learn into a Torah of life, we have no choice but to translate. Every person, every student, must ask, "Where am I? What is my place?" For example, we cannot study Rabbi Nahman's writings the same way that Rabbi Koenig[50] studied them and taught them in his lectures. If we tried to do so, we would just end up with a poor imitation of Rabbi Koenig, one that misses the whole point. At the same time, a Breslov Hasid might not sense the same deficiency we feel when it comes to staying within the world of the holy language.

We should note that not every language external to Torah can serve as a language of translation. The language of academic study cannot necessarily be a language of translation, because it is often an objectifying language – it constrains the holy language rather than encouraging it to bloom. Every now and then it flickers, but in general it cannot express the world of holiness.

To deeply understand the meaning of the "holy language" and the "idolatrous language," and the unique function of translation, we must turn to Walter Benjamin. In his essay, "On Language as Such and on the Language of Man,"[51] he puts forward a concept of language based on the first chapter of Genesis, which describes God creating by way of speech – "God said 'Let there be light'" (Gen. 1:3). Benjamin

ence to the seven medieval fields of study: Grammar, Rhetoric, Logic, Arithmetic, Geometry, Music, and Astronomy. In traditional Jewish writings, the term became a generic term for secular knowledge.]

[*] Based on a draft written in 5764 (2004) and a lecture on *Likkutei Moharan* I, 19 delivered in 5765 (2005), edited by Netanel Lederberg and published in *Expositions on Likkutei Moharan*, vol. 1, 227–229.

50. Rabbi Elazar Mordechai Koenig (1945–2018) was the spiritual leader of the Breslov hasidic community in Safed.

51. Walter Benjamin, "On Language as Such and on the Language of Man," in *Walter Benjamin: Selected Writings*, ed. Marcus Bullock and Michael W. Jennings (London: Belknap Press, 1997), vol. 1, 62–74. The essay reworks a letter from Benjamin to his friend Gershom Scholem, who dealt extensively with the significance of the Hebrew language in Kabbala.

distinguishes between two types of language. The language of God is pure language, wherein every word expresses the essence of what it names. However, there is also the language of man, which came about later due to the primordial sin and the multiplying of languages after the Dispersion. This fall shifted language from describing things as they are in their essence, to denoting different objects in a strictly functional, instrumental manner. Hence scientific language, which sees this world as nothing more than a collection of objects.

With this distinction in mind, we can see that Rabbi Nahman does not understand the holy language as a specific language, "Hebrew," but as a type of speech. The holy language is that same, world-creating divine speech. This language does not use speech to convey information – like mystical language, it creates a relationship. It expresses the world as it is, without bias.[52] Benjamin formulated this wonderfully in the following lines: "What does language communicate? It communicates the mental being corresponding to it. It is fundamental that this mental being communicates itself in language and not through language.... The answer to the question, 'What does language communicate?' is therefore, 'All language communicates itself.'"[53]

In light of this, we can say that translation itself is not a fall – the sin of Adam made translation necessary in order to rectify the idolatrous language. The holy language exists in oneness, without the duality of a person and his surroundings, so it cannot fall into the trap of "I will reign!"[54] – damaging the covenant by reducing everything that exists into tools of the speaker, nihilistically refusing to let language speak or

52. See the following formulation: "The other conception of language [as names], in contrast [to the "bourgeois" conception], knows no means" (ibid., 65). And further on he writes: "Language, and in it a mental entity in it, only expresses itself purely where it speaks in name.... In stepping outside the purer language of name, man makes language a means" (ibid., 65–71).

53. Ibid., 63.

54. A common term in hasidic thought, originating in the school of Rabbi Dov Baer ben Avraham of Mezeritch. See his *Magid Devarav LeYaakov* (Jerusalem, 1990), 125 (§73). The Tzemaḥ Tzedek notes the origin of this term in the *Idra Rabba* section of the Zohar (Menachem Mendel Schneersohn, *Derekh Mitzvotayikh*, 170b). See footnote 23, (p. 98) to the chapter, "Screen for the Spirit, Garment for the Soul" above, as well as Rabbi Shagar, *Faith Shattered and Restored*, 34.

let the event take place. The holy language does not reflect reality, but is itself reality. In this sense, it parallels Jewish existence – "Israel arose in thought."[55]

The concept "speech of faith" refers not to speech about faith, the content of which deals with faith, but to speech that is itself faith. The teachings of Breslov do not function as "speaking about" – the speaking fundamentally comes from a place of oneness, of speech that precedes reality. The same is true of Torah study: its holiness derives not from its content, but from its source in oneness.

Despite this, we still need translation, because ultimately, we live in a dualistic world.[56] We are not one with reality – we gaze at the world from the outside. This state has both advantages and disadvantages. Translation takes place in rectified speech and in reflective Torah study. The idolatrous language is dangerous because it brings with it desire, adultery, and an alienated, interest-focused gaze – what Rabbi Nahman called "damaging the covenant." In truth, there is not much difference between merely gazing at something from the outside and objectifying it in order to control it. In any case, while studying reflectively, we may lose our grasp on mystical language and our deep Jewishness, but we gain a depth and realism which does not exist in "speech of faith."

This understanding of translation does not emphasize transferring the original language into the language of translation. As per Benjamin, translation means attempting to discover elements of the original language – of the divine language itself – within the language of translation and drawing the two close together. In this way, the source itself, pure language, gains reality in the dualistic world. In the context of Torah study, the process certainly must include studying Torah reflectively, but this duality itself must be elevated. This means

---

55. See Rabbi Nahman, *Likkutei Moharan* 14 and 74. Rabbi Shneur Zalman of Liadi discusses this at length in the second chapter of the *Tanya*.
56. In Fichte's terminology, the language of God parallels the primordial state wherein only the infinite subject exists. The hard, alienated, external world takes form only after the subject forgets himself. See Samuel Hugo Bergman, *History of Philosophy – Vol. III: Jacobi, Fichte, Schelling* (Jerusalem: Mossad Bialik, 1979), 42–57 (Heb.). Regarding oneness and duality in our existence, see Rabbi Shagar, "Between East and West," in *Tablets and Broken Tablets* (Alon Shevut: Mekhon Kitvei Harav Shagar, 2013), 106–135.

shifting from searching for meaning – which puts the "I" at the center and tends to turn the text into an object – to receiving inspiration, where I give myself over to the text, to holiness, to the word, and where my "I" becomes nothing more than a vessel.[57]

---

57. For more on Benjamin's understanding of translation, see Walter Benjamin, "The Task of the Translator," in Benjamin, *Writings*, 253–263. There, Benjamin writes that pure language forms through the encounter between the original and the translation. For more on this, see Jacques Derrida, "*Des Tours de Babel*," in *Difference in Translation* (Derrida analyzes Benjamin's essay). For this idea in the thought of Franz Rosenzweig, see Franz Rosenzweig, *The Star of Redemption*, 366, as well as elsewhere in the *Star*.

Purim

Laugh and Be Free

T he happiness of Purim is an ecstatic happiness, differing significantly from the typical happiness associated with other Jewish holidays. Hasidic texts explain that this ecstatic happiness is joy (*sason*), a word used many times throughout the Bible to refer to a joy that is bound up with eros, with the happiness of a bride and groom:

> As a youth espouses a maiden, your sons shall espouse you; and as a bridegroom rejoices (*masos*) over his bride, so will your God rejoice (*yasis*) over you. (Is. 62:5)

> Who is like a groom coming forth from the chamber, like a hero, eager (*yasis*) to run his course. (Ps. 19:6)

Conveying a similar idea, the expression, "The sound of joy (*sason*) and the sound of happiness, the sound of a groom and the sound of a bride" appears in the prophecies of Jeremiah, as well as in the context of salvation.

Based on a draft written in 5765 (2005), edited by Eitan Abramovich and published on the website of the Institute for the Advancement of Rabbi Shagar's Writings (shagar.co.il).

The Mitteler Rebbe of Chabad (Rabbi Dovber Shneuri) said that the difference between the happiness of the other holidays and the happiness of Purim is like the difference between happiness contained in a vessel and happiness above and beyond any containment.[1]

The happiness of the other holidays is the *simḥa shel mitzva*, the happiness of commandment, a Jewish happiness that flows from a sense of security, of *bitaḥon*, in Jewish existence and its value. We feel secure not necessarily in what will happen to us, but in the value of what we do. This deep happiness contains fullness and satisfaction, faith and security in the value of our life. This happiness finds its clearest expression in acts of kindness. The act of giving, not receiving, is what makes us truly happy, because giving willingly is a gesture that expresses a deep faith in its own value. Through giving, we create our existence as a worthy existence of infinite value. We gain this satisfaction by doing good, by believing in Jewish destiny and the value of our life. Thus, the happiness of the holidays is the happiness of both commandment and kindness. This happiness comes from a sense of fullness and concrete reality; it is the happiness of existence in its very existence, and of the Jew in his Jewishness.

In contrast, the ecstatic joy of Purim comes from loss, "And if I am to perish (*avadeti*, from the root of 'loss'), I shall perish!" (Est. 4:16). Within this loss and absence, we discover an unlimited presence, even more than in the fullness of presence itself. The terror that underlies the joke of the Megilla, the very ability to turn this capricious and frightening story into a joke, creates this ecstasy.

Ecstasy is ignited by an encounter in which both parties are strongly present. It is experienced as a fleeting moment, as an experience of "Whom else have I in heaven? And having You, I want no one on earth" (Ps. 73:25). More than anything else, a person desires presence itself, a presence embodied in a fleeting, non-existent moment which cannot be held onto and which defies all vessels. A person wants to dissolve in a love that is as strong as death. This event arises from the transience of the encounter, from how today we are here and tomorrow

---

1.   Rabbi Dovber Shneuri, *Shaarei Ora* §99.

we are not, with no sense of security. In this lack of security, there is an existence much deeper and more infinite.

Ecstasy comes from the happiness of the encounter contrasted with its fleeting background and its basis in loss. It also derives itself from overcoming the nothingness and terror that come with these factors. This ecstasy reveals the infinite nature of human existence exactly because of its transient nature and lack of a need to be anchored. In experiencing ecstasy, we discover that we can turn arbitrariness into fate and accept it.

The writings of Rabbi Isaac Luria depict Purim as an exceptional situation, occurring specifically against the background of the crisis of exile. The word "*megilla*" alludes to "*hitgalut*" – revelation. The Purim story's combination of random events and opportunity enables the temporary and transitory revelation of what is generally concealed and hidden.

The happiness of a life that draws on the nothingness, the revelation that "we are here," the presence of the moment in its momentariness, all turn into joy. After this, when the present turns into the past, joy turns into a home, into being-with-yourself. However, the moment of the encounter contains an infinity that transcends the home, and which, in turn, sanctifies the home (just as the "ecstasy" of the death of Aaron's sons was the condition for the creation of the Tabernacle). Rabbi Nahman writes similarly regarding the holiness of Shabbat, which is stronger for our awareness of its temporary nature, of the loss that threatens it: "Due to the immense pleasure of the extra soul that arrives on Shabbat, we immediately begin to feel pain and yearnings over the loss of the soul with Shabbat's departure."[2]

In ecstasy, I find out that I can be free and independent. Discovering this very real possibility is enough to ignite me with "darts of fire, a blazing flame" (Song. 8:6), with the joy of "a bridegroom rejoicing over his bride." Overcoming the self by way of the joke, the greatest form of self-sacrifice, structures the life and the self around a center of lightness, not weightiness.

In this manner, the *orot hatohu*, the lights of chaos, are gathered in the vessels of rectification, which do not see themselves as independent entities but rather as representing something beyond themselves.

---

2. Rabbi Nahman of Breslov, *Likkutei Moharan* I:126.

Just as God exists while not in existence, we believe in God without believing. This deeply personal paradox is vital for creating the feeling of at-homeness, keeping the home from becoming a prison.[3] Only then will the finished Tabernacle be fitting for the *Shekhina* to descend into it, thereby satisfying the desire of He who spoke and brought the world into being.

The joke of Purim is a joke of negation and nullification, embodying the complete opposite of the affirmative fullness of the rest of the year. In contrast to the forbidden wickedness and nihilism of mockery, the rest of the year is characterized by moral intelligent speech.[4] On Purim, however, we turn the mockery towards the Amalekite mocker himself, making it a negation of negation, a joke about Haman's joke. This self-overcoming and double negative create a positive, an affirmation that appropriates for itself the power of the negativity of nothingness.

---

3. [Editor's note: The original Hebrew for "personal paradox" is *"perversiya,"* literally, "perversion," a reference to Slavoj Žižek's idea that disbelief actually intensifies observance. See Žižek, *The Puppet and the Dwarf,* 53–54. The book was translated into Hebrew by Resling Press as *The Subject Supposed to Believe.*]
4. While it is generally forbidden to mock others, idolatry is an exception to this prohibition. See Megilla 25b.

The Story of the Palace –
The Joke as Nullifying
Existence

"T he Story of the Palace," one of Rabbi Nahman of
Breslov's tales, is a version of a more famous story that also appears
in the collection of stories known as *One Thousand and One Nights*. In
Rabbi Nahman's version, however, the ending is changed. Rabbi Nahman loved stories like these, which he heard from his followers, and he
typically adapted them and retold them in new versions. This is his version of the classic story:

> Once there was a king who built himself a palace, and called for
> two men to paint the palace. He divided the palace between them,
> with the first man responsible for painting one half of the palace,
> and the second man responsible for painting the other half. He
> set a deadline for them, by which time they were required to have
> painted it. And the two went to work.

Edited by Odeya Tzurieli and published in *Lottery is Destiny* (Efrat: Yeshivat Siach
Yitzhak, 2005), 93–100 (Heb.).

The first man strove and struggled greatly and taught himself the art of painting and frescoing well, until he had painted the half for which he was responsible, with a very beautiful, wondrous painting. He even painted it with pretty, wondrous depictions of animals, birds, and the like.

The second man paid no mind to the king's decree and did nothing. When the deadline by which they were supposed to have finished their work drew near, the first had already finished his labors, and the paintings on his half were very beautiful and wondrous. The second man began to look at himself and what he had done in wasting all his time, rather than heeding the decree of the king.

The second man began to think about what to do, for certainly the few, limited days that remained were not enough to teach himself the art of painting and to paint his half in such little time, because it was very close to the deadline. He focused himself, taking a moment to think, and he went and covered his half with a shiny tar, which he had made entirely black. The tar was like the lens of a real mirror, such that you could see yourself in it like in a real mirror. He went and hung a curtain in front of his half, dividing his half from that of the first man.

When the king's deadline arrived, the king went to see the products of the labor they had done in that time. He saw the first half, which was painted with very beautiful, wondrous paintings. There were paintings of birds, etc., painted in wondrous ways. The second half was covered with a curtain, with darkness beneath it, and you couldn't see anything underneath it.

Suddenly, the second man arose and pulled back the curtain, and the sun shone and all of the wondrous paintings shone in his half, because of the tar which shone like a mirror. This meant that all of the birds, along with everything else painted in the first half, all of them appeared in the second half. Everything the king saw in the first half, he also saw in the second. Additionally, all of the wondrous vessels, all of the furniture, etc. that the king had brought into the palace, could all be seen in the second half. So too anything that the king might want to bring into the palace would all be reflected in the half of the second man. The matter was pleasing to the king, etc. [More than this, I do not remember.][1]

THE IMPORTANCE OF THE STORIES

While Rabbi Nahman believed that folk stories contain a hidden layer, he also believed that the stories had become distorted and therefore needed to be fixed and told anew:

> In the stories that the world tells, there are many hidden things and very lofty matters – but the stories have been spoiled because much is lacking from them and they are also mixed up, and they do not tell them according to the order, telling at the end what belongs in the beginning and vice-versa, and so on. But really in the stories that the world tells there are very lofty concealed matters.... In addition, sometimes he [Rabbi Nahman] told a story from the stories the world tells but he added much to them, exchanging and repairing the order.[2]

He further claimed that he thought this form of literary creativity was a mystical act:

> And the Baal Shem Tov, of blessed memory, was able via a story to perform unifications (*yihudim*). When he would see that the upper channels were spoiled and it was not possible to repair them via prayer, he would repair them and unify them via a story.[3]

Repairing the story is an act of mystical repairing, a rectifying of upper worlds! Rabbi Nahman also claimed that the ancient Kabbala was learned by means of stories.[4]

---

1. Note from Rabbi Natan of Nemirov, author of the book. Story is from *Ḥayei Moharan* §98.
2. From Rabbi Natan of Nemirov, Introduction to *Sippurei Maasiyot*.
3. Ibid.
4. Ibid.

Thus, in the case of the "The Story of the Palace," Rabbi Nahman rectifies its ending. In the original ending, the king "takes care of" the protagonist. The king reverses the protagonist's "scheme" and pays his reward not with real money, but with a reflection of money in a mirror, fighting fire with fire. While this ending is unquestionably wittier and more elegant than that of Rabbi Nahman's version, Rabbi Nahman changes the ending: "The matter was pleasing to the king, etc."

Why does Rabbi Nahman "ruin" the end? Why "was the matter pleasing to the king" at all? Is this not unjust to the first man who "strove and struggled greatly"? Why does the second man receive reward? Rabbi Nahman seems to ignore the ethical problem caused by his version of the story's end.

RABBI NAHMAN TELLS STORIES ABOUT RABBI NAHMAN

We must realize that in the gallery of characters in Rabbi Nahman's stories, the king is always the King of kings, God. Meanwhile, as with all Rabbi Nahman's characters, the time-wasting character is Rabbi Nahman himself. As someone once said, Rabbi Nahman only tells stories about Rabbi Nahman. In this way, our story unquestionably depicts Rabbi Nahman's self-conception.

Why? Rabbi Nahman felt himself to be a clown, a copycat of a true "rebbe," an imposter. Like the second man, he believed himself incapable of painting a real painting, rectifying true rectifications; his rectifications reflected only what he was not. Knowing this, we might more boldly say that the two characters, the serious man and the clown, are both Rabbi Nahman. He lived both what he was and what he was not. This, in Sartre's language, is the fundamental human failing.[5] In any case, Rabbi Nahman, in his unique way, turned this failure into victory, through a joke: Behold, the king validated it!

Dialectics like these are common in Rabbi Nahman's teachings. In one passage (*Likkutei Moharan*, I, 6), Rabbi Nahman teaches that a

---

5. Jean-Paul Sartre claimed that a person by nature is never where he is. A person's consciousness always transcends to a space in which he is not, and this is why he lacks any essence. See Jean-Paul Sartre, *Being and Nothingness*, translated by Hazel E. Barnes (New York: Philosophical Library, 1956), pp. 47–70.

repentant person must always repent for his repentance. This second repentance originates in the idea that the first repentance was not "serious." This is not in the regular religious sense of insincerity, but rather the very fact that it is defined as "repentance of this world," regular religious repentance, is what makes it not serious. It is simultaneously something you have to do and something you have to grin about doing. This is how Rabbi Nahman overcomes the Sartrean-Amalekite dualism.

In another passage, Rabbi Nahman reiterates this dialectic in a different manner.[6] This passage discusses the wings with which a *tzaddik* flies. The wings are "an instance of revealing a handbreadth and concealing a handbreadth":

> Sometimes, with regard to people, he [the *tzaddik*, meaning Rabbi Nahman] is the aspect of revealing: he reveals himself and draws closer to people. Other times he is the aspect of concealing…. And not only does he distance himself and keep aloof from them … but he also becomes the subject of questions and doubts. In time, because he has greatly distanced himself from them, their minds become twisted and confused…. He must therefore conceal and cloak himself in small matters [i.e., acts of foolishness].

The flight of the *tzaddik* emerges from the dialectic of revelation and concealment. In this passage, however, the posture is exactly the opposite of that in our story. Ultimately, the "true" Rabbi Nahman is the Rabbi Nahman that we cannot grasp. The way he reveals himself to his followers is by "concealing and cloaking himself in small matters," until "their minds become twisted and confused." Only through shattering social norms and blowing up the serious, dignified image of the "rebbe," was Rabbi Nahman able to keep flying.

THE CONCLUSION OF THE STORY

There are three possible endings the story could have had. In the first, the king gets angry and punishes the protagonist. In the second, the reverse happens and the king is pleased – this is Rabbi Nahman's ending. In the

---

6. Rabbi Nahman, *Likkutei Moharan* 63.

third ending, the ending of the story in *One Thousand and One Nights*, the king pays the protagonist with fictitious money, an ending that provides a fitting resolution to the inner dilemma of the story.

A closer examination renders the first option invalid. The king cannot punish the protagonist; the latter was too clever for that. The protagonist effectively set a trap for the king with his scheme. If the king gets angry and punishes him, it would expose the king's own lack of a sense of humor, lack of benevolence, and so on. The supremacy of the protagonist over the king on display is intolerable. The king has no way out but to accept the joke. The lesson of the story: the *tzaddik* can lead God into a vicious circle, thereby forcing his will upon God.

In the original ending, in *One Thousand and One Nights*, the king escapes the situation by turning the tables on the lazy artist. He overcomes the latter by using his cleverness against him. The money, the lazy artist's reward, is exactly as fictitious as the service he performed. This is the sweet vengeance of the king, enabling him to come out on top.

Rabbi Nahman fixes the story's ending, making it so that the king is willing to accept the joke. Moreover, he accepts the joke happily, as if the artist had really performed the job he was assigned. Why?

On a preliminary level, we might say that the king was just as willing to accept the funny joke and the protagonist's ingenuity and inventiveness as he would have been to accept serious work. The goal was to please the king, and that can be achieved through a joke as much as through serious labor and toil. What makes one better than the other?

However, there is a deeper level, which is revealed from the story's personal context. This is the true story, the story about Rabbi Nahman himself, about the *tzaddik* and God. In this context, the king clearly prefers Rabbi Nahman not just because of his humorous ingenuity, but because his clever joking is itself a higher realization of the divine.

The *tzaddik* exists in crisis, sensing the deep falsity of his existence. In this world, he can never realize the divine truth for which he so longs. His ability to turn his crisis into a joke expresses the divine infinitude much more than any attempt to shrink the gap between human and divine through serious service of God. The spirituality of the world and its infinitude are, therefore, specifically expressed through the fictitious *tzaddik*.

The joke is a variation of the famous hasidic concept of *bitul hayesh*, nullifying existence. Ultimately, God does not need concrete reality. Indeed, according to Hasidism, reality itself does not really exist. God thus prefers the *tzaddik*, whose service is not on the level of concrete reality. Choosing to emphasize the fact that concrete reality doesn't exist, the *tzaddik* makes a joke out of it. The clearest expression of this is the mockery involved in making a farce out of the king's command. The prerequisite to ensure that this mockery is indeed *bitul hayesh* and not a desecration of the holy, God forbid, is the *tzaddik's* tireless and subversive ingenuity. Ingenuity is an outcome of bold spirit and heroism, manifest in the ability to turn a crisis into a joke. In making the joke, one is thus breaking free from the shackles of the world.

In seeing what he is, Rabbi Nahman sees what he is not. His readiness to accept this is itself *bitul hayesh*. Undoubtedly, this idea challenges the serious, dignified perspective of religion. *Bitul hayesh* is not something that exists, it is something that does not exist. It is an "unbearable lightness" (or so it seems to his followers), and the joke is its clearest expression. This is also the solution to the ethical problem of how the con artist can receive a reward just like the hard worker who put in the real effort (the analogy here is, of course, effort in the service of God). From an internal perspective, the light, unserious effort of the former is no less effort than the second, and it is no less – and perhaps even more – risky and sincere.

This story is just one of a series of Rabbi Nahman's stories dealing with "self-less self," such as "*The Indik*," "*Maase MiBitahon*," "*Maase BeMargalit*," and others.[7] The lesson of all of these stories is about rejecting the idea that a person's self has a solid core.[8] Hasidism classically places great importance in searching for yourself, and the crushing, frustrating labor of *bitul hayesh*. In these stories, this is achieved through

---

7. See the analysis of "*Maase MiBitahon*" in *The Remainder of Faith: Postmodern Sermons on Jewish Holidays*, 35–41, and the analysis of "*Maase BeMargalit*" in *We Will Walk in Fervor*, 139–146.
8. [Hebrew Editor's note: Rabbi Nahman famously said that a person's level of spirituality does not depend at all on the root of his soul, and that the primary difference between a *rebbe* and a hasid is not in the inner quality of their souls but in their willingness to work hard (*Shivḥei HaRan*, 25–26).]

the approach that sees the self as *ayin*, as nothingness, and because it is nothing, it can be shaped. This frees the hasid from the inescapable entanglement that his consciousness places in front of his will to nullify his concrete existence.[9]

Rabbi Natan, Rabbi Nahman's disciple, writes that he does not remember the end of the story. It is therefore possible that according to Rabbi Nahman, as in *One Thousand and One Nights*, the *tzaddik* is paid with fake money. However, for Rabbi Nahman, this fake money is truly real. God answers the *tzaddik's* joke with His own – not out of competitiveness or a test of wills, but as part of a good-hearted game.

Even if Rabbi Nahman did not end the story like this, he certainly had it in mind. In any case, we are allowed to fix even Rabbi Nahman's own ending, and that is my joke.

THE JOKE AND *MESIRUT NEFESH* IN CHABAD HASIDISM

Significant portions of Chabad Hasidism today have developed a rigid metaphysical ideology and seriousness. However, originally, Chabad also included moments of jest. We will quote a few lines from the Baal HaTanya's *Torah Ohr*:

> The word "Yitzhak" derives from a language of jest, "*tzhok*," and enjoyment, which is the revelation of the supernal enjoyment

---

9. [Hebrew Editor's note: The regular hasidic path contains a paradox, which the leaders of Chabad pointed out long ago: the service of *bitul hayesh* is perhaps the only service where putting in effort causes failure. If a person makes a big deal out of the act of self-nullification, this means that he takes himself seriously, that "there is what to nullify," and the attempt at nullification itself inflates his existence. Rabbi Nahman releases us from all of this: you don't need to nullify your essence. *You simply do not have an essence.* The moment you gain this recognition – which can only be achieved by making a joke of yourself – you achieve oneness with God. Elsewhere, Rabbi Nahman suggests a reason why the Baal Shem Tov never succeeded in reaching the Land of Israel and the high spiritual levels attainable there, unlike him. The reason, he says, is because the Baal Shem Tov was not able to bring himself to the level of smallness as Rabbi Nahman did when he himself was on the way to the Land of Israel (*Hayye Moharan* §140). As explained in *Shivhei HaRan* (9–13), the primary element of smallness is lowering your self-image through acting foolishly and in a degraded manner.]

to the righteous in the future yet to come, as it is written, "You created the Leviathan to sport (*lesaḥek*) with" (Ps. 104:26)…. The matter is that "the Lord God (*YHWH Elokim*) is a sun and a shield" (Ps. 84:12). The name "*Elokim*" is a shield, a sheath for the name "*YHWH*" that creates something out of nothing…like the analogy of the light and glow of the sun through a screen and curtain…. Because of this sheath and shield, the creations are rendered an instance of concrete existence and a separate thing…. Thus, the soul has descended below in order to serve and rectify the aspect of darkness and concealment…. This is through *bitul hayesh*, turning *yesh* into *ayin*, nothingness…. This is through *mesirut nefesh*, self-sacrifice, in prayer and through Torah and mitzvot. This is "God (*Elokim*) has made laughter for me" (Gen. 21:6), for the essence of supernal jest and enjoyment is drawn down through the name "*Elokim*." This is like the laughter of ministers over a new thing; like a lion's struggle with another animal. For from the renewal derives the jest and enjoyment. Such is an instance of *bitul hayesh*…[10]

In short, the Baal HaTanya is saying that creation has no ontic reality of its own. It resides within its root in the supernal source, the divine infinite, and the name *YHWH* constantly gives it life. Only the name *Elokim* conceals this ontological truth. This name is the source of both the concealment and the ignorance that allows us to take ourselves to be independent beings. Created beings are responsible for returning existence to nothingness, returning the world to its original state, where there was no concealment, objectification, or alienation at all. Then creation and the individual within it will return to being immersed in the pure, divine inwardness that is free and infinite.

This process of concrete reality dissolving into nothingness is the meaning of *mesirut nefesh*, self-sacrifice, in the work of Torah and the commandments. In this dissolving, a person gives up on his narcissistic ego in favor of a higher, infinite awareness. He dies – so to speak – in his yearning for God. However, this yearning is the root of the jest and

---

10. Rabbi Shneur Zalman of Liadi, *Torah Ohr*, 17b-18a.

enjoyment. And it unquestionably contains an erotic element, as the Baal HaTanya continues later in the passage to expound the verse, "Isaac was laughing (*metzaḥek*) with Rebecca his wife" (Gen. 26:8).

Like a ridiculous occurrence wherein we discover the full nothingness and insignificance of something that had previously seemed so serious or important, so too the nullification of existence reveals the true ridiculousness, the joke, of concrete reality. Both the jest and the enjoyment come from this nullification of existence. This is not the space to explore the enjoyment that comes along with jest. It is sufficient to note that the jest is symbolized by Isaac, who is depicted in Kabbala as symbolizing *paḥad*, fear. Isaac is the one who was bound on the altar to die, according to the divine command. Isaac, the one who suffers, is also the person who laughs with both *mesirut nefesh* and enjoyment, thereby showing that Thanatos and Eros walk arm-in-arm at this level of *bitul hayesh*.

The Joke of the Megilla

A SHARP CRITIQUE

The Megilla is unquestionably a parody. The author of the Megilla shoots his sharp arrows of irony in every direction.[1] He aims them first and foremost not at Haman, but at Aḥashverosh. There are many examples of this, such as the exaggerated description of Aḥashverosh's feast that opens the Megilla:

> At the end of this period, the king gave a banquet for seven days in the court of the king's palace garden for all the people who lived in the fortress Shushan, high and low alike. [There were hangings of] white cotton and blue wool, caught up by cords of fine linen and purple wool to silver rods and alabaster columns; and there were couches of gold and silver on a pavement of marble,

---

Based on a draft written in 5765 (2005), edited by Yishai Mevorach and published in *The Remainder of Faith*, 109–120. Rabbi Shagar composed this sermon against the backdrop of the decision by Ariel Sharon's government to enact "The Disengagement Plan" from northern Samaria and the Gaza Strip. The plan brought the meaning of law and justice, as well as their very legitimacy, to the forefront of communal debate.

1. In light of this ironic characteristic, the serious way in which the halakha relates to the Megilla is basically a second-order joke. In order to notice this joke, one simply has to look at people sitting in *shul*, with me among them, reading and listening to the Megilla, terrified of missing a single word and thereby failing to fulfill their obligation, for "it is a mitzva to read all of it" (Maimonides, *Mishneh Torah, Hilkhot Megilla* 1:3).

alabaster, mother-of-pearl, and mosaics. Royal wine was served
in abundance, as befits a king, in golden beakers, beakers of varied design. And the rule for the drinking was, "No restrictions!"
For the king had given orders to every palace steward to comply
with each man's wishes. (Est. 1:5–8)

The mocking description of the feast reaches its crescendo when the king
is not satisfied with "displaying the vast riches of his kingdom and the
splendid glory of his majesty for one hundred and eighty days" (v. 4),
for half a year, no less. His ostentatious urges lead him to command:
"Bring Queen Vashti before the king wearing a royal diadem, to display
her beauty to the peoples and the officials, for she is beautiful" (v. 11).

At the center of the Megilla's critique stands the law, called "*dat*"
throughout the Megilla. This critique first arises in the Vashti narrative.
Drawing on the Purim-esque spirit of the Megilla, we can describe it
like this: an urgent cabinet meeting is called together in Aḥashverosh's
palace, with the highest legal forum of the seven officers of Persia and
Medea, all well-versed in the laws and procedures, in order to determine
"what the correct procedure is for dealing with Queen Vashti" (Est.
1:15). Aḥashverosh acts exclusively within the framework of the law, of
course. The legal debate reaches the almost too meaningful conclusion,
"that every man should wield authority in his home and speak the language of his own people" (v. 22). This is such an important decision, of
course, made by such important people and of such great significance, to
be distributed via all means of communication available to the empire:
"Dispatches were sent to all the provinces of the king, to every province
in its own script and to every nation in its own language" (v. 22). The
dramatization here is ridiculous and makes fun of itself. They are legislating something unbelievably trivial and self-evident. The Persian empire
was multi-national, "a hundred and twenty-seven provinces from India
to Ethiopia" (v. 1), so linguistic pluralism was the status quo, and these
events took place well before feminism.

The author of the Megilla is thus mocking and deriding
Aḥashverosh's devotion to the law, a devotion that stands in total con-
trast to the caprice and hedonism he displays throughout the Megilla.
The king's hedonism comes out in the ridiculous description of the

young women being brought to Shushan and waiting in line, cleansing in "the twelve months' treatment prescribed for women. That was the period spent on beautifying them: six months with oil of myrrh and six months with perfumes and women's cosmetics" (Est. 2:12). All of this is in order to pleasure the king.[2]

IN THE THEATER OF THE ABSURD

Exacting in law and acting exclusively via legislation and government, Aḥashverosh exemplifies exaggeration, lack of proportion, and kitsch, alongside caprice and unrestrained indulgence. The Megilla returns to this depiction throughout the book, combining Aḥashverosh's fastidiousness with the lauded Persian bureaucracy, which itself does not escape the irony and joke of the Megilla unscathed. The runners and riders of the king's steeds go to-and-fro, carrying messages from Haman one time and from Mordekhai the next. This state is a state of law and "an edict that has been written in the king's name and sealed with the king's signet may not be revoked" (Est. 8:8).

The only problem is, this joke is not at all funny. A deep terror lies at its foundation. Aḥashverosh's caprice, anchored in law, is lethal to the point of absurdity. The scariest piece of it all is that the different actors in the Megilla – from Mordekhai and Esther to the young girls and the eunuchs who guard the gates – do not seem to notice how absurd it all is. They think that the law is as serious and as logical as it gets. The Megilla's parodic depiction only amplifies the dread. A frivolous and mundane story about a feast, a banished queen, another crowned in her place, and a man who will not bow, leads to the harshest of penalties, way out of proportion to the frivolity of the story, yet enshrined in

---

2. The irony is expressed in a comparison between the verses of the Megilla and their parallels in the Torah. David Henshke finds a playful example in the formulation, "for that was the full period spent on beautifying them" (Est. 2:11), which shows up only one other time in Scripture: the death of Jacob in Egypt. "For that was the full period of embalming" (Gen. 50:3). Putting these two verses together creates the impression that the women are being embalmed in their perfumes. See David Henshke, "*Megillat Esther*: Literary Disguise," in *Hadassah is Esther: Essays on Megillat Esther*, ed. Amnon Bazak (Alon Shevut: Tevunot, 1997), 93–106 (Heb.).

serious law, "to destroy, massacre, and exterminate all the Jews, young and old, children and women" (Est. 3:13).

The joke of the Megilla is a response to a deep, bitter despair over an absurd situation: the author of the Megilla discovers that what ought to be serious (the law) is a parody, and the parody, incredibly, makes it all the more funny and absurd. The price of entry into the Megilla's theater of the absurd is life and death. Where does this lead? To laughter, or, perhaps, despair.[3]

SO SHALL BE DONE

The story of the Megilla is not funny. On the contrary, even if the Jews are ultimately saved, the threat of genocide inspires more fear than laughter. So why does the Megilla make all of this into a joke? The danger is tangible and serious; Esther's fear, Mordekhai's cries, the mourning, and the sackcloth…these are not nothing. Where did the author get the ability to turn the frightening into the funny? To tear away the mask and reveal the ridiculous in the foolish?

The Megilla seems to provide a clear answer.[4] The ability to laugh at all of this comes from the knowledge that the actors are just puppets controlled by a hidden puppeteer, shaping the performance according to His own intentions. However, this knowledge does not override the awful human experience of chaotic happenstance and of the total absence of any guiding hand behind the events of the Megilla. In fact, the reverse is true. Paradoxically, the divine decree highlights the human happenstance rather than erases it.

The story teaches about the incidental and unstable nature of Jewish existence specifically, and of human existence in general. For example, regarding Mordekhai, the Jew who sits at the gate of the king: Who is the "man whom the king desires to honor" (Est. 6:11), Haman or Mordekhai? The clear answer would seem to be Mordekhai. He

---

3. Here we must ask, is it possible to look at the Nazis with a parodic gaze and turn them into the object of a joke? Is it possible that, despite the terror that wells up within us when we remember them, they are simply ridiculous, and that this ridiculousness makes their actions even more terrifying and absurd?

4. Particularly in its inclusion as one of the holy books of Tanakh.

wears the king's royal clothing, he is led around on a horse, and he is ultimately chosen to be the king's right hand. However, is he guaranteed a secure and redeemed existence after he rises to greatness? Various verses indicate a parallel between Haman's position before his fall from grace and Mordekhai's position after his rise, suggesting that he is anything but secure.

Furthermore, the phrase, "So shall be done for the man whom (*kakha ye'ase la'ish asher*) the king desires to honor" (Est. 6:11), describing Mordekhai as he rides on the king's horse, shows up in only one other place in Tanakh, Deuteronomy 25:9:[5] "His brother's widow shall go up to him in the presence of the elders, pull the sandal off his foot, spit in his face, and make this declaration: 'So shall be done to the man who (*kakha ye'ase la'ish asher*) will not build up his brother's house.'" In light of this, should we not read "*kakha ye'ase la'ish*" as spitting in Mordekhai's face? "Here today, gone the next," as they say – yesterday Haman, today Mordekhai, and tomorrow, who knows?

Indeed, hasidic texts see the phrase, "*kakha*," "so" or "such," as central to the Megilla: "'So shall be done for the man whom the king desires to honor' – the use of 'so' is not accidental."[6] Furthermore, "When reading the '*Kiddushat HaKeter*' liturgy,[7] one should keep in mind '*KaKhaH*,' an acronym for 'the crown of all crowns (*keter kol haketarim*).'"[8]

The fickle caprice of this world, with its baseless and meaningless rises and falls, merges with the absolute divine decree. There is no attempt to explain the different steps of the narrative individually, but rather the entire story is shifted to a different plane. Human happenstance does not reign in the story, nor a lofty meaning that is hidden from human eyes, but the decree of the King of the Universe: "A king's command is

5. This was also noted by Henshke.
6. Rabbi Menachem Mendel Schneerson (*Tzemah Tzedek*), *Yahel Ohr Al Tehillim* (New York: Kehot, 1953), 533.
7. [Hebrew Editor's note: "*Kiddushat HaKeter*" is a prayer said on Shabbat and holidays by the community during the repetition of the *Amida* and is considered one of the high points of the service: "We will crown you, Lord our God; the angels, the hosts above, with your nation Israel, the masses below."]
8. Said in the name of the Baal Shem Tov. See "Things I Heard from my Teacher," in Rabbi Yaakov Yosef HaKohen of Polonne, *Toldot Yaakov Yosef* (Warsaw, 1941), 209.

authoritative, and no one can say to him, 'What are you doing?'" (Eccl. 8:4). Why does he do what he does? It is "so" (*kakha*) – because it is what he wants. Citing their founder, Chabad Hasidism says regarding the divine meaning of, and reason for, creating the world: "*Oyf a tayva iz ken kashya nit*" – you can't ask questions about a desire.[9]

Opposite the kingdom of Persia, ruled by the capricious Ahashverosh, stands the kingdom of God. As R. Yohanan taught: "Anywhere [the Megilla] simply says 'king,'" it is referring to the King of kings."[10] The writer of the Megilla is not thinking of the happenstance that reigns in the kingdom of Persia, but the absolute "*kakha*" of the King of kings.

How does this focus lead to the unrestrained joke about the terrifying situation of the Megilla? Isn't the only laughter possible in this situation the laughter described in the verse, "He who is enthroned in heaven laughs; the Lord mocks at them" (Ps. 2:4)? God sits and laughs because, from heaven, the events really are funny. However, here on earth the joke is not funny at all: "The heavens belong to the Lord, but the earth He gave over to man" (Ps. 115:16).

For the writer of the Megilla, the events happen in a different plane, that of the absolute divine decree, and the joke exists on that level. This is an ecstatic joke, which opens our awareness to the possibility of its liberation, occurring when the individual accepts the arbitrary "*kakha*" quality of his life. Deep pessimism leads a person to the ecstasy of liberation from the need for proof, liberation from teleological support for reality. Pessimism can liberate us from dependency because we have despaired of everything.

The divine decree does not comfort, nor does it make the Megilla's joke less painful. It does not explain or grant meaning to the events that happened or will happen, and it cannot guarantee that Haman's plans will not come to pass in the future. The joke is fully aware of fate,

9. Quoted in Rabbi Menachem Mendel Schneerson (Lubavitcher Rebbe), *Torat Menachem: Hitvaaduyot* (Brooklyn: Otzar HaHasidim, 1953), 31.

10. "R. Yudan and R. Levi in said in the name of R. Yohanan: Anywhere in *Megillat Esther* where it says 'King Ahashverosh,' the text is referring to Ahashverosh; anywhere it simply says 'king,' the text is referring to the King of kings" (Midrash Aba Gurion [Buber edition], 1, on Esther 1:10).

leading to an ecstasy in which negativity, bitter despair, and suffering are lived as they are. In the crises of life, a person discovers that there is no way to deal with how things turn out. However, there's also no need to deal with them, since life happens for itself, entirely for itself.

IF I AM TO PERISH

The religious idea of trust, *bitaḥon*, like the joke, accepts within it the reality of arbitrariness and dread. Hasidism teaches that this sense of trust is the result of passionate commitment and sacrifice. In other words, trust comes after the terror and fear of the incidental and the absurd, not before; it cannot be achieved without them. Moreover, trust is not a support that lends a person strength, turning the whole game into something predetermined. From a certain perspective, this trust is itself the terror: "If I am to perish, I shall perish" (Est. 4:16), says Esther. What she does not say is, "I am certain of my success." On the contrary, she expects to die, because of her trusting, passionate commitment. This trust is not free of terror; it is present in the terror itself, since it is open to anything that might happen.[11]

Mordekhai also does not promise Esther anything. He does not say, "I am certain that you will succeed," but, "Who knows, perhaps you have attained to royal position for just such a crisis?" (Est. 4:14). He is certain that salvation will come for the Jews from somewhere, but he is not at all secure in his and Esther's personal attempt at salvation. He says, "Who knows?" not, "I know."

Mordekhai and Esther's responses inspire astonishment, and perhaps even a challenge: if they could see divine providence before their very eyes, shouldn't they have believed fully? Esther, unbelievably, was selected as queen at exactly the right moment. Everything that was happening pointed to the fact that God "gives the medicine before the disease" and enthroned her in order for her to save the Jews, and yet, despite this, the doubt persists: "Who knows?" This is because "who

---

11. If we turn this discussion to the actual situation that crouches by our door, Esther would not have said, "I am certain, the 'disengagement' definitely won't come to pass...."

knows" is the flip side of *kahka*, just "so." In a place where things happen just "so," the "who knows" persists.

The response to the divine "*kakha*" is the human "*kakha*," things are just so, creating the feeling of *bitaḥon*. This is the secret of Purim: passionate commitment without any security, with nothing upon which it can rely – that is where *bitaḥon* can be found. The trust in God does not come from some tangible protection and goodness that He gives. On the contrary, the lack of security, normally something from which people flee, actually provides an individual with the opportunity to commit and to feel secure in God no matter what He does.

The Midrash says, "The apple tree is shunned by all people when the sun beats down, because it provides no shade. So too all the nations refused to sit in the shade of the Holy One, blessed be He, on the day of the Giving of the Law."[12] The lack of security that comes from the divine "*kakha*" creates the human ability for passionate commitment. It creates a sense of *bitaḥon,* of trust in God that does not provide any security regarding the future, nor any sense of meaning or ultimate purpose. This is because the divine is beyond human comprehension – not because a person's perspective is so narrow that it cannot encompass the divine, but because the divine will itself lacks meaning. Correspondingly, trust in and devotion to God are illogical processes.

Life's arbitrariness represents an opportunity for passionate commitment which can enable a person to escape the human frameworks that bind him and to cling to the divine essence. A person who accepts the divine "*kakha*" overrides his conceptual, human consciousness that demands explanation and justification. He accepts his life as it is, in its arbitrariness. Why? Just so!

APPENDIX: THE LAW AND THE JEW

The author of the Megilla emphasizes how Mordekhai's position within the space of the narrative is in direct relationship with the law of the procedures of Persia and Medea. For example, the scene that motivates Haman's genocidal plot:

---

12. Song of Songs Rabba 2:1.

All the king's courtiers in the palace gate knelt and bowed low
to Haman, for such was the king's order concerning him; but
Mordekhai would not kneel or bow low. Then the king's courtiers who were in the palace gate said to Mordekhai, "Why do
you disobey *the king's order*?" When they spoke to him day after
day and he would not listen to them, they told Haman, in order
to see whether Mordekhai's resolve would prevail; for he had
explained to them that *he was a Jew*. When Haman saw that
Mordekai would not kneel or bow low to him, Haman was filled
with rage. (Est. 3:2–5)

Why do the king's servants get involved? If Haman himself did not notice
Mordekhai's disobedience (or perhaps he simply was not so bothered
by this behavior), why was it so important for the king's servants to
direct Haman's attention to this problem? Moreover, since they seem so
motivated by their commitment to upholding the dignity of the king's
decree, they should have turned to the king himself.

The explanation for the servants' process is explicit in the text:
"They told Haman, in order to see whether Mordekhai's resolve would
prevail; for he had explained to them that he was a Jew." Mordekhai disrupting the order of the kingdom is what bothers them. He tells them
that he is a Jew and therefore does not obey and bow. In this, the Jew
functions as one who disrupts the law and the proper order.

Not by accident is the term "Jew" repeated throughout the
Megilla; here we find the first development of the place of the Jew, his
identity and his role in relation to the world. Here we find the roots of
antisemitism. The Jew is the remainder that cannot be accommodated,
as his very existence represents that which does not enter the symbolic
order. In this, he destroys and undermines the order itself.[13] Indeed,
why did Mordekhai endanger the Jews by refusing to bow? Why didn't
he just leave the king's gate? Did he have provocative aims? Either way,

---

13. See also the sermon, "Seventy Bullocks and One Sukka," in Rabbi Shagar, *Faith Shattered and Restored*, 173–192.

this is his identity as a Jew, and in this Haman and the king's servants are correct: Mordekhai has a loyalty that precedes his loyalty to the king.[14]

To be exact: Mordekhai's disloyalty is complex, manifesting as a pure disruption of the order of the kingdom. On the one hand, Mordekai is loyal to the king and reports on Bigtan and Teresh, the two royal servants who attempt to assassinate Aḥashverosh. On the other hand, Mordekhai ultimately has a greater loyalty to his nation and his God, and in this he shatters the law. This is a disloyal loyalty, something that disturbs more than anything else a law and order that attempts to determine, "Are you one of us or of our enemies?" (Josh. 5:13).

Esther also presents this way, validating Haman's claim to Aḥashverosh that "there is a certain people…whose laws are different from those of any other people and who do not obey the king's laws" (Est. 3:8). She enters the court of the king without receiving the king's permission. Vashti refuses to come, and Esther comes uncalled; Vashti is entirely outside, while Esther is simultaneously inside and out.

In general, the Jew who does not bow disrupts the orderly world of "servants of the king," with Haman being chief among them. Because these servants are devoted to the law of the kingdom by virtue of it being law, they cannot tolerate the anomaly of Jewish existence. This is Haman's basic claim: difference and lack of obedience threaten and reject the decree of the king.

The Megilla states: "That day Haman went out happy and light-hearted. But when Haman saw Mordekhai in the palace gate, and Mordekhai did not rise or even stir on his account, Haman was filled with rage at him. And Haman controlled himself and went home" (Est. 5:9–10). Haman's serenity is disturbed not because the Jew does not obey but because the Jew rejects the entire principle upon which his happiness is based: the king's decree. This is why it was not enough to just get rid of Mordekhai alone; the problem is the very presence of the Jew – "He disdained to lay hands on Mordekhai alone; having been told who Mordekhai's people were, Haman plotted to do away with all the Jews, Mordekhai's people, throughout the kingdom of Aḥashverosh" (3:6).

---

14. Similarly, Esther remains loyal to Mordekhai and follows his commands even after she marries Aḥashverosh.

Further, the Megilla notes that Haman "controlled himself." As angry as he was with Mordekhai, he did not respond immediately. Why was it important to the writer of the Megilla to note this? Was Haman afraid that if he killed Mordekhai in anger he would be punished? Seemingly, Haman knew that if he did that, he would not succeed in freeing himself from the Jew, and Mordekhai's death would chase after him.[15] Only if he arranged Mordekhai's destruction in the framework of the law would he succeed in ridding himself of Mordekhai and the disruption that he embodies.

Law fights by way of the law itself, via legislation. One cannot ignore the violence inherent in the legislation. The Megilla reveals, in a painful and sarcastic form, the very basis of sovereignty, the violence that founds its laws:

> What manifests itself as the law's inner decay is the fact that rule of law is, in the final analysis, without ultimate justification or legitimation…. At its foundation, the rule of law is sustained not by reason alone but also by the force/violence of a tautological enunciation – "The law is the law!"[16]

As far as I am concerned, the mindset of the writer of the Megilla lays bare the foundation that underlies the events we will undergo this summer. For me, the disengagement plan symbolizes the crime that is in legislation, the violence subsumed within it – the recognition that the violence of transgressing the law is less than the crime of legislating the law. The inner decay that exists in the rule of law comes forth in the claim repeatedly heard from supporters of the removal law: this is the law, the law is the law, and therefore it must be respected. The tautology of the law is strengthened by the arbitrariness of its legislation. The "judicial wisdom" that would be able to justify it is entirely lacking. Now its justification is simply the legality of the process, and the process is legal:

---

15. Just like the Oedipal killing of the father, that traps the son through guilt.
16. Santner, *On the Psychotheology of Everyday Life*, 56–57. See also Walter Benjamin, "Critique of Violence," in *Reflections. Essays, Aphorisms, Autobiographical Writings*, trans. Edmund Jephcott (New York: Schocken, 1986), 286.

it is confirmed and organized in the Knesset. The law is justified not by ethics or judicial wisdom, but by the simple fact of its legislation at the hands of the majority. The violence required to enact this law, removing people from their land, is not the extraneous remainder of the process, but the very heart of law: the violent claim that the law is law.

If he was with us today, how would the author of the Megilla write the story that we are a part of? Where would he aim the sharp arrows of his irony?

Pesaḥ

"This Is for You a Sign":
Miracles and Faith

*"Further, when you understand the true meaning
of faith, then you will know that someone who sins
regarding faith should properly be enslaved,
and someone who merits faith should properly
be free."*[1]

MIRACLES AS PROOF FOR FAITH

Close study of the Bible confirms that the Exodus is a foundation of
the Jewish faith. The first of the Ten Commandments, the commandment of faith, makes this particularly clear. It says, "I am the Lord your
God who took you out of Egypt from the house of bondage" (Ex. 20:2).
Many medieval Jewish interpreters saw the Exodus as establishing faith
in God based on the many miracles that accompanied it.[2] According to

---

Based on a draft written in 5753 (1993), edited by Yishai Mevorach and published in
Rabbi Shagar, *The Time of Freedom*, 78–85.

1. Rabbi Yehuda Loew of Prague, *Gevurot Hashem*, ch. 9.
2. See, for example, Nahmanides on Exodus 13:16: "And now I shall declare to you a
    general principle in the reason of many commandments. Beginning with the days
    of Enosh when idol-worship came into existence, opinions in the matter of faith fell
    into error. Some people denied the root of faith by saying that the world is eternal;
    'they denied the Eternal, and said: It is not He' [Who called forth the world into

this approach, miracles demonstrate the truth of faith and its corollaries, such as creation, providence, and reward and punishment. To quote the German poet Goethe, "Miracle is really the favorite child of belief."[3]

The rabbi character in Rabbi Judah HaLevi's *Kuzari* also gives miracles a central role in the context of faith. However, rather than framing miracles as proof for faith, he says that they create a connection to faith. The rabbi chooses to present himself to the Khazar king as "believing in the God of Abraham, Isaac and Israel, who led the children of Israel out of Egypt with signs and miracles... who sent Moses with His law."[4] The king is confused by this confession and asks, "Shouldn't you have said that you believe in the Creator of the world, its Governor and Guide, in He who created you and keeps you?"[5] In response to the king's shock, the rabbi emphasizes the miracle of the Exodus from Egypt as the basis of faith. The Exodus from Egypt demonstrates God's direct, personal relation to the Jew, a relation that transcends nature. This

---

existence]. Others denied His knowledge of individual matters.... Some admit His knowledge but deny the principle of providence 'and make men as the fishes of the sea,' [believing] that God does not watch over them and that there is no punishment or reward for their deeds, for they say 'the Eternal hath forsaken the land.' Now when God is pleased to bring about a change in the customary and natural order of the world for the sake of a people or an individual, then the voidance of all these [false beliefs] becomes clear to all people, since a wondrous miracle shows that the world has a God Who created it, and Who knows and supervises it, and Who has the power to change it. And when that wonder is previously prophesied by a prophet, another principle is further established, namely, that of the truth of prophecy, 'that God doth speak with man,' and that 'He revealeth His counsel unto His servants the prophets,' and thereby the whole Torah is confirmed.... And because the Holy One, blessed be He, will not make signs and wonders in every generation for the eyes of some wicked man or heretic, He therefore commanded us that we should always make a memorial or sign of that which we have seen with our eyes, and that we should transmit the matter to our children, and their children to their children, to the generations to come, and He placed great emphasis on it.... And many other commandments are like them which are a memorial to the exodus from Egypt" (trans. C.B. Chavel, *Ramban: Commentary on the Torah* [New York: Shiloh, 1974], vol. 2, 171–173).

3. Cited in Franz Rosenzweig, *The Star of Redemption*, 93.
4. Rabbi Judah HaLevi, *The Kuzari*, trans. Hartwig Hirschfeld, I:11, with minor emendations.
5. Ibid., I:12.

personal relation creates the Jew's connection to his God and his Torah.[6] This great, revealed miracle demonstrates real, divine closeness, and this closeness is itself the primary revelation of faith. As far as the Kuzari is concerned, miracles are not some momentary "hocus pocus." Instead, they are events that carry within them the sensation of direct encounter with the wondrous, the mystical. This is the religious significance of miracles, without which they have no meaning.

In contrast to the approach that makes miracles central to the life of faith, Maimonides puts forward a different religious approach in the *Mishneh Torah*:

> The Jews did not believe in Moses, our teacher, because of the wonders that he performed. Anyone whose belief is based on wonders, there is a flaw in his heart, because it is possible to perform a wonder through magic or sorcery. All the wonders performed by Moses in the desert were not intended to serve as proof [of the legitimacy] of his prophecy, but rather were performed for a purpose.[7]

Maimonides teaches that using miracles as proof can never lead a person to inner certainty, because doubt will always rush to fill the space between the miracle and what it is meant to prove, with the skeptic declaring, "It is possible to perform a wonder through magic or sorcery." Miracles could perhaps lead to faith, but this will always be "a faith that allows for suspicions and doubts."[8]

THE SELF OF FAITH AND DEPENDENCE ON MIRACLES: A STUDY IN THE MAHARAL'S *GEVUROT HASHEM*

The Maharal took the same approach as Maimonides, entirely rejecting miracles as signs or proofs that lead to faith:

6. Ibid., I:19–27. See also Rabbi Shagar's essays, "The Memory of Creation and the Memory of Egypt: A *Shabbat HaGadol* Sermon," and "*Matza* in the Teachings of the Baal HaTanya: A Class on Faith and the Way of Life," in *The Time of Freedom*, 46–50 and 137–145.
7. Maimonides, *Mishneh Torah*, Hilkhot Yesodei HaTorah 8:1.
8. Ibid.

Pesaḥ

The proofs and demonstrations [of the philosophers] will not be demonstrative. They bear witness that the philosophers have turned from truth and uprightness. Indeed, they have confused Scripture for us, and distorted its interpretation, and they have given a reason for the miracles that indicate God's deeds. This, they say, is why miracles are called "signs" and "demonstrations," for they are signs and proofs of God's awesome deeds. This is not a good reason, as it introduces weakness into signs and wonders, which God primarily brought into the world in order to strengthen those who believe in Him.[9]

The Maharal opposed seeing miracles as proofs for faith due to his unique understanding of the nature of faith:

The explanation of this matter is that the beginning of Abraham's examination was when his faith was tested in being thrown into the fiery furnace. If he is strong in his faith, "a bulwark of silver will be built upon him" (cf. Song. 8:9). This silver bulwark is the construction of the world that was built upon Abraham…. For the only person fitting to be a beginning is someone who has firm existence, therefore it was because of this faith that he was fitting to conquer this world and the World to Come. Since he was firm in his faith, he has a firm existence, and fitting to be the primary root of existence in this world and the primary root of existence in the World to Come. However, someone whose existence is infirm in his faith, he is not fitting to be the primary root of existence in this world, nor in the World to Come. As the Sages said, Israel only merited redemption by virtue of faith, which is because slavery indicates a lesser existence, for the slave is subjugated to others and therefore dependent on the other, and that which is dependent cannot be considered an existence. When Israel had faith, they had a firm existence, and therefore were not fitting to be subjugated to others and dependent on something other than themselves. Thus, it was because of their firm faith that they went

---

9. Rabbi Yehuda Loew of Prague, *Gevurot Hashem*, Second Introduction.

forth to freedom, and this is a very deep matter.... This is because the faith with which he has a firm existence is a divine virtue, for the material things, infirm of existence, receive constant change and have no strength.[10]

According to the Maharal, faith does not rely on anything. This connects it to redemption, and is also why it expresses freedom and lack of subjugation: "When Israel believed, they had a firm existence, and therefore were not fitting to be subjugated to others and dependent on something other than themselves." True redemption is a certainty that does not depend on anything, not even on the demonstrations of wondrous miracles. Faith is therefore a condition for freedom, which is nothing other than a person's independence.

To illustrate Maimonides' and the Maharal's ideas, imagine a table right in front of you. Suddenly, wondrously, the table turns into an angel and begins to fly around the room. Would you suddenly become a greater believer? A better person? I assume the flying table would lead to a certain degree of excitement, but that would dissipate with time. Moreover, someone who was opposed to faith from the start would certainly find an explanation that could include the "miracle" within his general world view – the scientific world view, for example. He could also just shrug and say that his inability to understand everything does not actually prove anything. This is exactly what Maimonides is saying in the passage above. The gap between the proving miracle and the proven faith will always be filled by doubt.

Further contemplation reveals that the problems with this way of thinking run even deeper. The Maharal teaches that even if a miracle stood before us like a gun pressed against our temples, forcing us to admit to whatever it indicated, it still would not make us into believers. Faith is a function of real recognition, recognition that comes from a person's self, which itself is not purely cognitive. It is based on the entire whole of one's personality, a whole that cannot be disconnected from the person's actions, character traits, and thoughts. Miracles do not emerge from within this whole; they are an external source of authority, and

---

10. Ibid., ch. 7.

they leave a person in a state of "his existence is infirm in his faith," for his self is not itself sufficient. Miracles, therefore, are "not fitting to be the primary root of existence in this world, nor in the World to Come."[11]

The Maharal's understanding of faith is rooted in the biblical etymology of the word faith (*emuna*), which is similar to "*omanut habayit*," meaning strengthening the home.[12] "A person of faith," "*ish emunim*," is not someone who believes, but someone trustworthy and reliable – someone who will not let others down. It is a person who is steadfast and will not mislead those around him: "An honest (*emunim*) witness will not lie; a false witness testifies lies" (Prov. 14:5). When the Maharal speaks about faith, he is speaking about exactly this fundamental element. For him, a person of faith is someone self-sufficient and independent. This diverges from how we typically look at things. We generally think that for us to believe, external factors must convince us of the truth of faith. In contrast, the Maharal claims that faith is the strength a person finds inside. In this sense, faith moves in the opposite direction. Faith is a psychological-mental-spiritual character trait, which rises from within and moves outward, forcing itself on the outside.

We might think that a believing Jew has a sort of insurance policy, as if he were tightly holding onto to someone, relying on that person. However, based on what we have said here, faith is you yourself. It is your ability to say "Yes," despite the hardships you experience, the contradictions and doubts that roll over your faith. It is the ability to say yes, rather than despair. "Someone who has faith has existence," as the Maharal puts it, has his own personal existence. Those who merit this experience feel an incredibly strong feeling. A person within whom sparks true faith in God – a personal, inner recognition rather than cognitive awareness – feels like he has entered a different world, even if just for a few seconds. We live in a world of distress, doubts, and uncertainties. When a person reaches the level of certain faith, he lives with a different sort of mindset, a steadfast mindset.

---

11. For more on this idea, see Rabbi Shagar, *The Time of Freedom*, 137–145.
12. See note 13 in the next chapter, p. 174.

In short, the Maharal asserts that to the degree that miracles can make us believers, we only become dependent believers, or masked heretics of a sort.

HE SHOWS HIMSELF

As we have seen, the Maharal opposes the equation of miracles and faith, because he sees faith as something personal and independent. However, he also opposes this equation because of how he understands miracles. The Maharal's concept of miracles is best expressed in his famous statement, "Miracles have an order":

> Someone who says that the miracles of God have no intelligent order whatsoever is entirely mistaken.... Rather, just as the natural world has an order that is arranged and behaves according to its nature, so too miracles have an order as well. For miracles appear in the world in that the world is connected, bonded, and unified with the transcendent world, and this has an arranged order, for cleaving only happens in an arranged order, and because of this miracles only happen at specific times and are not constant. When God gave the manna to Israel, one should not say that this was not the fitting order for reality, that the world strayed from the reality according to which it should properly behave. Just as it is fitting for the world to behave according to its nature and guidance, so too it is fitting for Israel, in that they cleave to the transcendent world, that they have orderly miracles. Indeed, miracles have an order arranged by God, and miracles are therefore not considered changes in creation, for we say that everything is in order as arranged by God.[13]

According to the Maharal, miracles are not arbitrary acts of God's will, coming from above as if from nowhere. Rather, they follow a set of laws with their own intelligent reasons, a supernal set of laws: "Just as the natural world has an order that is arranged and behaves according to its nature, so too there is a miraculous order as well." In this sense, miracles

13. *Gevurot Hashem*, Second Introduction.

do not derive from the highest divine realm. According to this fundamentally kabbalistic way of thinking, divine activity follows the sets of
rules of systems from different levels and worlds. We see something as
miraculous because we live in a system where miraculous activity seems
like it shatters the system's typical order and behavior. By way of analogy, imagine a person from antiquity who sees a modern device such
as a computer or telephone. For this person, the device is like a miracle,
because he does not have the categories for explaining the device's activity to himself. He is not intellectually deficient, it is just not a part of
his world. Miracles are similarly wondrous for a material person who
cannot understand them.

The Maharal understands regular miracles in this manner, but the
Exodus from Egypt was different because "it is as significant as all the
other miracles combined."[14] It comes from a higher root and relates to
the highest *sefira*. In several places, the Maharal explains the Haggada's
midrashic interpretation, "And God took us out of Egypt, not through
an angel, nor a seraph, nor a messenger, but God Himself in His glory,"
as teaching that the Exodus from Egypt was a personal divine activity.
The Exodus belongs to the highest existence, not to an angel or a messenger. The miracle of the Exodus is distinct from other miracles because
the Exodus from Egypt constitutes a great wonder, the creation of the
nation of Israel as a unique nation – the creation of the nation's self.[15]
This is a process only a divine revelation itself could enact:

> Perhaps you will ask how great and lofty an exodus of that sort
> must be that it was not possible except through God Himself,
> and could not be attributed to any other agent…. It is like if a
> person resides in a city and a wise man comes and tells him to
> leave the city because war is coming to it, and the person goes
> to another city and is saved, and has children and grandchildren
> there, people wouldn't say that the wise man saved this person
> and his descendants. Instead, the wise man saved the person, and
> the salvation persisted to his descendants. This was not the case

14. Ibid., ch. 3, based on Mekhilta Yitro.
15. Ibid.

in Egypt. God did not merely take out that generation; He took stock of all of Israel, the earlier and the later generations, and took them all out. This is something uniquely fit to God, for He is all-inclusive. Thus, all of Israel was taken out, corresponding to God's level as inclusive of all generations.[16]

The act of creating the selfhood of an entire nation, of all of Israel, "the earlier and the later," is an act of the all-inclusive divine essence. The Exodus is therefore not a proof that points toward God's existence, but rather is itself a manifestation of the divine. Selfhood is the greatest miracle, because it transcends any known rules; it creates rules, rather than obeying them. The great wonder of the Exodus from Egypt was that it did not occur as an external act of divine force, through an angel or a seraph. Rather, reality itself reflects the divine intimacy and self-dwelling immanently within it. The miracle is itself the reality that is proven.[17] The miracle of the Exodus from Egypt is thus not a proof of God's existence, as initially suggested, but simply a picture of reality, a picture of divine revelation. Miracles reveal the divine rather than pointing toward it or proving it.

---

16. Ibid., ch. 52.

17. [Hebrew Editor's note: Maimonides seems to suggest similarly in the halakha quoted above, regarding Mount Sinai: "What is the source of our belief in [Moses]? The revelation at Mount Sinai. Our eyes saw, and not a stranger's. Our ears heard, and not another's. There was fire, thunder, and lightning. He entered the thick clouds; the Voice spoke to him and we heard, 'Moses, Moses, go tell them the following:....' Thus, Scripture relates: 'Face to face, God spoke to you' (Deut. 5:4), and it states: 'God did not make this covenant with our fathers, [but with us, who are all here alive today]' (v. 3). How is it known that the revelation at Mount Sinai alone is proof of the truth of Moses' prophecy that leaves no shortcoming? Scripture states: 'Behold, I will come to you in a thick cloud, so that the people will hear Me speaking to you, [so that] they will believe in you forever' (Ex. 19:9). It appears that before this happened, they did not believe in him with a faith that would last forever, but rather with a faith that allowed for suspicions and doubts."]

The Name of the Father

A Sermon for the Days Between Pesaḥ and Shavuot

IT CANNOT BE CONTAINED

> On the third day, in the morning, there was thunder, and light-
> ning, and a thick cloud upon the mountain, and a loud horn
> blast; all the people who were in the camp trembled. (Ex. 19:16)

> From the day on which you bring the sheaf of elevation offer-
> ing, the day after the Sabbath, you shall count seven weeks. They
> must be complete; count until the day after the seventh week,
> fifty days. Then you shall bring an offering of new grain to the
> Lord. (Lev. 23:15–16)

The passage from Exodus depicts the event of revelation as a loud thunder and lightning, like sparks flying and striking human comprehension.

In this sermon, I will attempt to convey something of this event
by elaborating on the tension expressed by the days of counting the
Omer daily – seven complete weeks – between the holiday of Pesaḥ
and the holiday of Shavuot, between the national and familial holiday of

Edited by Yishai Mevorach and published in *The Remainder of Faith*, 121–140.

identity and the holiday of the Revelation in which the Torah was given. Instead of going in chronological order, I will begin with Shavuot, move on to Pesaḥ, and then return to Shavuot, from revelation, to identity, and back to revelation.

As we shall see, a tension exists between revelation and identity. This same tension exists between the Christian mindset and the Jewish mindset, between an existence totally free of the past and an existence found entirely within the nourishing and sustaining memory of the past.

Borrowing an idea from the work of Alain Badiou, I would like to distinguish between an "illumination" and an "event."[1] An illumination is connected to the *sefira* of *Ḥokhma*, which is the beginning of existence, the "first cause" in the language of philosophy, or the beginning of the "process of emanation" in the language of Hasidism. In contrast, an "event" is rooted in the *sefira* of *Keter*, and thus connected to the Real, to the absolute reality that is beyond the process of emanation.[2] The relationship between event and illumination can be seen as the relationship between will and wisdom: the event is an act of will, where reality itself changes. Something that did not exist before appears, like a lightning bolt of reality, what the kabbalistic mythos describes as the birth of new souls emerging from the divine infinite. Illumination, in contrast, explicates what already exists, improving the situation and deepening its constituent parts. This improvement is bound up with *conatus*, with the need to persist and self-sustain that is fulfilled by the meaning and explanation given to reality.[3]

---

1. Alain Badiou, *Ethics: An Essay on the Understanding of Evil*, trans. Peter Hallward (London and New York: Verso Books, 2001). Badiou discusses the "event," which I am contrasting with "illumination." [Translator's note: In Hebrew, these two terms are spelled differently, with different derivations, but are homophones, pronounced "*heh-ah-ra*."]

2. [Hebrew Editor's note: In kabbalistic terminology, the *sefira* of *Ḥokhma*, the first that is counted, is identified as the first created thing, and it is called "the beginning of wisdom." The *sefira* of *Keter*, the first that is uncounted, is "pure, refined, light," identified with the will of the Creator, the Infinite.]

3. [Translator's note: *Conatus* means effort or impulse. In seventeenth-century thought, it meant the desire of each specific thing to persist in, self-sustain, and strengthen its existence.]

Revelation is an event, not an illumination. When it occurs, it is a vibration that shakes up, rather than clarifies, what already exists. What is the receiving of the Torah? It is those events wherein a person suddenly experiences an explosion of truth: "For My words are like fire, says the Lord, and like a hammer that shatters rock" (Jer. 23:29). "Something that happens in situations as something that they and the usual way of behaving in them cannot account for."[4]

The giving of the Torah is possible only when a person is ready to think about and experience the world differently, to open up to "a new way of being," in Badiou's words.[5] The revelation of an event that occurs within a reality that is already given – what there is – and wherein nothing else can appear, is dependent on this readiness. A person "needs something to have happened, something that cannot be reduced to its ordinary inscription in 'what there is.'"[6]

There is no specific revealed content at the center of revelation. The event of revelation is not an idea, but rather "the name of the void" that in its nature "cannot be named entirely."[7] This is where the need for a covenant arises in revelation: "The Lord our God made a covenant with us at Ḥorev" (Deut. 5:2), a covenant that was concretized with the declaration, "We will do and we will listen." This covenant is the response to the "name of the void," the requirement for uncompelled loyalty that creates "a new way of being and acting within the situation," because "the event was excluded by all the regular laws of the situation."[8] The heart of revelation is therefore universal in that it is free of any named content, leaving only singular loyalty to it; creating new laws and approaches, through which a person enables a "way of being" for the new event. This is true for more than just the giving of the Torah: scientific revolutions, like Einstein's, for example; political revolutions, like the French Revolution; the revolution that is in the constantly innovative artistic creativity;

---

4. Badiou, *Ethics*, 41.
5. Ibid., 42.
6. Ibid., 41.
7. Adi Efal, "Introduction: On the Function of Ethics in Creating Reality in the Thought of Alain Badiou," in Alain Badiou, *Ethics: An Essay on the Understanding of Evil* [Hebrew], trans. Adi Efal (Tel Aviv: Resling Publishing, 2005), 9 n.10.
8. Badiou, *Ethics*, 41–42.

and religious and spiritual revolutions. These all express constructive loyalty to a revelatory event, creating a new language for the "name of the void." These illuminations come from the "primordial intellect,"[9] a dimension that precedes the intellect and renews it.

The combination of revelation and loyalty to that revelation is, as per Badiou, how truth appears – in the commitment of the subject to the event. The event demands loyalty since it itself appears only as an excess, as a void with no place in language and disconnected from everything. The lightning flashes without context and disappears as if it had never been. It is to this lightning that we must be loyal, and this loyalty constructs the lightning as truth. This is what the kabbalists and Hasidim call raising *Malkhut* to *Keter*, an instance of "the crown of sovereignty," "*keter malkhut*." *Keter* is the lightning bolt of reality, and *Malkhut*, which has no independent content, is the loyalty and decisiveness that realize the event.

THE FATHER AND THE SON

I know that I am not being entirely faithful to the meaning of Badiou's words. Badiou describes revelation as a revelation-freedom that nullifies what was in order to create something new: "The essential characteristic of the event is that it creates a break in the world, that it interrupts the flow of things."[10] Specifically, as Eli Schonfeld claims in his afterword to the Hebrew edition, Badiou's words present the Christian-Western mindset wherein revelation, the truth, necessarily involves nullifying the existing situation – the particular – in order to bring about the new and the universal.

To me, as a Jew, revelation does not cancel out what already was; it is the identification of freedom within what already exists (for example, in Jewish particularism). Jewish revelation – as minimally as it exists after the destruction of the Temple – is not a creation from nothing. It is

---

9. For more on this concept see Gershom Scholem, "The Unconscious and the Concept of the Primordial Intellect in Hasidic Literature," in *Explications and Implications: Writings on Jewish Heritage and Renaissance* (Tel Aviv: Am Oved, 1976), 351–360 (Heb.).

10. Eli Schonfeld, "Is Truth Really Universal? An Afterword to Alain Badiou's *Ethics: An Essay on the Understanding of Evil*" (Heb.), in Badiou, *Ethics*, 113.

not a revolution like all the revolutions that we mentioned, but rather it reorganizes the elements of the situation to create new understandings. Only in the future yet to come, as Rabbi Isaac Luria taught, will "new souls" be born and a "new Torah" be revealed.

Is this utopia of "new souls" and a "new Torah" parallel to Badiou's thought process? In order to respond to this question, I want to play a little with the Jewish-Christian tension and present two possibilities for the revelation of truth, as they are reflected in the tension between the holiday of Pesaḥ and the holiday of Shavuot. The holiday of Pesaḥ presents us with the truth of the Jewish family, a truth that is not "something from nothing" but "something from something," a mindset of continuity. Meanwhile, the holiday of Shavuot presents a truth that in many senses undermines the truth of Pesaḥ and represents something of a break and a revolution. As such, the truth of Shavuot corresponds to the event in the thought of Badiou, an event that is *"ex nihilo."*

This is how Schonfeld presents Badiou's position:

> The particularistic father must retreat in order for the universalistic son to rise. According to Badiou's understanding, and faithful to a long tradition, in order to save the event, the truth, we have to erase the name of the father. The father, the past, the existing situation, must make room for the present, the new order, the son. New is always better than old…. The subject, as the son of truth, is the son of no one. Patricide.[11]

Killing the father, according to Badiou's understanding of Christianity, is necessary for the establishment of truth: "The father must retreat in order for the son to rise." The father, the law and order that appears as a yoke hindering a person from freedom, must be unwound so that it will be possible to be free from him. The establishing of truth, Badiou's "truth event," asserts a binary way of thinking. A person is either given over to the constantly repressive paternal law, or he frees himself from it to create a new and revolutionary truth. Identifying with the law (the father) means repression.

11. Ibid., 116–117.

Is this really the case? Are the options available to a person really limited to these two poles? As Schonfeld suggest, Jewish truth differs from this: "A Jew relates positively to the father.... A Jew is connected to the father just like he is connected to the past; like he is connected to the generous and fertile Creator."[12] Fatherhood, and therefore the past and the present situation, appears as rootedness – as generosity, as a promise for the future, as covenant and commitment. A Jew, therefore, starts from obedience, from belonging to covenant with the paternal law, the commandment. It is from this that Jewish truth sprouts forth. Therefore, Jewish truth does not require killing the father, since the Jew is connected to and identifies with him – he trusts the father's promise and is loyal to him: "He trusted God and it was considered a merit for him" (Gen. 15:6).[13] This loyalty is, first and foremost, loyalty to the paternal law imprinted in the identity of the son; selfhood is achieved in the eternal return, in the fact that "you are what you are" – a Jew. This is the acceptance of a yoke that in practice is the acquisition of a personal identity – "this is me and I am this." The truth event that derives from this is a revelation that appears as a new possibility within a given context. On the one hand, it means the ability to belong to a world, but on the other hand, without the constraints imposed by the world, escaping from the external appearance of the world (the paternal law) to the substantial possibilities within this world-law itself. The revelation of truth is the openness to the range of possibilities within the present order of things. I am not speaking about the son's attachment to the existing situation, but about the son's freedom within this situation. Schonfeld writes: "Identifying the connection between the I and the past as a positive connection means recognizing the virility of the father, in a fatherhood

---

12. Ibid.

13. As noted in the previous chapter, in Hebrew, the word for "faith," "*emuna*," is similar to "*omanut bayit*," meaning strengthening the home. An "*ish emuna*" is not a man who has faith, but a man who can be trusted that he will not betray you, a man who is stable and does not trick the people around him: "An honest (*emunim*) witness will not lie; a false witness testifies lies" (Prov. 14:5). Faith is that reliable stability of security and authority, as well as loyalty to that authority.

relationship that does not constrain the I, that is not a burden, but is a source of liberation, of freedom."[14]

PHENOMENOLOGY OF FAMILY

The clear difference presented here between the truth of Badiou and Jewish truth originates in different and opposite family structures. Does familyhood begin with castration – to which circumcision could allude – when the child is forced to give up his selfhood in order to join the culture, the language, and the given order? This, as Freud taught, leads to the child abandoning the burdens placed upon him, and to a patricide that subjugates the son to the paternal law with exponentially greater force by way of guilt. Or, perhaps, is the foundation of family-hood a covenantal partnership, meaning loyalty that comes after the event of the revelation-birth? This is an act that creates being itself as being part of the tradition.

It seems like the traditional Jewish[15] family contains a different possibility for the role of the father in relation to the son – the role of the father thus differing from the Freudian-Western depiction that stands in the background of Badiou's words. It seems that we must build a traditional Jewish psychological model of the image of the father, wherein the father does not represent an external compulsion and which therefore likely does not contain the Oedipal complex. A phenomenological depiction of the laws of the Seder night, the night of the Jewish narrative, can illuminate the difference between the two possibilities.

This is what Maimonides wrote in the chapter dealing with the Seder night in his code of Jewish law, the *"Mishneh Torah"*:

---

14. Schonfeld, "Is Truth Really Universal?", ibid.
15. [Hebrew Editor's note: The intention behind the term "traditional Jewish" is not the sociological demographic in contemporary Israeli society, but an existence that is found deep within the flowing of the Jewish tradition, without the self-reflection that keeps the tradition from flowing. Zygmunt Bauman said regarding this: "The paradox of tradition is that the moment we speak about tradition it is no longer what we are claiming that it is" (cited in Avi Sagi, *The Challenge of Returning to Tradition* [Jerusalem: Hakibbutz Hameuhad, 2003], 15 [Heb.]). Therefore, it's not enough for familyhood to be religious-Jewish in order for it to fit the phenomenon proposed here, but rather, it must be "traditional." Regarding this see below.]

He should make changes on this [Seder] night so that the children will see and ask: "Why is this night different from all other nights?" until [the father] answers them that such and such happened and such and such was. What changes should be made? He gives them roasted seeds and nuts; the table is taken away before they eat; and they snatch matzot from each other; and the like.[16]

Rabbi Abraham ben David of Posquieres (Raavad) adds in his commentary to the *Mishneh Torah*: "'They snatch matza' means to eat quickly so that they do not fall asleep."

The commandment to tell the story in the form of questions and answers, the laws that are intended to keep the children from falling asleep, as well as diverging from the norm during the meal – this structure is intended to inspire spontaneous questions in the child, like "Why is this different?" This question is essentially interested participation. The story is not truly passed on to the son unless the son becomes interested in and immersed in the story. Moreover, the story is not "speaking about" but rather leads to taking part in what is spoken. We do not just tell the story through the Haggada, we also say that we are telling the story. The message is passed on not just by the full and interested participation of the child but also in his being a part of the message itself – "God said to Moses, 'Go to Pharaoh'... so that you can recount in the hearing of your sons and of your sons' sons how I made a mockery of the Egyptians and how I displayed My signs among them – in order that you may know that I am God" (Ex. 10:1–2). We don't just recount what happened; what happened happened "so that you can recount!"[17]

If so, the Haggada is the story of telling a story. It realizes itself while telling about how it is realizing itself – an instance of a story within a story. We are not recalling a story about something that happened, we are performing the story of the Haggada in the telling of the story of the

---

16. Maimonides, *Mishneh Torah, Hilkhot Ḥametz UMatza*, 7:3.
17. Similarly, we should note that the partnership and belonging that a child has in the story of leaving Egypt "on this night" also surrounds the learning Torah and observing the commandments that are central in the child's life, and involvement in those things is itself the content of the message, as quoted in the Haggada: "Initially our fathers were idolaters and now God has drawn us close to His service."

the Exodus itself. The object of the story is therefore also the subject of the story. This is even clearer in the Haggada because of how, among other things, part of the story includes repeated references to the situation of the participants, references found in the body of the text itself: "Why do we eat this matza?"; "Why do we eat this maror?" Similarly, the references to the obligations imposed upon them – "Pesaḥ, matza, and maror" – are not procedural guides leading to saying the three obligatory things, but are part of the storytelling procedure itself.[18]

There is a duality here. On the one hand, the spontaneous question of the son in the story of the Seder night, and the elements that accompany it, construct the passing on of the tradition with partnership, interest, and belonging at the center. On the other hand, the question of the son creates something else. It is not a dialogue between two equals, but rather an unbalanced dialogue between asker and answerer, a dialogue that essentially strengthens the authority of the father. Therefore, we have here again the same vital duality of partnership and authority. The father is the bearer of a tradition that gives him his authority, while the son belongs to this same tradition and participates in it. As such, the image of the father appears not as the coercive representative of a society alienated from the son, but as an authority that grants space, security, and liberty.

The elderly father in this discourse represents the tradition and the culture. Fatherhood is the source of knowledge and authority, and this is on display in the joint Torah study and in the son's question about the customs and conventions of each season and holiday. Here the son turns to the father as the one who passes on the tradition. The father,

---

18. Regarding the dimension of the "story within a story" in the Haggada, I draw on Ido Dickman, *The Ontology of the Book of the Torah as Mise en abyme* (M.A. thesis at Hebrew University; Jerusalem, 2004). In light of his words, we can see the circularity that we're discussing as a unique ontological phenomenon of holy texts in Judaism. We find an example of this phenomenon in the biblical verses that tell us about Moses writing the Torah scroll: "Moses wrote down this teaching and gave it to the priests, sons of Levi, who carried the Ark of the Lord's Covenant, and to all the elders of Israel" (Deut. 31:9). If so, the Torah says that Moses wrote the Torah, in which itself it says that Moses wrote the Torah, etc. This is a book within a book, where the outer edge of one book overlaps into the inside of the second inner book.

from his perspective, stands as the source of the command – not the Freudian command that suppresses the liberty of the son, but a command that gives him his identity and his context, and thus, his liberty. This command begins from interest and partnership. The father, in this depiction, does not create obsessive compulsivity but appears as the source of authority upon which the world is founded, the foundation stone of the personality. The actual truth is much sharper and deeper: the father does not only transfer tradition and culture – his image is the tradition! The father signifies the tradition itself in his lifestyle, in his observance of the commandments, Jewish customs, and in his Torah study. Without a father there is no tradition,[19] and without a father there is no personal identity or liberty. This is the great difference between the modern-Christian-Western father and the traditional-Jewish father.

In the modern Western world, the son sees the image of the father as bound up with alienation, duality, and discomfort. The father, whose role "is to enforce the law and impose the order"[20] of the society and the culture, hinders the liberty and freedom of the son; therefore, only removing the father will enable the son to exit these constraints. To this, Sartre says, "There is no good father, that's the rule…. Had my father

---

19. Victor Frankl's words are quite fitting for this: "From a theological perspective, the god is not a father figure but rather the father is a figure of God. According to this understanding, the father is not an example of divinity but rather the opposite: God is an example of fatherhood. From a biographical and biological perspective, the father comes first; from a theological perspective, God comes first. From a psychological perspective the connection between child and father precedes the connection between a person and God; however, from a theological perspective, my natural father, and in this sense my creator, is simply the first representation of the supernatural father, the creator of heaven and earth." See Victor Frankl, *The Unconscious God: Psychotherapy and Religion*, trans. Shimon Levi (Jerusalem: Dvir Publishing, 1985), 61 (Heb.).

20. Dylan Evans, *An Introductory Dictionary of Lacanian Psychoanalysis* (London and New York: Routledge, 1996), 63. [Translator's note: Rabbi Shagar was working from the 2005 Hebrew translation published by Resling Publishing. The original English sentence, in full, seems to have been: "This function is none other than that of imposing the Law and regulating desire in the Oedipus complex, of intervening in the imaginary dual relationship between mother and child to introduce a necessary 'symbolic distance' between them."]

lived, he would have lain on me at full length and would have crushed me." Only the death of the father, he continues, "gave me freedom."[21]

What is more, in modern discourse – which in many senses guides Jewish-religious familyhood today and certainly brings about its complexes – the paternal "you" emerges and appears in full view, strengthening the alienated presence of the father. This is entirely opposed to the traditional discourse, wherein the "I" and the "you" do not stand opposite each other but as part of a "we" (tradition), concealed within the "together" by means of partnership and "being with," as in, "All of you stand today before the Lord your God – the leaders of your tribes, your elders and your officers, every man of Israel" (Deut. 29:9). This is the context in which the Haggada asserts, "Even if we were all scholars, we were all wise men, we were all elders, we all knew the Torah, we would still be obligated by the command to tell about the Exodus from Egypt." This is an anti-elitist, populist position. From this perspective, the scholar is equal to the layman, and he too must participate in the story.

This difference emerges sharply in the words of the wicked son in the Haggada who asks, "What is this service to you?" The Haggada notes that he says, "to you," excluding himself, through which he has "removed himself from the collective" and thus "rejected an essential principle." Because faith, the paternal law, is a function of belonging, someone who "removes himself from the collective" has automatically rejected an essential principle. What this means is that the son has freedom only in relation to his father, not freedom from his father. The son belongs to the tradition of the father, and this enables his interpretive freedom regarding his father.

The main question that stands before the believer is, "Do I identify with the image of the father, which is the tradition and my personal identity?" If the answer is in the affirmative, then the father no longer seems alienated from me, but rather creates identity and security. The father is the center that shapes the world, not an imposing, external entity, like the one reflected in Western discourse. Of course, a model such as this constructs an entirely different psychology from the psychological systems which Freud and Badiou propose. This is a model where

---

21. Jean Paul Sartre, *The Words* (New York: Vintage, 1981), 19.

you can identify "in the law – or in the command – liberty."[22] Patricide is thus not inevitable, since the appearance of truth does not require a revolutionary, reactionary event. Rather, it is an event that *from the perspective of the son* is understood as continuing the past and not opposed to it. I say from the perspective of the son, since, for those around him, his freedom in regard to his father could be construed as rebellion and deviation – but the father and son know well that this is not so. Furthermore, the father even seeks the son's freedom in relation to him: "'For the leader (*lamenatseyaḥ*); with instrumental music. A psalm of David' (Ps. 4:1). R. Kahana said in the name of R. Ishmael the son of R. Yosei: Sing for the one who is happy when they defeat (*shemenatzeḥim*) him."[23]

CALLING BY NAME

What happens if this identification with the father dissolves? Does the father lose his authority? Does the familyhood as it is expressed in the Haggada crumble? What happens when the father is called by his name (as happens in certain families in our day), in violation of the halakha that "he cannot be called by his name, neither while he lives nor after his death"?[24] Does calling the father by his name necessarily kill him? Or, could it perhaps be a different way of taking your place in the "Big Other," a new arrangement of the given order?

    We can find answers to these questions by studying the writings of Rabbi Isaac Luria (known as the Ari) and diving into the depths of his symbolic and semantic space. We can thereby illuminate the relationship between two aspects of Jewish truth – the truth of interpretive freedom and the higher truth of inspiration and creation.[25]

---

22. Schonfeld, "Is Truth Really Universal?" 117.
23. *Yalkut Shimoni* II:627.
24. Maimonides, *Mishneh Torah*, Laws of Rebels 6:3.
25. [Hebrew Editor's note: For the ease of reading, we will clarify some points from the Lurianic teachings so that the reader has some basis from which to proceed: Lurianic Kabbala is enormously concerned with the divine faces (*partsufim*). Kabbalists before the Ari were primarily concerned with the divine *sefirot*, meaning the powers with which the Godhead acts or the traits with which it is characterized, while seeing each power or trait separately and not as part of a whole. The Ari, in contrast, speaks primarily about "the collectivity of the *sefirot*," meaning the networks of multiple powers and traits working together – a face (*partsuf*). The Ari's project attempted to

In the Ari's writings we find two types of inspiration, what he called "drawing down vitality." These are the two forms of "spiritual coupling," one which is constant and uninterrupted while the other is sporadic. In one, we find that the spiritual energy (*shefa*) comes from the divine faces (*partsufim*) of the father and the mother. In the other, the spiritual energy comes to the son not by way of the father and mother but straight from the *sefira* of *Keter*. This is how it is described by Yosef Avivi, a scholar of Lurianic Kabbala:

> The first coupling is a *fixed coupling*, to sustain everything....
> This coupling is in the father and mother (*Hokhma* and *Bina*),
> and only in them... they therefore give the creations limited and
> constrained energy.... This coupling draws down to reality a fixed
> vitality, *what is necessary for the existence of the creations*. The fixed
> coupling ensures that reality will not return to chaos, ensuring
> that the vessels will not shatter again.
>
> The sporadic coupling [in contrast] *draws down the souls*....
> The sporadic coupling includes couplings in all the faces (*part-
> sufim*) of the emanation (*ha'atsilut*), from *Arikh Anpin* [=large
> faces] (*haketer*) to *Ze'ir Anpin* and *Nukvah*.[26]

The Ari speaks about "coupling." This refers to the drawing down of spiritual energy-light (insemination) leading to pregnancy and birth. "The fixed coupling" is connected to the *conatus* of existence – to its persistent existing rather than evaporating into non-being. It would be a mistake to think that the coupling sustains creation as an impermeable object

---

characterize the faces. In this the Ari does not just talk about divine powers or traits, but also about divine personality; a personality made up from a broad spectrum of character traits and powers of action. The Ari depicts divinity that has a personal character, that has many expressions that communicate to us many relational stances of God to the world. Each of these stances is composed from a collection of traits and characteristics. The divine faces discussed by the Ari are presented in his writings as five family members: *Arikh Anpin* (the grandfather), *Abba* (the father) and *Ema* (the mother), *Ze'ir Anpin* (the young groom), and *Nukva* (the young bride). These faces are parallel to the *sefirot*: grandfather-*Keter*, father and mother-*Hokhma* and *Bina*, the boy-*Tiferet*, the girl-*Malkhut*.]

26. Yosef Avivi, *The Kabbala of the Gra* (Jerusalem: Kerem Eliyahu, 1993), 38 (Heb.).

that lacks vitality. Indeed, this energizing gives the creation-family its vitality. Specifically an energy that sustains it so that it does not return to the silent chaos, impermeable and dark. "The sporadic coupling," by contrast, breaches the *conatus* rather than being connected with it, and in this sense it "shatters the vessels." This is an instinctive-creative illumination that opens creation up to new horizons, beyond what was given to it initially. This illumination is referred to as the drawing down of new souls.

Connected to this, the Ari (in his composition of contemplative intentions for the prayers of the holiday of Shavuot) teaches that the holiday of Shavuot is a day when there is a coupling-illumination that corresponds to "the sporadic coupling." This is the time when the son receives straight from the *sefira* of *Keter*:

> When morning arrives [on the day of Shavuot], just before daybreak, when the sky in the east is just starting to lighten (*mashḥirin*), that is called "the doe of the dawn (*hashaḥar*)" as is known, then you must immerse in the ritual bath (*mikve*) and contemplate the upper *mikve*, which is *the highest Keter of Ze'ir Anpin*, flowing to him on this night... through this we receive additional holiness from this aspect of the crown... then through the morning prayer and the additional holiday prayer of *Shavuot*, that is exactly when she (*hamalkhut*)[27] ascends like him and they are coupled together.[28]

The coupling under discussion is that of the *Keter* of *Ze'ir Anpir* with *Nukva*, the *sefira* of *Malkhut*. The *sefira* of *Keter*, as we saw, is a lightning bolt of absolute reality. It is a will that has never shone before. *Ze'ir Anpin*, the adolescent son, is the divine face that symbolizes the divine space of the Torah, the space of the divine concepts. It is the paternal law – not the father, but his symbolic space – that is imprinted on the son. This is the face of the young son that is not the source (that is, the father and the mother), but already the offspring. If so, this is the

---

27. *Nukva D'Ze'ir Anpin; The Malkhut of Ze'ir Anpin.*
28. Rabbi Isaac Luria, *Sha'ar Hakavvanot*, Sermons for the holiday of Shavuot §1.

illumination of the *sefira* of *Keter* that is in *Ze'ir Anpin*, which inseminates the female, the bride, bringing a new lightning-flash to the world. This is an illumination of *Keter* in the context of *Ze'ir Anpin* – the world of Torah and the paternal law. In the context of our discussion, this means that we can have two different experiences in relation to our Torah (the paternal law). One option is that during our learning, inspiration flows like a river and with it we discover additional aspects of Torah, added possibilities for understanding, and more horizons of depth. This is an inspiration of understanding. It is the illumination that clarifies the pre-existing reality, improving the way things already are, an illumination of *Ḥokhma*. This is what the Ari said was a constantly flowing illumination, sustaining the situation and keeping it from returning to chaos. This is a father-son relationship of the type reflected in our discussion here. The father is the foundation of possibilities that will come later – possibilities that exist within the symbolic context of the father. However, it is also possible that there will be a revelation, an event of the birth of new souls. This revelation is already the appearance of a "new Torah," an intermittent, rather than constant, spiritual energy.

The *illumination* is a constantly flowing spiritual energy. According to the Ari, it gives critical vitality and liveliness to the religious world. Without this illumination, this world would become an alienated law that oppresses the son, a law that leads to the killing of the father. The *event*, however, is a shattering – an illumination from the *Keter*-lightning and therefore sporadic. According to the Ari, the situation on the morning of Shavuot is that of an event, not an illumination.

Of course, we are not just talking about the morning of Shavuot, but rather of any moments where the sky lights up in the east, moments primed for a coupling of new souls – moments of erotic creativity in relation to the "paternal law." These moments are when a person opens up not just to his interpretive freedom but to the fact that he has the ability to create the substance of reality – "If the righteous wanted they could create worlds."[29] In hasidic thought, such moments are understood as "a time to act for God," and they inherently include "they have rejected your Torah": "It is a time to act for God, they have rejected your Torah"

---

29. Sanhedrin 65b.

(Psalms 119:126) – "Any place where it is a time to act for God, it is an allusion to the command to reject the Torah."[30] The new Torah does not appear as a possible interpretation of the existing paternal text, but as a real religious moment that shapes the paternal law anew without getting rid of it.[31] In other words, rejecting the Torah is itself the Torah. The paternal law's concept of the truth itself changes, and "nullifying it is upholding it."[32] Getting rid of the law, breaking it, is internalized into the law itself. Indeed, the necessary activity of getting rid of the Torah and rejecting it is recorded within the Torah itself. Specifically, in the sons'[33] twisting of the meaning of the biblical verse. No longer does it mean, like the plain meaning of the verse, a time to enact the judgment of God on those rejecting his Torah[34] – a false prophet, covenant-breakers, etc. Rather "it is a time to act," the entire essence of which is rejecting the Torah. The rejection that the exegete is teaching about is written into the law of the Torah without overriding it!

If so, Jewish truth has two aspects: illumination and the event of revelation. Illumination is the interpretive liberty that the son possesses by virtue of his at-homeness and loyalty. As a member and

---

30. Rabbi Mordekhai Yosef Leiner of Izbica, *Mei Hashiloaḥ* vol. 1 (Bnei Brak: Mishor, 2005), Parshat Yitro s.v. "Anokhi."

31. There is a degree of unmediated immediacy here; it is not possibility but substance. The illumination of *Keter* in *Ze'ir Anpin* means that the possibility leaves the realm of interpretation and becomes a real, concrete, religious option; the possibility becomes halakha – "the halakha is in accordance with him in every place" (based on Bemidbar Rabba 13:1).

32. [Like the statement of Rabbi Shimon ben Lakish – "Sometimes nullifying Torah is how you uphold it, as it is written [regarding the tablets of the Ten Commandments], 'that you broke' (Exodus 34), God said to Moses: 'You did well that you broke them'" (Menaḥot 99b). This is what is called "transgression for its own sake"; an action of truth that overrides the law validates it and is faithful to it simultaneously. Regarding the concept see: Nazir 23b; Horayot 10b; Sermons of Rabbi Tzaddok Hakohen of Lublin, Leiner's student, *Likkutei Amarim*, §16. Regarding this see at length Nahum Rackover, *The End Sanctifies the Means* (Jerusalem: Mmoreshet Hamishpat Beyisrael, 2000), 35–110 (Heb.).]

33. In our case these "sons" are the talmudic sage Rabba and the hasidic leader and teacher Rabbi Mordekhai Yosef Leiner of Izbica.

34. See the commentary of the *Metsudat David* on this verse, as well as the opinion of "some say" in the commentary of Ibn Ezra ad loc.

partner in the traditional way of life, the son feels comfortable with it. Therefore, he does not construct it as a narrowly object-like, alienated world, but as a world that enables him to interpret it and expound it, to speak it as a language game.[35] In contrast, the event is of another order entirely. Here freedom toward the tradition is discovered – the freedom to create the tradition differently (but not a different tradition), to change the combinations of its letters. Religious breaches like the appearance of the teachings of Hasidism of Rabbi Israel Baal Shem Tov or the birth of Rabbi Abraham Isaac Hakohen Kook's teachings are examples of such events. The revelation event is not bound to the grammar of the language-tradition and can create a language of the unseen – the hidden Torah. The sentences it creates are meaningless not because they have been cut loose from the vocabulary of the language, but because they transcend and escape its logic, and they reorganize it anew.[36] This is a moment of "new Torah," because the revelation enables a paradigm shift in the foundation of the religious reality of the paternal law. It opens new possibilities for the son that were not there before, notwithstanding the interpretive freedom that the son possesses in relation to the father, because despite the many possibilities it has, this freedom ultimately participates in the grammar and rules of the language of the father.

This illumination of the birth of new souls is bound up with what the Ari described as the ascent of *Ze'ir Anpin*, the boy, to the level of the father[37] so that he may receive illumination from *Keter*. This is a situation where the sons reach the level of the fathers-tradition-law and receive their inspiration directly from *Keter*. Doesn't this ascension teach that the sociological phenomenon of calling a father by his name presents a powerful option for innovation? Clearly, this occur-

35. Additionally, the son who enters into unity with the paternal law does not experience it as an external limit, and therefore his space within this law does not stand in enmity with different spaces – the law does not constrain him since it does not stand as a limit to other realities.
36. See Rabbi Shagar, "Faith and Language According to the Baal HaTanya of Chabad," in *We Will Walk in Fervor*, 173–206.
37. "We find that *Ze'ir Anpin* has already grown to the size of the father and mother" (Rabbi Isaac Luria, *Sha'ar Hakavvanot*, ibid.).

rence appears as shattering and crushing, as spoiling, and therefore we should guard against it. But what is necessary for innovation and revelation of Torah as described here? It can express a revelation of creative freedom in relation to the father and within his law. Furthermore, in a certain sense, this indicates that "calling by name" is not necessarily killing the father. Instead it could point to an exciting religious option that will come as a result of the connection and love between parents and children – connection, not rebellion. Is the exegete who inverts the text-father and punctuates it anew – thus nullifying and upholding it – necessarily motivated by feelings of rebellion? Do not love and connection make their marks here?

> "He brought me to the banquet room, and his banner of love was over me" (Song of Songs 2:4) – R. Yissakhar said: "and his banner of love was over me," even a person who sits and is involved in Torah and skips (*medaleg*) from law to law and from verse to verse, God says: I love him. "And his banner (*diglo*) of love (*ahava*) was over me (*alai*)" – his skipping (*dilugo*) is lovely (*ahava*) to me (*alai*).
>
> Rabbi Brekhayah said: Even the skippings that our father Jacob skipped with his father. [As it says,] "And the skins of the goat kids" [with which Jacob disguised himself in order to deceive Isaac] (Genesis 27), God's presence dwelled within them, as it says, "and ten curtains of goat hair" [for the tabernacle] (Exodus 26).[38]

In an age when the "you" is no longer hidden beneath the surface of the "we," we must open a dialogue between the paternal "you" and the young "you." Speech must achieve liberty. This liberty is the ability to speak with children and with parents, an ability that we generally do not possess. This speaking will enable us to become familiar with both the children and the parents. This ability could arise from the question: who is this person – the father, the son – that is simultaneously so close to me and so far from me? Although this question is asked from

---

38. Numbers Rabba, 2:3; Yalkut Shimoni, Song of Songs, 2:986.

an alienated position, it could act as a jumping-off point for deep and close familiarity. It can also serve as an entry to a new familyhood, and a new offering to God on the holiday of Shavuot.

> Behold, I will send the prophet Elijah to you before the coming of the great and fearful day of God. He shall reconcile parents with children and children with their parents. (Malachi 3:23–24)

Iyar

Muteness and Faith

A Sermon for Yom Hashoa

MUTE MEANING

When tragedy strikes, believers typically ask, "What does this mean?"[1] The Holocaust denies any possibility of asking such questions, representing a total shattering of the world and its cultural construction. It falls outside the constructive world and the realm of discourse.

This is how I experienced the meaning of the Holocaust regarding my parents (of blessed memory), if it even makes sense to say such a thing. The Holocaust tore apart their youth and they carried that with them for the rest of their lives. They almost never spoke about that time, going on with their daily lives based on a sort of stubborn muteness. Concealing the irreparable, they remained victims for their entire lives. They could never speak, for the Holocaust forced them into an incurable muteness. They trusted neither reality nor people, a situation which left my parents incapable of accepting the other or addressing them with an open heart. They were barred from experiencing that sense of well-being which Tanakh describes as "everyone under his own vine

---

Based on drafts written in 5758 (1998) and 5761 (2001), edited by Yishai Mevorach and published in *On That Day*, 64–77.

1. See Rabbi Shagar, *On That Day*, 256–259.

and under his own fig tree" (I Kings 5:5). In a certain sense, I continue to carry this burden.

This idea reminds me of the kabbalistic and hasidic commentaries on Pesaḥ and the Exodus from Egypt. Here we see the word "*Pesaḥ*" as breaking down into "*peh-saḥ*," "the mouth that speaks," speech itself leaving its exile.[2] Speech generally enables us to turn a harsh, traumatic event into processable human suffering, an act that is the first step toward redemption from that suffering. The Holocaust, however, is not just suffering: it is suffering that lacks speech and becomes muteness. Because there is no conceptual framework that could render their experience as suffering, in this sense, my parents never left the Holocaust. The Holocaust was not just murder, but the murder of murder itself. It is not an injustice or suffering that took place within the normal circle of human existence; it somehow transcends and refutes it. The Holocaust cannot be conceptually rendered into any other thing, so it cannot achieve any sort of conciliation. This is how I explain my parents' muteness: they lived their lives in the empty space split open by the Holocaust. The meaning of the Holocaust typifies Lyotard's concept of "the differend,"[3] or "an unsayable debt." He states, "Auschwitz was the death of death. In this death, even the possibility of mourning over what was lost is itself

---

2. See, for example, Rabbi Isaac Luria, *Pri Etz Ḥayim*, Gate of the Holy Scriptures, ch. 4; Rabbi Nahman of Breslov, *Likkutei Moharan* II 74. This is how I understand a famous statement by the Ḥiddushei HaRim of Ger: "'And you shall know that I, the Lord, am your God who freed you from the sufferings of the Egyptians' (Ex. 6:7) – 'Sufferings,' so that they no longer suffer from the practices of Egypt" (quoted in *Sefat Emet*, vol. 2, *Va'era*). In Egypt, when speech was in exile, a person simply continued to suffer, unable to free himself from the sufferings imposed on him.

3. [Hebrew Editor's note: "Differend" is a term coined by the French philosopher Jean-François Lyotard in order to refer to a situation wherein a victim is rendered incapable of expressing the injustice done to him, for the very act of expressing it would deny the injustice had ever occurred. Moreover, even staying silent fails to convey the intended accusation or claim. The aggressor thus injures his victim twice over: first, in the injustice itself, and second, in denying his victim the ability to express that injustice. The clearest example of such a "differend," for Lyotard, was the existence of Holocaust survivors.]

dead. The process of mourning cannot take place, so it is impossible to continue forward and move on."[4]

When I discuss the Holocaust, I do so not from the perspective of someone who had experienced it firsthand, but from the perspective of a second generation who had inherited an incurable genetic disease. In a certain sense, members of the second generation are no less victims of the Holocaust than members of the first; they also experience the Holocaust as an absolute lack of security in existence. Their reality fundamentally lacks any basis or foundation, a metaphorical "black hole" waiting to swallow everything up. Due to the presence of this black hole, they experience a persistent sense of threat in the background of their lives.

For me, the Holocaust is a black hole of non-existence that nonetheless exists. It is a horror on display in the noonday sun that should have annihilated everything, taking place in a world that continues to turn exactly as before. A reality of non-existence, it nevertheless exists in that it leads only to being stuck, without any ability to escape or even to disappear.

I seek to present an incredibly powerful religious response to the Holocaust. First however, I will lay out two opposing theories on how the collapse of systems of humanity led to the horrors of Nazism.

POWER OR ORDER?

Generally speaking, we can say that philosophy puts forward two frameworks for thinking about the horrors of the Holocaust. First, there is the theological idea of Satan and his will to power. Second, there is a theology that, while inverse of the first, is no less satanic: the theology of the machine and of Satan as a technocrat.[5]

---

4. See Adi Ophir and Ariella Azoulay, "Standing In: In Conversation with Lyotard," in Jean-François Lyotard, *The Postmodern Condition* (Tel Aviv: Resling Books, 1999), 127–128 (Heb.). Indeed, I often find people's pronouncements about the Holocaust dubious, not because I think they are insincere, but because I see them as foolish attempts to conquer the unconquerable.
5. I will note that such a theological discourse is very fitting for Nazism, which always brimmed with religious symbols and maintained a consciousness of chosenness and messianic purpose. See Rivka Schechter, *The Theological Roots of the Third Reich* (Tel Aviv: Ministry of Defense, 1990) (Heb.).

The theology of "Satan and his will to power" posits that Satan requires a human sacrifice to strengthen himself. Because he draws vitality from the blood of others, he must annihilate them. Blood, which contains the soul within it (Deut. 12:23), provides greater sustenance than any other material. Because murder is stronger and more energizing than any other act, murder is how Satan nourishes his existence. In this understanding, "the will to power" is what drives Satan and underlies his annihilation of the other. Satanic evil is not the result of maliciousness: it exists because it cannot tolerate any constraint. Much in the same way that Hitler (may his name be erased) saw culture, satanic evil sees all culture as degrading simply in that it is culture. Hitler believed that culture limits man's activities by creating and asserting values of good and evil.[6] This sort of satanic evil is inhuman; it does not represent human evil, insofar as it lacks any goal. It does not intend to achieve anything. Instead, the battle itself strengthens its existence: "Destruction is not a means to elevation, but rather is elevation itself."[7] Similarly, the relationship between Jews and Germans was not seen as antagonistic due to some specific quality of the Jews, or for that matter of the Germans, who denied the Jews their right to exist. If that were the case, then we could describe this as a human evil. Instead, the antagonism was simply antagonism itself. Here we see a fundamental duality between Nazism and satanic evil; just as Nazi antagonism was for its own sake, so is satanic evil not a means but an end in and of itself.

Thus, the "Satan of Power" must free itself from humanity and culture in order to receive power. It is a deliberate evil, an evil for the sake of evil. As an evil which tries only to free itself from anything human, it is destruction for the sake of destruction. However, to the same degree that this Satan tries to destroy the other, he also turns his venom against himself. He must free himself even from himself, so that nothing can limit him. Otherwise, he cannot exist. Ultimately, Hitler took his own

---

6. Nazism hated the Jews because, for them, the Jews symbolized culture and ethics, which the Nazis thought degraded the race.

7. Adi Ophir, *A Language for Evil: Toward an Ontology of Ethics* (Tel Aviv: Resling, 2001), 384, §9.252 (Heb.), and see also ibid., 371, §9.210; 385, §9.255. See also Adi Ophir, *The Order of Evils: Toward an Ontology of Morals*, trans. Rela Mazali and Havi Carel (Cambridge: Zone Books, 2005).

life because he fed on himself until there was nothing left to consume. He killed himself, and took the German people with him, due to this same will to power.

Alongside this explanation, some adhere to the theory of the well-oiled machine and of technocratic evil. This facet of the Holocaust came to the fore in the trial of Adolf Eichmann.[8] Eichmann said, "I was just following orders." He understood this obedience, in Kantian terms, as fulfilling the ethical categorical imperative. Eichmann saw himself as just part of the efficiency of the machine. From this perspective, the Holocaust should be understood as modernity's rotten fruit. The sterility of the modern relationship with the other, which could be paradoxically seen as the ethical puritanism of following orders, becomes itself inhuman. This is not the inhumanity of Satan's will to power, but rather the inhumanity of the machine, where violence is not human sacrifice but rather merely the cleansing of disease. The "pure alienation" of the industrial-technological mindset, which derives from the idea of the individual as nothing other than a means to an end, creates a "death industry" wherein people are the raw material. Here the industrial mindset, which typically wants to create, and uses technology to achieve its ends, suddenly makes a 180-degree turn and desires only technocratic efficiency, without making anything and without any purpose.[9]

The extermination camps were nothing more than efficient slaughterhouses, plain and simple, only slaughtering people instead of animals. The unbelievable organization of the slaughterhouse machines, the power of the laws and regulations, and the famed German obedience and efficiency, all came together to make it possible to turn human beings into raw material to be gathered into freight trucks for the sake of the final solution to the "problem" of their existence. In this way, it was made possible to exclude Jews from the universal humanistic discussion concerning pain, suffering, wrongdoing, and injustice. While we do not feel a sense of inhumanity in a slaughterhouse, without question, the animals suffer. The pain of animals, and even their awareness

---

8. See Hannah Arendt, *Eichmann in Jerusalem: A Report on the Banality of Evil* (New York: Viking Press, 1963).

9. See Ophir, *A Language for Evil*, 456 n. 57.

of this pain, does not exist in the same discussion as that of a human being. From the human perspective, their pain does not exist. Human consciousness cannot access this otherness; therefore, this otherness does not exist from the human perspective.

In this way, the Jew is not just a victim, but a victim who is not recognized as a victim. This is Lyotard's differend. Turning people into raw material without any humanity requires actively excluding them from the human realm, by sterilely estranging them from their existence and by putting their pain into other categories inaccessible to human discourse, just like the pain of animals. Thus, the Jew was excluded from the realm of humanity even in his own eyes. Jews themselves began to believe in their own non-humanity. Perhaps this is what led to the muteness of many survivors. Their suffering had been excluded from the realm of humanity and culture, and so, hurting them was no longer considered criminal or inhuman.[10]

It is important to understand that many of the commanders of the camps, "the monsters," were just regular people who ran ordinary businesses before the Holocaust. If not for the war, they would have lived their lives like any other person. They were normal in every way. Moreover, they were not the only people involved in the scourging of "the Jewish disease," as thousands of Eastern Europeans collaborated as well. Every person contains within them the possibility of taking part in grave, inhuman injustice. In specific situations, every person could find themselves confronted with this possibility. In one sense, the evil of the Holocaust was deeply inhuman. In a different sense, it was very human indeed.

To emphasize this point, let us apply our position to a neighbor who is, for whatever reason, excluded from our world. I recommend

---

10. See Lyotard's own words in the first chapter of *The Differend*: "The 'perfect crime' does not consist in killing the victim or the witnesses (that adds new crimes to the first one and aggravates the difficulty of effacing everything), but rather in obtaining the silence of the witnesses, the deafness of the judges, and the inconsistency (insanity) of the testimony. You neutralize the addressor, the addressee, and the sense of the testimony: then everything is as if there were no referent (no damages)" (Jean François Lyotard, *The Differend: Phrases in Dispute*, trans. Georges Van Den Abbeele [Manchester: Manchester University Press, 1989], 8 [§9]).

imagining a specific neighbor who is excluded from our discourse due to their religion, nationality, etc. Could we participate in sending them to the slaughter? We intuitively want to answer, "Of course not!" However, the Holocaust ought to challenge our confidence in our own ethical nature. Good, upstanding people played active roles in the Nazi death machine. This fact requires us to examine anew our intuitions about ourselves and humanity.

To be more precise, I am not talking about indifference to our neighbor's fate. We encounter this sort of indifference on every street corner. Do we care about the fate of the downtrodden beggar we pass in the street? Do the horrifying images which are broadcast on TV every now and then shake us from our comfortable, everyday lives? Do they keep us up at night? Rwanda, Bosnia, Tibet, Burma, the list goes on. Additionally, I am not talking about choosing indifference or involvement based on fear or duress. I am talking about intentional collaborators acting out of a belief that they were fulfilling an ethical imperative. Many Europeans collaborated in a variety of ways because they identified with Nazism. This is the real question we must be asking ourselves.[11]

Relatedly, I think we should see post-modernism as a response to Nazism in both the power it sought and the mechanical precision with which it acted. Against the long lines of infinite, obedient Nazi soldiers marching in identical lockstep with their arms raised in salute to the Führer, post-modernism has given us a society of individualists who are wild, colorful, and entirely undisciplined, who totally disregard any seriousness that might cross their path. These qualities dissipate the will to power until it is a total lack of will, a dispirited, pretense-less "chill." Moreover, since Hannah Arendt defined totalitarianism as terror that not only invalidates the other but actually removes them from discourse entirely, thereby making them an excess, post-modernism denies this possibility in principle because it validates any and all discourses.[12]

---

11. This raises another question: has humanity undergone a radical change following the Holocaust? Can oppressed people today rely on their fellow humans to help them? The answer is, not always and not enough. Despite this, we should not look askance at the real changes the Holocaust inspired in the human race's sense of mutual responsibility.

12. See Ophir, *A Language for Evil*, 343, §8.550; 380, §9.241. See also Hannah Arendt,

Every person has a place not because the space can include everyone, but because each person is their own space: "He is the place of the world."[13]

Whether it was Satan and his will to power, or Satan as a technocrat, the Holocaust provided a revelation of evil and injustice that breached the boundaries of humanist discourse. This evil silenced the inner lives of the survivors, forever denying them the comfort of "Let me speak, then, and get relief; let me open my lips and reply" (Job 32:20).

DECISIVENESS BEYOND THE DIVINE:
THE KLAUSENBURGER REBBE

The great question raised by the Holocaust is ultimately addressed not just to the human spirit but also to religious faith: does the latter not fall apart in the face of the Holocaust? People say the Holocaust killed not just humanity and the human spirit but also faith in God. Religious people have responded to this catastrophe in a variety of ways. Religious Zionism claims, to use the language of Rabbi Zvi Yehuda Kook, that the Holocaust was part of a process of "disconnecting" the Jews from the exile.[14] Rabbi Yissachar Shlomo Teichtal, author of *Em HaBanim Semeḥa*, similarly claimed that the Holocaust was a result of the Jews sinfully and intentionally ignoring Zionism.[15] Representing the other side of the spectrum, Rabbi Menachem Shach claimed that the Holocaust was punishment for the sins of the Enlightenment, Zionism, and secularization movements that had spread throughout the Jewish communities of the day.[16]

I wish to examine the deep, surprising religious response found in the life story of the hasidic Rebbe, Rabbi Yekusiel Yehuda Halberstam of Sanz-Klausenburg, also known as the Klausenburger Rebbe. Born

The Origins of Totalitarianism (London, San Diego, Orlando, New York, Austin: Houghton Mifflin Harcourt Inc., 1973).

13. Genesis Rabba 68:9.
14. See Rabbi Eliyahu Bazak, *Talking Justice: Lectures on Rabbi Tzvi Yehuda Kook's Discourses on the Holocaust* (Eilat: Yeshivat Ayelet Hashachar, 2000) (Heb.).
15. See Rabbi Yissachar Shlomo Teichtal, *Em HaBanim Semeḥa* (Jerusalem and Mevaseret Zion: Kol Mevaser, 1998) (Heb.).
16. See Rabbi Shagar, *On That Day*, 48–51.

in 1905 (5665) and raised in occupied Hungary,[17] he lost his mother, all his siblings, his wife, and all eleven of his children in the holocaust of Hungarian Jewry. The Klausenburger Rebbe endured long journeys, suffered in both concentration and labor camps, and walked in death marches. During his many sufferings, no matter how bad things were, he took it upon himself to never transgress any law of the Torah or eat any non-kosher food. For example, during all seven days of Pesaḥ, he gave up his ration of bread, refused to eat anything cooked in the kitchen of the camp, and lived off just a few potatoes he cooked for himself in a pot he *kashered* before the holiday.[18] He also made sure to continue living a thoroughly Jewish life. He prayed, put on tefillin, delivered hasidic discourses with great passion during the third meal each Shabbat, and intensely maintained various customs, such as eating apples on the night of Rosh HaShana.[19] In short, he was willing to sacrifice his life for his Jewishness.

The Klausenburger Rebbe's response to the Holocaust differed from other religious responses such as that of the Piaseczner Rebbe,[20] who dealt at length with the issue of the seeming meaninglessness of the suffering. The Piaseczner Rebbe attempted to attribute religious significance to the human suffering of the Holocaust, viewing it as the sufferings of the *Shekhina*, to the point where he said that Jews should pray not for the *Shekhina* (as hasidic thinkers had long instructed), but for the Jewish body groaning in pain. In contrast, the Klausenburger Rebbe's suffering and the suffering of the people around him aroused in him no questions of faith. On the contrary, he took pride in how he came through the calamity without ever questioning God's actions.[21] His response to the Holocaust boils down to commitment to the point of total self-sacrifice, to observance of the Torah and the commandments even as the depths of hell swallowed him whole. He saw his fight

---

17. The discussion below is based on Aharon Surasky's biography of Rabbi Halberstam, *A Flame from the Fire: The Wondrous Life of the Exemplar of the Generation, the Sanz-Klausenburger Rebbe* (Bnei Brak: Y. Sh. Frankel, 1997).

18. Surasky, *A Flame from the Fire*, 242.

19. Ibid., 231.

20. See Rabbi Shagar, *On That Day*, 51–62.

21. Surasky, *A Flame from the Fire*, 227, 264.

for Torah as a fight for the very existence of Judaism. He did not direct his efforts toward theological reflection like the Piaseczner Rebbe, but poured all his energy into the decision and struggle themselves, toward making a decisive commitment to fight for Torah.

It is important to note that the Klausenburger did not arrive at the decision not to transgress any religious prohibitions because he thought he was obligated to keep those prohibitions even at the risk of his own life. In fact, he instructed other people that "since the enemy intends to destroy the Jewish body, in addition to the soul, he gives you no choice but to rescue yourself from what he has decreed upon you, and therefore it is a mitzva for us to do the exact opposite. This is not the time to avoid eating and thereby endanger our lives."[22] For himself, however, he insisted: "Master of the World, I am all alone, I have nothing. You took everything from me…. I am laid bare, exposed, and now you want me to eat *treif*? I don't want to eat *treif*! I will not eat it!"[23] Making this decision did not lessen his suffering. His life story does not tell of a man without worries or fears. Indeed, the man suffered greatly: "The *Shekhina* is in exile, the Congregation of Israel is in exile, and his [i.e., the Klausenburger Rebbe's] fate would be no different, as the Sages said, 'Anyone who is not subject to His hiding of the face is not one of them. Anyone who is not subject to: "And they shall be devoured" (Deut. 31:17) is not one of them' (Ḥagiga 5a-b)."[24] However, even though he was fully aware of his fears and vulnerabilities, the Rebbe did not let them guide his actions, choosing rather to accept them, yet override them via his decisive commitment.

The Rebbe's insistence on refusing to question God and committing to the Torah and the commandments, often to the point of near death, was an expression of his personal rebellion against the Nazis.[25] Despite this, his faith and commitment to his God actually gave him a certain degree of freedom in relation to a God who had "betrayed" him, or, to use religious language, a God who had "hidden His face

---

22. Ibid., 172
23. Ibid.
24. Ibid., 227.
25. Ibid., 236–237, 242.

from him." In this way, the Rebbe's rebellion was a rebellion against a God who wanted him to question divine justice. The Rebbe's personal struggle to maintain his Judaism exceeded his faith in God. God surely had not commanded him to keep Shabbat or only eat kosher in this terrible situation! His decision to live as a Jew and not violate any religious prohibition stemmed from him experiencing his Judaism as the totality of existence, transcending beyond even the divine command itself. In the terrifying reality of the Holocaust, the Klausenburger Rebbe revealed that he would rather die than be forced to live without Judaism. For him, life would be meaningless without the Torah and commandments. In acting beyond any commandment as he did, he placed Judaism's devotion, intimacy, and ultimately holiness itself, beyond God: "You took everything from me... and now You want me to eat *treif*?" The Rebbe did not arrive at this decisive commitment as the result of a halakhic calculation on whether or not he was obligated to martyr himself in a time of Jewish persecution. He made this decision with full consciousness of a divine will that took everything from him, even commandedness itself.

Moreover, the Rebbe's devotion to his Judaism took form in his self-understanding as a "Rebbe," or a righteous person. This means understanding the self as absolute, as if God were subordinate to him: "A righteous person decrees and God fulfills." Such self-understanding led him to paradoxical moments, like when he gave thanks to God that he merited to fulfill the commandment of lighting Ḥanukka candles in the camp, putting himself in mortal danger: "Even if I give thanks to God my entire life... I will not fulfill my obligation of thanksgiving to God for the fact that I was able to truly fulfill the commandment of the Ḥanukka candles, in every aspect, under the reign of evildoers. Moreover, I escaped alive and sound despite the great danger that hovered above me [due to my lighting the candles]."[26] If God did not command him to fulfill the commandment in these conditions and did not want the Rebbe to do so, how could the Rebbe put himself in danger just to light the candles? How could he then give thanks for being saved afterward? Throughout this process, the Rebbe displayed a devotion to Judaism based on a faith beyond his faith in God, a faith based on the revelation

---

26. Ibid., 226.

of essence itself. The Rebbe was overwhelmed with the awareness that if he could not maintain the practices of his forefathers, he did not want to live. Without these practices, he reasoned, his life would not really be *life*. This was a revelation of the very essence of his life, and as a righteous person, he forced God to accept it.

Indeed, the Rebbe's life *was* Judaism, devotion, and rootedness. In other words, the Klausenburger Rebbe totally identified his "I" with Judaism; there was no difference between his faith and himself. The divine manifested in his life in an immanent manner rather than in the inherently transcendent form of halakhic thinking, exhibiting a sort of *quality* rather than a *command*. His God was not the God of halakha but the God of Jewish intimacy, the God of the covenant. Even if his God broke the covenant with him, he would not break his covenant with his God.

However, we should not view this as a heroic position. We must see it simply as it was: a decision that it would be better not to live than to live non-Jewishly, as a Jew lacking faith and Torah. Similarly, it would be better to be a victim than to join in the slaughter, better to be persecuted than to take part in the persecution. More than anything, it would be better to believe in God even if this belief cannot be supported or justified objectively, rationally, or religiously. This decision creates a *quality* that makes its difficult price easier to bear – a quality that can only be created by a person's total freedom.[27]

"WITH THE BEGINNING" – GOD'S CREATION

The Kabbala says that the revelation of God is not the beginning itself: "In the beginning God created" (Gen. 1:1) – "With this beginning, the unknown concealed one created the palace. This palace is called *Elokim*, God. The secret is: '*Bereshit bara Elokim*,' 'With beginning, _____ created God' (Gen. 1:1)."[28] With the beginning, the concealed and unknown created God. What does that mean? In Ezekiel's prophecies,

---

27. This is where the Klausenburger Rebbe and the Piaseczner Rebbe essentially agree: The Holocaust leads to "*bitul hayesh*," "nullifying existence," thus turning faith into a decision rather than a divine command. In a situation like the Holocaust, it would be unjustifiable as a command.
28. Zohar I:15a. Translation from the Pritzker edition by Daniel Matt.

we read about the divine throne: "Above the expanse over their heads was the semblance of a throne, in appearance like sapphire; and on top, upon this semblance of a throne, there was the semblance of a human form" (Ezek. 1:26). In Tanakh, God wears a human face, "the semblance of a human form," when revealing Himself to humanity and addressing people. Moreover, the human being draws his very humanity from this divine face and address. Because this divinity is the beginning of the created human world, the Zohar's "palace," as such humans can access and know it. The Holocaust revealed something beyond the material world, the inhuman divine, "the unknown concealed one" who is beyond both the Torah and our human existence and who therefore cannot be expressed in language – "the differend." Perhaps this was what the Lubavitcher Rebbe meant when he said, "We cannot explain or clarify (based on the wisdom of the Torah) anything about the Holocaust. All we know is the fact that 'thus it arose in thought before Me' and 'it is a decree from before Me.'"[29] Not only can the Holocaust not be explained, but the very language and terminology of Torah also denies any explanation of the Holocaust. This is because the divine that manifested in the Holocaust is not part of the human-divine discourse which the Torah creates. Similarly, the Klausenburger Rebbe's decisive commitment can be understood neither as part of human discourse, nor even as part of "the wisdom of Torah," as the latter does not demand such total commitment. The Klausenburger Rebbe's faith embodies a reality that transcends both the human and the divine – it is a manifestation of essence.

The divine face was not the only thing that broke in the Holocaust. The human spirit, which derives from the image of man on the divine throne, broke just as decisively. This does not mean that there is no human spirit after the Holocaust: "Truly it is the spirit in men" (Job 32:8). However, this spirit is not an absolute nature that is eternal and unchanging. The Holocaust shattered the myth of human progress no matter how you define it: reason, freedom, the free subject, etc. In the Holocaust, humanity was revealed to be inhuman, to be "something else entirely."

---

29. Rabbi Menachem Mendel Schneerson, *Hisvaaduyos: Shenat 5751* (New York, 1992), vol. 2, 120. See Rabbi Shagar, *On That Day*, 48–51.

Regarding God, the Holocaust revealed the *"nora ha'eloki,"* the "terrifying divine" that is above the "image of man." Does this divine face leave us unprotected, exposed to arbitrariness? Can God act capriciously? Doesn't this mean that a godless world has somehow invaded God's territory? Religion teaches otherwise: far be it from God to do injustice! "A faithful God, never false, true and upright is He" (Deut. 32:4). But what sense is there to meaningless meaning? If there is any meaning, it comes in the form of the "differend": it cannot be humanly comprehended, but the human cannot transcend the human in order to somehow grasp a meaning that is foreign to him. What does it mean to say that there is meaning "over there," other than the acknowledgment of that simple fact without actually comprehending it? Was this what the Lubavitcher Rebbe meant when he said, "We cannot explain or clarify (based on the wisdom of the Torah) anything about the Holocaust. All we know is the fact that 'thus it arose in thought before Me'"? Does this meaningless statement function in the same way as "negative attributes"? Does it function as the "differend"? "In the differend, something 'asks' to be put into phrases and suffers from the wrong of not being able to be put into phrases right away."[30] Could a meaningless statement about meaning constitute an encounter with something that seeks expression but cannot attain it?

I conclude with these questions.

---

30. Lyotard, *The Differend*, 13 (§23).

On That Day:
Natural and Mystical,
Zionist and Post-Zionist

> *Mystical perception is based on the inner clarity*
> *of the omnipotent, on the unlimited possibilities*
> *of the infinite strength…. There is no limit to the*
> *power within the mysterious, and freedom is not*
> *revealed within the revealed.*[1]

"And it will be on that day" (Amos 9: 11). The prophets once prophesied of the day, "*that day*," when the redemption will take concrete form. On Yom HaAtzma'ut, I often feel as if I can sense "the future yet to come." I do not mean that the hoped-for redemption is here among us, but rather that an echo of that time, of "that day" that will come in the future, rings in our ears around this time of the year. When we celebrate the return of the people of Israel to the Land of Israel, we hear this echo. It raises

---

Based on drafts written in preparation for Yom HaAtzma'ut in 5757–5759 (1997–1999). Edited by Yishai Mevorach and published in *On That Day*, 164–189.

1. Rabbi Abraham Isaac HaKohen Kook, *Orot HaKodesh* (Jerusalem: Mossad Harav Kook, 1985), vol. 1, 103.

the question: What will be the nature of "that day," the echo of which we can hear even now?

MIRACLE OR MYSTERY?

I will begin by exploring the debate between the statements of the rabbinic Sages and Maimonides' teachings on the nature of the End of Days, a debate many scholars and researchers have already noted. I will not explore the different nuances and definitions of the various stages of the Messianic Era and the World-to-Come in the words of the rabbis and Maimonides.[2] What I intend to do here is portray the spirit that moves within each of the different opinions and try to determine how each spirit leads to a different vision of redemption.

In their different depictions of the Messianic Era, we find two mutually exclusive ways of thinking. The first, that of the rabbis, is utopian and miraculous, giving rise to a world of wonder and wondrousness. The second, that of Maimonides, refuses to grant any space for miracles. As far as he is concerned, in the Messianic Era the world will run as it normally does: "There is no difference between this world and the Messianic Era, other than our subjugation to the gentile kingdoms."[3]

The Sages depict the future redemption through fantastical-miraculous images. For example, they say that "in the future, God will create ten new things":

> Another explanation: It is written: "Behold, the former things are come to pass, and new things do I declare" (Is. 42:9). Will there be "new things" in the Time to Come? Is it not written: "That which hath been is that which shall be... and there is nothing new under the sun" (Eccl. 1:9)? We do, however, find ten things which the Holy One, blessed be He, will renew in the Time to Come. The first is that He will illumine the whole world .... When a man

---

2. See Rabbi Shagar, "History and Messianism According to Maimonides," *We Walk in Fervor*, 75–96; idem., "The Torah of the Land of Israel," *On That Day*, 146–163; idem., "Faith Girding his Waist," ibid., 217–225; idem., "The Messianic Era," *Your Face, I Seek*, 163.

3. Maimonides, *Mishneh Torah, Hilkhot Teshuva* 9:2; *Hilkhot Melakhim UMilḥamotehem* 12:2.

shall be sick, God will order the sun to heal him.... The second thing is that He will bring out living water from Jerusalem and heal therewith all those who have a disease.... The third is that He will make trees yield their fruit each month, and when a man eats of them he will be healed.... The fourth is that they will rebuild all the waste cities so that there shall not be one waste place left in the world; even Sodom and Gomorrah will be rebuilt in the Time to Come.... The fifth is that He will rebuild Jerusalem with sapphire stones.... These precious stones will shine like the sun, and the heathens will come and see the glory of Israel.... The sixth is that "the cow and bear shall feed" (Is. 11:7). The seventh is that He will bring all the wild beasts, birds and creeping things and make a covenant with them and with all Israel.... The eighth is that there will be no more weeping or wailing in the world.... The ninth is that there will be no more death in the world, for it says: "He will swallow up death for ever; and the Lord God will wipe away tears from off all faces; and the reproach of His people will He take away" (Is. 25:8). The tenth is that there will no longer be any sighing, wailing or anguish, but that all will be rejoicing, for it says: "And the ransomed of the Lord shall return, and come with singing unto Zion" (Is. 35:10).[4]

To understand these wondrous, otherworldly, and magical depictions, we look to a somewhat parallel literary phenomenon: science fiction. Both science fiction and the statements from the rabbinic Sages about the future redemption describe alternate worlds. The primary purpose of these alternate worlds, if we can speak of such a thing, is to lay bare the mystery of our lives. This encourages the collapse and destruction of our banal, boring everyday lives. The two have similar effects on their readers, and, at least for me, often inspire mystical sensations.[5]

4. Exodus Rabba 15:21. Translation from Soncino edition.
5. [Hebrew Editor's note: "Mysticism" is a concept with many meanings, interpretations, and uses. In this sermon, Rabbi Shagar is using it less in terms of mystical *experience* and more in terms of a mystical *mindset*, meaning a mindset of contradiction and impossibility.]

Iyar

In the rabbis' days, there were no rockets; therefore, their eschato-
logical homilies do not talk about distant galaxies or about worlds full of
robots and beyond-human creatures like those in science fiction. However, they contain magic and wonders just as great. They provide their
audience with the realistic possibility of a substantive alternative to this
world, an alternative that the rabbis certainly thought would arrive one
day: "Today, if you obey His voice."[6] In this way, the miraculous and the
wondrous burst into the world and disrupt its factual, scientific stability.

Facing the future miracle that fractures fixed reality led the rabbis
to believe that redemption cannot take place in this world. This world, by
nature, is finite, constricted, and banal. According to the rabbis, there can
be no continuity between this world and redemption because the latter
depends on the destruction of the former. Only an apocalyptic catastrophe can lead a person to the world of the miracles, to the redeemed
world. The rabbis called the Messiah, "Son of the Fallen,"[7] because when
the miraculous permeates this world, it causes the natural order to crack
and crumble. The Messiah's coming signifies, as the Maharal put it, "a new
reality" that causes the world to crumble rather than to be built upon it:

> Any reality in the world comes into being one little bit after
> another, as you can see with all the realities of animals and plants,
> which come into being one little bit after another.... When you
> look into the words of the rabbis, you should pay attention to
> this. In [Sanhedrin 96b] it says, "R. Nahman said to R. Yitzhak:
> Have you heard when the Son of the Fallen will come? R. Yitzhak
> said to him: Who is the Son of the Fallen? R. Nahman said to
> him: He is the Messiah. R. Yitzhak asked him: Do you call the
> Messiah the Son of the Fallen? R. Nahman said to him: Yes, as it
> is written: 'On that day I will establish the Tabernacle of David
> that is fallen' (Amos 9:11)".... They said that the coming of the
> Messiah, when the realities will be renewed, will cause the loss
> of the former reality. Therefore, the week when the son of David

6. Sanhedrin 98a.
7. Sanhedrin 96b.

comes, in being close to the new reality, will cause the loss of the former reality.[8]

The rabbis' homilies present us with a miraculous yet apocalyptic vision of the Messianic Era. We find an oppositional response to this in Maimonides' rulings in the *Mishneh Torah*: "Maimonides became a mouthpiece for all those who wanted to do away [with apocalypse]."[9] It is almost as if Maimonides reacted against the utopian trends in rabbinic homilies when he writes, "A person should not occupy himself with the *aggadot* and homilies concerning these and similar matters, nor should he consider them as fundamentals, for study of them will neither bring fear or love of God. Similarly, one should not try to determine the appointed time for the Messiah's coming. Our Sages declared: 'May the spirits of those who attempt to determine the time of the Messiah's coming expire!'"[10]

Resolutely citing the talmudic dictum of Shmuel, "There is no difference between this world and the Messianic Era, other than our subjugation to the gentile kingdoms,"[11] Maimonides seems to imagine the Messianic Era as a world wherein the prosaic everyday remains as it is. The only change will be the reign of a Jewish king, wherein he and the rest of the Jewish people spend their time studying Torah. However, a truer reading of Maimonides paints a picture of a world without any banality at all:

> Do not presume that in the Messianic Age any facet of the world's nature will change…. The world will continue according to its pattern…. Israel will dwell securely together with the wicked gentiles…. They will all return to the true faith and no longer steal or destroy. Rather, they will eat permitted food and be at peace with Israel….

8. Rabbi Yehuda Loew of Prague, *Netsaḥ Yisrael*, ch. 32.
9. Gershom Scholem, "Concluding Thoughts," in *The Messianic Idea in Israel: A Conference for the Occasion of Gershom Scholem's 80th Birthday*, ed. Yair Zakovitz (Jerusalem: The Israel Academy for the Sciences, 1982), 257.
10. Maimonides, *Mishneh Torah, Hilkhot Melakhim UMilḥamotehem* 12:2.
11. Sanhedrin 99b.

Our Sages taught: "There is no difference between this world and the Messianic Era, other than our subjugation to the gentile kingdoms".... At the beginning of the Messianic Age... a prophet will arise to inspire Israel to be upright and prepare their hearts.... He will come... only to establish peace within the world.... In that era, there will be no famine no war or envy or competition, for good will flow in abundance and all the delights will be freely available as dust. The occupation of the entire world will be solely to know God. Therefore, the Jews will be great sages and know the hidden matters, grasping the knowledge of their Creator according to the full extent of human potential, as Isaiah 11:9 states: "The world will be filled with the knowledge of God as the waters cover the ocean bed."[12]

For these reasons, all Israel, [in particular] their prophets and their Sages, have yearned for the Messianic Age so they can rest from the [oppression of] the gentile kingdoms who do not allow them to occupy themselves with Torah and mitzvot properly. They will find rest and increase their knowledge... because the king who will arise from David's descendants will be a master of knowledge.... Therefore, he will teach the entire nation and instruct them in the path of God.[13]

Miracles and the supernatural may be absent from this vision of the End of Days, but excitement and enchantment (natural enchantment, of course) are on full display.

What was the vision of redemption for which Maimonides hoped? Imagine a world that is not capitalist, whether in the financial, social, or psychological realms. Imagine a world that is driven not by the desire for power or for material profit; a world where people will not worry about their livelihoods or about quality of life. In this world, apathy toward the other would disappear and deep affection would reign between all creatures.

---

12. Maimonides, *Mishneh Torah, Hilkhot Melakhim UMilḥamotehem* 12:1–5.
13. Maimonides, *Mishneh Torah, Hilkhot Teshuva* 9:2.

Furthermore, Maimonides overlays this whole shift in humanity with knowledge of God, showing us a world of people living good lives overflowing with "knowing." Such "knowledge of God," of course, does not mean Torah study in the typical sense. Maimonides understands "knowledge" as love and devotion rather than as study, as it is commonly understood. Knowing God means knowing a secret which overflows with the erotic tension of love, just as an artist's knowledge of his own work is, at its core, love. This is how Maimonides speaks about love: "What is proper love? That a person should love God with a very great and exceeding love until his soul is bound up in the love of God. Thus, he will always be obsessed with this love as if he is lovesick, such that his thoughts are never diverted from the love of that woman.... This concept was implied by Solomon when he stated, as a metaphor: 'I am lovesick' (Song. 2:5). Indeed, the totality of the Song of Songs is a parable describing this love."[14] This love results from knowing God and from contemplative meditation. We should see this loving knowledge not as a mysticism interested in "supernal worlds," but as devotion focusing on the mystery of this world and the physical and metaphysical secret it contains, the secret of creation: "What is the path to love and fear of Him? When a person contemplates His wondrous and great deeds and creations and appreciates His infinite wisdom that surpasses all comparison, he will immediately love, praise, and glorify Him, yearning with tremendous desire to know His great name."[15] In the world of redemption, knowledge will cover everything like water, and the reality principle, the *conatus*[16] (which focuses on maintaining existence), will no longer reign supreme. Instead, the pleasure principle, which is best expressed in the imagination and in the aesthetic dimensions of reality, will be dominant.[17] It will be a world of pleasure and happiness, where "the good" – that is human, physical good – will be bountiful.

---

14. Maimonides, *Mishneh Torah, Hilkhot Teshuva* 10:3.

15. Maimonides, *Mishneh Torah, Hilkhot Yesodei HaTorah* 2:2.

16. For a definition of "*conatus*," see p. 170, note 3 above.

17. See Rabbi Shagar's discussion of "The Torah of the Land of Israel" in Rabbi Shagar, *On That Day*, 146–163.

Maimonides feels no need to see this world destroyed for redemption to arrive, nor does he feel any need for a miracle to experience enchantment. He depicts the Messianic Era as "a new Middle East," a world of international peace, booming economies, and societies typified by generosity and positivity. All of this will be achievable within our natural world. What will people do with their time, when they no longer need to struggle to earn a livelihood? When social conflicts dissipate? When competition and social pressure disappear, leaving people to pursue only the activities they desire? What will citizens do when they do not need to go to work every morning and when they do not need to be concerned about politics or the news? People will spend their days immersed in thinking about God, in "knowledge of God" – devotional meditation, if you will. What a wondrous narrative this is! It is a divine romance wherein I forget myself and experience the holy enchantment, the prophetic pleasure, and yet it will not just be a story or a dream. It will be reality itself.[18]

Maimonides was not drawn in by the drama and flare of supernatural miracles. He sought out the good and the secret contained within the natural. The everyday will remain a natural everyday; it will be a day-to-day of good, devotion, and love in the service of the Creator amidst global peace.

THE LAND OF ISRAEL

Just as the rabbis debated the nature of redemption, whether it will be wondrous and mystical or enchantingly harmonious, so too did they debate the nature of the land of the redemption: the Land of Israel.

What does the Promised Land mean to us? What does "the land of the redemption" promise? Does it promise the miracle that shatters nature, or the wonder that shines from within nature itself? I want to shed light on this question from within three distinct sources: the

---

18. We can experience a minimal version of this during prayer today. Maimonides' description recalls those "masters of prayer" sitting in the forest from Rabbi Nahman's stories: "The master of prayer and his men would sit outside the town and spend their time only... praying, singing, and praising God" (*Sippurei Maasiyot*, "The Story of the Master of Prayer").

teachings of Rabbi Nahman, those of Rabbi Kook, and the philosophy of Franz Rosenzweig.[19]

Rabbi Nahman said of himself, "Anywhere I go, I am going to the Land of Israel," while Rabbi Kook confessed, "Living eternally in our hearts is the faithful belief in the return to our Holy Land, to the city where David encamped."[20] While these statements seem similar, the two thinkers had very different Lands of Israel in mind. Rabbi Kook saw the Land of Israel as a platform for the drama of redemption, for the redemption and realization of nature itself. Rabbi Nahman, in contrast, saw it as a utopia of the wondrous. While they both spoke of returning to the land itself, Franz Rosenzweig, on the other hand, saw the Land of Israel as the destined land of eternal yearning: "The nations do not tend to see themselves as immigrants… [but] our history begins with the command to the father of our nation: 'Go forth from your land, to the land which I will show you…. Exile stands at the door of this history in its entirety."[21]

Rabbi Kook asserted, "The holiness that is in nature is the holiness of the Land of Israel…. When we arrive at this highest apprehension of the perfect holiness in nature… all inclines toward kindness. All of the powers in a person manifest in their elevated refinement, as they are in their nature."[22] Like Maimonides, who saw the mysteriousness of the world revealing itself within the world as the redemption, Rabbi Kook sought nature itself, the nature of the land, rather than the shattering of this nature: "Holiness that fights against nature is not perfect holiness, and it must be subsumed within the highest essence of the highest holiness, which is the holiness in nature itself, as well as the foundation of the rectification of the entire world and its total elevation."[23] Moreover, holiness that opposes nature cannot bring the redemption because, for

19. For more on Rabbi Kook and Rabbi Nahman's different understandings of the Land of Israel, see "The Torah of the Land of Israel" in Rabbi Shagar, *On That Day*, 146–163.
20. Rabbi Abraham Isaac Kook, *Orot HaRe'aya* (Jerusalem, 1985), 99.
21. Franz Rosenzweig, *Naharayim: Selected Writings*, trans. Yehoshua Amir (Jerusalem: The Bialik Institute, 1977), 65 (Heb.).
22. Rabbi Kook, *Orot*, 77–78, §28.
23. Ibid.

Rabbi Kook at least, such holiness is inherently exilic: "Only in the time of the destruction [of the Temple] and immediately thereafter, when Israel began to be distanced from its land…there took root in certain individuals a guidance toward ascetic distancing from temporal life in favor of eternal life, and even this was met by a heavenly protest."[24] It is no wonder that he says that "political and social regulations [in the Land of Israel]…are themselves the body of Torah. The more the practical elements will expand and develop, the more the spirit full of holiness and true life will act on the world and on life, and the light of Israel will shine on the world in all its splendor."[25] Nature expresses itself to the point of building institutions and political regulations, bringing out and revealing its hidden powers. The world building itself with might and power is the great drama of redemption, and an intoxicating, addictive drama at that.

Rabbi Nahman taught something very different. To him, the Land of Israel represents the greatest possible shift – a venture into openness and possibility. He spoke of "the song of the natural order, of the design of the heavens. This is an instance of the songs and praises with which God is praised for His current providence, for guiding the world through the natural order."[26] However, this song is not the hoped-for melody of the future, an honor which is reserved for the melody of the Land of Israel, "but in the future, a new song that is an instance of wonders will burst forth…. This new song that will burst forth in the future is…the concept of kindness, through which the world will be renewed in the future, as in, 'The world will be built on kindness' (Ps. 89:3)…. Renewal of the world is an instance of the Land of Israel…. And then the song of divine providence and miracles will burst forth."[27] This is the song of the Land of Prayer, the Land of Hope that is open to all possibilities, because God actively manages it at all times: "Now, prayer is an instance of miracles, for it is not according to the natural order. Sometimes, the

24. Ibid., 77, §27.
25. Ibid.
26. Rabbi Nahman of Breslov, *Likkutei Moharan* II 8:10.
27. Ibid. For more on this teaching, see Rabbi Shagar's essay, "Joseph the Dreaming *Tzaddik*" in Rabbi Shagar, *We Will Walk in Fervor*, 133–136.

natural order necessitates one thing, whereas prayer overrides nature's course. And the essence of miracles, which is the essence of prayer, is only in the Land of Israel, as in, 'Dwell in the land and cultivate faith' (Ps. 37:3). And faith [in the verse] is prayer."[28]

BETWEEN THE CITY AND THE FIELD

These different aspects of the Land of Israel all played out within me, comingled and interchanging, during the Pesaḥ that just passed. Rabbi Kook, Rabbi Nahman, and Rosenzweig's various approaches all crossed my path.

I spent Ḥol HaMoed in two places this year; that is, in two different worlds entirely. I sought the beloved, about whom we read in the Song of Songs, in the field:

> For now the winter is past, the rains are over and gone. The blossoms have appeared in the land, the time of pruning has come; the song of the turtledove is heard in our land. The green figs form on the fig tree, the vines in blossom give off fragrance. Arise, my darling; my fair one, come away! (Song. 2:11–13)

> Come, my beloved, let us go into the open; let us lodge among the henna shrubs. Let us go early to the vineyards; let us see if the vine has flowered, if its blossoms have opened, if the pomegranates are in bloom. There I will give my love to you. The mandrakes yield their fragrance, at our doors are all choice fruits; both freshly picked and long-stored have I kept, my beloved, for you. (Song. 7:12–14)

There is nothing lovelier than celebrating the festival of spring in the fields of the Land of Israel, in the shade of the fig tree listening to the

---

28. Rabbi Nahman, *Likkutei Moharan* 9:5. Of course, Rabbi Nahman's corpus contains statements that resonate more with Rabbi Kook's assertion. For example, see *Likkutei Moharan* II 116. Similarly, Rabbi Kook has statements that echo Rabbi Nahman's approach as discussed here. Below, we will see that for Rabbi Kook these two approaches should not be seen as in tension, but as two stages of a larger redemptive vision.

song of the nightingale. The powerful bloom, the intoxicating scents, and the chirping of the birds surround us as we hike through nature. They create a sense of Shabbat. Kabbalistic texts describe Shabbat and the Land of Israel as parallel. Indeed, the Land of Israel is an aspect (*beḥina*) of Shabbat. In both, physical reality ascends to God. The air and the dirt, the base material itself, are all holy. The beloved is in the field. The king is in the field.

We experience the world differently on Shabbat than we do during the week. Existence shines with a different light: the room is the same and the people are the same, but a different light emanates from them, the moment Shabbat starts. We experience the Land of Israel similarly. The soil is the same soil as all other places, the air is the same air, and the animals are the same animals, but they all take on a different light when we hike this land. It fills us with a sense of beauty, illumination, and freedom like we feel on Shabbat – "a microcosm of the World to Come."[29] This illumination emerges from nature itself rather than transcending or opposing it. It emerges from the very rocks of the earth, from the steps trodden upon it, and from touching the wet grass, just as the light of Shabbat emerges from matter itself, from eating and from bodily pleasure. According to Rabbi Kook, the light of the land permeates not just the act of hiking under fig trees but even the crude processes of setting up the state and its institutions.[30]

This experience of the land tracks closely with the biblical description of God's providence over the land: "It is a land which the Lord your God looks after, on which the Lord your God always keeps His eye, from year's beginning to year's end" (Deut. 11:12). Moreover, the very rocks of this land contain the history of divine providence. Furthermore, the renewed contact with the land has laid bare this reawakened history.[31] As Moshe Dayan, who grew up in Kibbutz Nahalal, wrote:

---

29. Berakhot 57b.
30. Rabbi Kook spoke of "sanctifying the mundane," which means the illumination of holiness within the mundane, an illumination that can be attained specifically through the mundane.
31. See Rabbi Shagar, *On That Day*, 81–94, 123–127.

It was not enough for me to see Israel with my own eyes and touch it with my own hands. I also wanted to make the ancient Israel, the Israel of names and verses, into a reality. Before my eyes, I saw not only the Kishon River passing through the fields of Nahalal and Kefar Yehoshua, but also the Kishon River which swept away Sisera's army.... I wanted to give my physical birthplace a spiritual-historical depth, to fill the ruins and archaeological tels with the soul of the past, to revive the Israel of the days of the Patriarchs, the judges, and the kings.[32]

Today, one of the ways this phenomenon manifests is in the revolution of the study of Tanakh. People are studying Tanakh in a new style, one which connects Tanakh with the Land of Israel and with the reality of nature in Israel.

I spent the rest of the holiday far from the field, in a different world that is the holy city of Bnei Brak.[33] In Bnei Brak, I experienced an entirely different Pesaḥ, one which was Jewish rather than Israeli. The holiness that surrounded me there was not the holiness that rises from flowers budding in the fields, as the last orchard in Bnei Brak, on the edge of Zichron Meir, which always gave off the nicest aroma this time of year, had been recently torn out. Instead, Bnei Brak gives off the scent of Torah. Though this scent lacks the tangy sweat of the hiker or the smell of fresh grass crushed under the soles of shoes, it is full of "oil of myrrh and women's cosmetics."[34]

Those days I spent in Bnei Brak were characterized by nice holiday clothing, as the Sages decreed: "A man is obligated to gladden his children and the members of his household on a Festival.... With what should he gladden them?.... Women...by buying them colorful clothes."[35] They were days of unhurried prayer, Torah, holiday meals, and time spent with family. The closest thing to a hike, if you could even

---

32. Moshe Dayan, *Living With the Tanakh* (Jerusalem, 1978), 9 (Heb.).
33. See Rabbi Shagar, *On That Day*, 205–206. For a different take on the tension between the city and the field, see ibid., 311–324.
34. Based on Esther 2:12.
35. Pesaḥim 109a.

call it that, was walking with my kids to Luna Park, which had different sections for each gender. The heads of the yeshivas had run a successful campaign against their students hiking during vacation.

While I was in Bnei Brak, I visited a friend who learned in Kollel. He told me about the novel Torah ideas he thought of while learning, as well as of strictures new and old. It was the same old chit-chat, one-dimensional and entirely predictable, repeating itself year after year.

In those days, I argued with my children about the essence of this holiday. They claimed it was boring. "We should be so lucky," I replied, saying that it was full, celebratory nirvana. I must admit, I was jealous of the Kollel member strolling slowly and speaking Torah with his kids. My children would not enjoy walking with me, certainly not like the Kollel member's kids, because my children feel pressured by time. Bnei Brak during Ḥol HaMoed exists in a different kind of time, a time without any worries. It is entirely faithful to itself and whole within itself, committed and harmonious. There is a suspension of time that takes place as eternity breaks into reality.

Rabbi Nahman's world of wonder emerges within this world, fracturing the everyday time that pressures us and imposing a different set of rules on reality. As we have seen, Rabbi Nahman teaches about the melody of nature, where there is a harmony within reality. A sense of order and lawfulness within this world, from which arises a song and a melody. This melody is an instance of, "The heavens declare the glory of God, the sky proclaims His handiwork" (Ps. 19:2), or, like we cited above, that "which is an instance of the song and melody of the natural order, of the design of the heavens. This is an instance of the songs and praises with which God is praised for His current providence, for guiding the world through the natural order."[36] In contrast, the melody of the redemptive future is the melody of the wondrous, or of the "unnatural." This melody has a positive aspect: the miracle and the connection with the power of "God's works," a power which is not bound to the law and order of reality. It also has a negative aspect: it means recognizing that the laws of nature, the orders and processes according to which reality operates, have a controller to which they are subordinate. This

---

36. Rabbi Nahman, *Likkutei Moharan* II 8:10.

recognition leads to discovering a distinct possibility: the laws of nature themselves are not absolute.

The time that is faithful to itself, the time which I found in Bnei Brak, invades everyday reality, upsetting its orders and opening it up to the possibility of an entirely different rhythm and order. However, it is not the same as time as Rabbi Nahman describes it, a time of "unnatural" wondrousness that sings from within nature itself rather than rejecting nature. Bnei Brak's form of existence within the Land of Israel does not strive to realize itself within the land. In fact, realizing itself in the land would be totally opposed to its nature, which is why Bnei Brak's form of existence comes off as specifically rejecting such a realization.

Let me put it like this: Jewish existence, like the kind you see in Bnei Brak, is an existence that steps out of real, concrete history by eternalizing memory and repeating it forever. The Jew exists in the Torah and returns again and again to the form of time it creates.[37] This pries him out of the real, constantly advancing historical time in which the rest of the world lives. Franz Rosenzweig described this form of existence quite powerfully:

> And here again the eternal people buys its eternity at the cost of its temporal life.... The moment petrifies and stands between unincreased past and immovable future, and so the moment is not fleeting.... The memory of its history does not form a point fixed in the past, a point which year after year, becomes increasingly past. It is a memory which is really not past at all, but eternally present.[38]

It is as if the Jewish world carries within itself a different form of time, the Jewish time of the Exodus from Egypt rather than clock time or the time of factual history: "While the myth of the peoples changes incessantly – parts of the past are continually being forgotten while others are

---

37. See above, "A Space for Faith," pp. 60–63. See also Rabbi Shagar, *On That Day*, 267–284, and *Commemorating the First Day: High Holy Day Sermons*, 104–105. For a criticism of this form of time, see Rabbi Shagar, *On His Torah He Meditates*, 216–221.
38. Franz Rosenzweig, *The Star of Redemption*, 303–304.

remembered as myth – here the myth becomes eternal and is not subject to change."[39] It also has its own system of laws – the just, righteous laws of the Torah rather than the laws of nature or the state: "And while the peoples of the world live in a cycle of revolutions in which their law sheds its old skin over and over, here the law is supreme, a law that can be forsaken but never changed."[40]

Thus, in contrast to Rabbi Nahman's Land of Israel, part of what characterizes the Jewish world is the way it exists as non-existent, as unattained. It is a world that does not realize itself, a metaphorical castle in the sky. This represents a further contrast with the factual world of everyday life: the Jew does not exist within space because he is not rooted in anything other than himself. His defining character trait is that he is not relative to any other nations: "There is a people that dwells apart, not reckoned among the nations" (Num. 23:9). This solitude, this singularity, does not position the Jew against the rest of the world, but rather seals him off beyond it.[41] In Rosenzweig's language, the Jew is an individual, not an individual among other individuals, but rather an individual who strives to be the entire whole itself:

> For us, land and language, custom and law, have long left the circle of the living and have been raised to the run of holiness. But we are still living, and live in eternity. Our life is no longer meshed with anything outside ourselves. We have struck root in ourselves…. What does this mean: to root in one's self?…. It means…that one people, though it is only one people, claims to constitute All.[42]

As an outgrowth of this, the Jewish world yearns for a Jerusalem frozen in eternity in the sacred past of the Temple, of "the place where the Lord your God will choose to establish His name" (Deut. 12:11). The earthly

39. Ibid.
40. Ibid.
41. In Rabbi Nahman's story, "The King's Son and the Maid's Son Who Were Exchanged," the protagonist's house is suspended in the air, providing a literary image of the detached rootlessness of the Jew.
42. Rosenzweig, *The Star of Redemption*, 305.

Jerusalem, which we see today rebuilt alongside other cities, cannot suffice to realize this Jerusalem. Any sort of realization would place the Jewish world alongside other worlds instead of beyond them, and would thus destroy its spirituality, rendering it realized within the physical:[43]

> The eternal people has not been permitted to while away time in any home. It never loses the untrammeled freedom of a wanderer who is more faithful a knight to his country when he roams abroad, craving adventure and yearning for the land he has left behind, than when he lives in that land. In the most profound sense possible, this people has a land of its own only in that it has a land it yearns for – a holy land.[44]

Even if the Jewish people lives in the unattained holy land, Rosenzweig continues, "it is not allowed full possession of that home. It is only 'a stranger and a sojourner'.... The holiness of the land removed it from the people's spontaneous reach while it could still reach out for it."[45]

Rosenzweig's Land of Israel is a world of wonder, a world with its own internal logic different from the logic of our normal lives. It is a world that will never come to be, which from the perspective of this world is an instance of, "See, the things once predicted have come, and

---

43. It is therefore unsurprising that ultra-Orthodox Jews, who live in the world of Torah, are not Zionists. Their manner of existing is not made to take possession of the land. Their approach steps out of history and avoids any contact with anything concrete. This is why the heads of the yeshivas are so opposed to their students hiking during summer break. It is not about modesty problems. The very encounter with nature and the actual land, with the soil and the streams, is what threatens them. They see hiking as taking leave of the holy cloud surrounding their unnatural, unreal world in Bnei Brak. This is also why when you do occasionally see yeshiva students who are, against the instructions of their rabbis, out hiking, they are not dressed in the classic yeshivish white shirt and black pants or frayed denim shorts like students from pre-military academies or pre-military yeshivas. Instead, they wear swimsuits, as if to signify that they are totally "outside the camp," in the realm of sin and the flesh.
44. Ibid, 300.
45. Ibid.

now I foretell new things" (Is. 42:9). It is the mystical wonder of Bnei Brak rather than the enchanted Land of Israel of the Song of Songs.

Thus, Rabbi Kook's Land of Israel is the land of the holiness of nature, while Rosenzweig's is the land of yearnings, of wonder that does not realize itself in the nature of the land but confines itself within the buildings of the city. Rabbi Nahman's Land of Israel is faith in the reality of wonder. For him, as for Rosenzweig, it is faith in the possibility of wonder regardless of whether it actually occurs, sufficing to disrupt the world of the believer and inspire powerful yearnings. However, Rabbi Nahman is not satisfied with this alone. Like Rabbi Kook, he also wants the land itself, but he wants the supernatural, rather than the natural, that it contained within it.

UNNATURAL NATURE

During the long years of exile, the Jew built his home halfway between heaven and earth. He maintained a careful system of balances that enabled him to avoid conflicts with the world around him and kept the world around him from imposing on his spirituality. As far as he was concerned, the outside world did not exist. The Zionist desire to return to the soil and to nature has returned the Jew to the physical land. This raises the crushing question: is it possible to return to the land, to build a real home not made of paper but of earth and slate, with real walls, without falling into physical banality empty of all spirituality and of wonder itself?

As we will see, the Maharal's writings depict a return to Zion, wherein the return to nature does not come at the cost of redemption's supernatural wonder. The Maharal teaches in many places that the nature of a nation necessitates that all the members of the nation gather together in one place; hence his confident faith in the redemption of the Jewish people within the Land of Israel.[46] However, he quite surprisingly teaches the exact opposite as well: the same natural law that connects each nation inherently with a specific geographical location itself does

---

46. Rabbi Yehuda Loew of Prague, *Netsaḥ Yisrael*, ch. 1. Regarding the nature of the Land of Israel in the thought of the Maharal, see Rabbi Shagar, "Seventy Bullocks and One Sukka," in Rabbi Shagar, *Faith Shattered and Restored*, 173–192.

not naturally apply to the Jewish people. This is the crucial point of his approach, which emphasizes that nature is not natural for the Jewish people: "The dispersion of Israel throughout the world demonstrates their divine status.... This is why they were dispersed throughout the world, for it is fitting that the place of the nation which is all the world should be throughout the world."[47]

The Jewish people have no singular, unique place. In other words, their place is throughout the world as cosmopolitans. This is exactly because of their lofty status. According to the Maharal, the exile signifies *status*. The Jew and the Jewish people possess natural spiritual aspirations, mighty yearnings that keep the nation from being able to settle in one specific place of primary importance. Their place transcends any specific place, and their identity transcends the narrow boundaries of the nation.

The Maharal seems to be tracing the very characteristic features of the Jewish world I found when I visited Bnei Brak, about which Rosenzweig wrote:

> The very difference of an individual people from other peoples establishes its connection with them. There are two sides to every boundary. By setting separating borders for ourselves, we border on something else. By being an individual people, a nation becomes a people among others. To close oneself off is to come close to another. But this does not hold when a people refuses to be merely an individual people and wants to be "the one people." Under these circumstances it must not close itself off within borders, but include within itself such borders as would, through their double function, tend to make it one individual people among others.[48]

Since the Jew is outside the world, he does not belong to any specific place. He does not realize himself in one spot and settle in within those

---

47. Ibid., ch. 56, and see also ch. 8.
48. Rosenzweig, *The Star of Redemption*, 305. It was not incidental that Rosenzweig opposed the political Zionism of his day.

borders. According to the Maharal, the whole world is his place, so he belongs throughout the world.

In contrast to Rosenzweig, however, the Maharal seems to leave open a path to the yearned-for utopia. The Maharal is unparalleled in his passionate belief in the return of the people to the nature of the land. Returning to nature might not be natural for the Jewish people as far as Rosenzweig was concerned, but he was certain it would take place. According to the Maharal, meriting the sort of landed existence that totally opposes the Jewish spirit takes a miracle. The Land of Israel is a miracle for the Jew, so nature itself becomes miraculous, developing a wondrous character and rising above the banality of this world. This is why the Maharal describes the Messianic Era and the End of Days as "a new reality." Wonder is not found only in the unnatural because the natural itself is wondrous.

The teachings of the Maharal present a complex relationship with the soil and the land. Exile is inherently part of the Jewish people, so we must build a home that will preserve exile, the broken heart of the Jew, and humanity within itself. It is a home based significantly on a degree of yearning.[49]

According to the Maharal, the Jewish people's utopian return to their land contains an astonishing internal contradiction: on the one hand, the nation will return to its homeland like a child to the arms of his mother, striking root in its beloved land. On the other hand, the land is not natural for the nation; they are foreign to one another, leaving the nation connected to the entirety of the globe. This national coincidence of opposites approaches a mysticism that can actually be realized in the land.

---

49. Just as in the personal realm, where a person's freedom precedes his choice (see Rabbi Shagar, *The Time of Freedom*, 163–168), so too does this occur in the national realm, where the universal element comes first and enables national uniqueness. The latter need not impinge upon the former; rather, as Rabbi Kook taught, it affirms it. As we will see, holiness appears as "nothingness" that enlivens and grants inner life to choice and creativity.

SHATTERING THE VESSELS *IS* RECTIFYING THEM

Another alternative to this mystical, wondrous naturalism can be found in the post-modern, post-Zionist crisis spreading through much of Israeli society today. If we go beyond the most superficial level, we can see that the "post-modern condition" is deeply connected to fantasy, wonder, and mysticism. The relativistic idea of language games and the absence of truth – absent not because we cannot access it but because there is no material from which we could make it – is just a small cognitive step away from the mystical idea that everything is true and that "the whole world is full of His glory" (Is. 6:3). I want to explore this step a little further.

Two significant political processes have been underway in the State of Israel for as long as it has existed: polarization and republican democratization (meaning, majority rule).[50] These two processes oppose each other on a fundamental level. In this model, the controlling majority imposes its values on the minorities living alongside it. The Jewish, nationalist, Zionist majority in the state receives control by way of democratic elections, and from this controlling position it shapes the state in light of Jewish, Zionist, and Western-democratic values. In doing so, it marginalizes minorities such as ultra-Orthodox Jews, and Arabs. This is opposed to the social and ethnic polarization that characterizes the state and intensifies the differences between the various minority groups.

Polarization within Israeli society has created far-reaching changes in the archetype of its ideal citizen. In the past, it was the *sabra*, the new Jew from an Ashkenazi background, the son of the land with his pioneering, nationalist ethos. The *sabra* was connected to the land's vistas and was ready to sacrifice himself for the collective. He was coarse, straightforward, and secular. He rejected the exile and believed in conformity. The ideal of the *sabra* still serves as a model for imitation and jealous self-evaluation among Religious Zionist youth. However, other ideal conceptions of "Israelis" have begun to emerge today.

The State of Israel currently contains three distinct cultures: Israeli, ultra-Orthodox, and Arab (each, of course, containing numerous subgroups with deep divides between them). This cultural multiplicity

---

50. The sociopolitical analysis presented here is based on Sami Semuḥah, "Changes in Israeli Society: After Fifty Years," *Alpayyim* 17 (1999): 239–261 (Heb.).

developed out of various ongoing societal trends as well as from the influence of post-modernist thought that disrupted the very existence of a cultural center-point that could dictate the proper places of all Israel's citizens. The post-modern idea that all human culture is no more than a possible, contingent narrative undoes any hierarchy of one culture over another. What makes the *sabra* any better than a Moroccan immigrant or a Soviet refugee? The unifying tendency within Israeli democracy must lead to conflict with the tendency towards multiplicity and polarization within society, as the former tendency always wants to impose the majority's values on minorities and deny the minorities' legitimacy.

We must therefore distinguish between Israeli democracy and multi-cultural democracy. The latter does not attempt to instill its values within the comprising sub-cultures. The only condition it poses is strict observance of the rules of the game.

The shift Israel must make from republican democracy to multi-cultural democracy, the sort so characteristic of the post-modern era, is itself the shift from Rabbi Kook's Zionist Land of Israel so deeply enmeshed in modernist narratives to the mystical, post-Zionist Land of Israel. The post-modern roots of this sort of democracy enable a center-less multiplicity of cultures and approaches. A democracy such as this operates not based on general principles, but by way of a conversation between the different parts of the society who desire to maintain its internal equilibrium. This sort of democracy is based on communication, which belongs to the world of speech. As opposed to rigid, stubborn *logos*, speech is open, flexible, and infinite. Dialogue does not require coherence. It begins somewhere in the middle and ends somewhere else in the middle, making it uniquely capable of connecting things that, logically or conceptually, would not otherwise be connected at all.[51] In its essence, this sort of democracy makes multiplicity possible.

This multiplicity, which leads not to the breaking of the vessels but to their construction, ultimately leads toward a mystical-faithful mindset. Multiplicity renders the vessels of human cognition more flexible.

---

51. This is in contrast to the position that claims there is such a thing as meaningless conversation, "nonsense" – meaning a form of speech which fundamentally refers to nothing and cannot offer a full accounting of itself.

Human thinking is typically solipsistic and only allows for the existence of one singular truth. One truth cannot contradict another; one of two conflicting ideas must simply be false. Mysticism, however, can bear the weight of multiplicity and contradiction, enabling us to use a different language of faith. Am I capable of believing without being bothered by my neighbor's lacking or entirely different faith? *Prima facie*, the answer would seem to be negative. For my faith to be true, it must necessarily rule out any other faith. Correspondingly, for his faith to be true, it must necessarily rule out my faith. Moreover, accepting all faiths, both mine and that of my neighbor, would seem to involve taking a relativistic stance toward reality that is implied in saying, "From my perspective, from within my own meta-narrative, my faith is correct, while from my neighbor's perspective, his faith is correct, based on the meta-narrative underlying his life."

Such a stance withers the experience of faith on a fundamental level. One of faith's defining characteristics is the way it presents itself as absolute. In saying something about what is taking place within himself, a person says something about what is taking place outside himself. As Ludwig Wittgenstein put it, "The statement that something is taking place inside me says that something is taking place outside me."[52] Faith is taken plainly as subjective perception, which refers to "the state of the subject." However, faith is not satisfied with saying, "I believe"; it yearns to say, "*Zeh hadavar*," "This is the thing" – "Just as Moses prophesied with the phrase 'So said the Lord,' so too the prophets prophesied with the phrase 'So said the Lord.' Moses exceeded them by saying, '*Zeh hadavar*' – 'This is the thing.'"[53] This is an absolute statement overriding any gap between internal and external. Relativism, in contrast, uproots the very possibility of this sort of absoluteness.

The post-modern experience could lead to a celebration of relativistic, spiritless (and therefore faithless) identities. However, it is important to recognize that the multi-cultural perspective need not be

---

52. Cited from Eliezer Malkiel, *Intention, Sensation, Emotion* (Jerusalem: Magnes: 2000), 63 (Heb.). See also, Rabbi Shagar, "Faith and Language According to the Baal HaTanya of Chabad," in *We Will Walk in Fervor*, 173–206.

53. *Sifrei, Matot* 153.

based on contingency and relativism. In fact, it could create an alternative perspective, that of "relative absoluteness."[54]

The post-modern crisis shatters human vessels and makes them flexible enough for new possibilities of inspiration and enlightenment. After the multi-cultural deconstruction, the believer can finally enter the realm of mysticism. He can recognize the inspiration, substance, and truth that each religious and faith position carries within it, a recognition that would have been impossible with normal human vessels. In opening up to the divine infinite, this recognition does not undermine the believer's religious life but actually fills it with enthusiasm.[55] The post-modern believer attains the deep recognition that "everything is founded upon the supernal capacity, which has no end,"[56] and that "from the perspective of holiness, reality is free of exaggeration."[57]

The deconstruction of homogeneous reality, accompanied by faith, is a "prescription" for a mystical life. Because he sees everything as merely human cultural constructs which are necessarily relative, the post-modernist lacks that which can be found in the faith that God is the one who vitalizes and gives rise to this construct. Divine holiness does not appear as a dogmatic absolute but as a "nothingness" that vitalizes and grants inwardness and existence to human choice and creativity. The believer is exposed not just to a multiplicity of absolute truths but also to the creative inspiration within his very existence. In this sense, a person has the power to create reality: "If the righteous wish, they create a world."[58]

The mystical believer will not see democracy's multi-cultural discourse as a mere means for balancing societal extremes. He will see such speech as accompanied by the wondrous recognition:

---

54. See Rabbi Shagar, *Broken Vessels*, 46.
55. This could be seen as, to use Chabad terminology, "the lights of chaos in the vessels of rectification."
56. Rabbi Kook, *Orot HaKodesh*, vol. 1, 103. Rabbi Kook also finds the supernatural nature to be the end of the process of redemption.
57. Ibid., 212. In a certain sense this is the implementation of a kabbalistic way of thinking wherein every nation has its own divinity. Kabbala grants a dimension of truth to other faiths, even though they differ from the Torah of Israel.
58. Sanhedrin 65b.

All statements are received from heaven, for all statements are there, as it is written, "The Lord exists forever; Your word stands firm in heaven" (Ps. 119:89).... Any statements that are received from there ... the person who receives them should not be denigrated even though the halakha does not accord with him, since he received it from heaven. Thus, in truth, "These and these are the words of the living God" (Eiruvin 13b), and the fact that the halakha does not accord with him is something that is impossible for us to understand or comprehend... for it is an instance of the ways of God which are impossible to comprehend.[59]

The world's increasing openness in advance of multi-cultural, multi-national democracy reveals itself as a possibility for elevating the religious world itself. Rabbi Nahman teaches us that there is a melody of nature and a melody of mystical wonder, and that the latter is also the melody of the redemptive future. We can thus imagine a process wherein the actualization of the mystical land is the next stage in the state's evolution. After the natural stage of modernity, which produced the Zionist Land of Israel,[60] the miraculous Land of Israel will sprout out of the post-modern crisis, a land of fantasy and mystical wonder that takes form without becoming crude or impinging on the wonder.[61]

---

59. Rabbi Nahman, *Likkutei Moharan* 56:9. For more on this teaching, see below, "The Folded Torah," pp. 257–266.

60. See Rabbi Shagar, *On That Day*, 162–163.

61. Will "relative absoluteness" necessarily lead the believer to paganism, which is the religious equivalent of cultural pluralism? Will the creative inspiration of post-modernist belief necessarily lead him to corrupt the covenant of his faith simply by recognizing the creativity and validity of someone else's faith?

I think there is no necessary connection between the relative-absolute and pagan viewpoints. This is because of another element of the encounter with the "nothingness" and the divine infinite. This element is the reality which is beyond, or precedes, faith (see above, "Muteness and Faith," pp. 202–204). I will explain. On the one hand, faith is described as deriving from creativity which grants itself absolute validity, "a righteous person decrees and God fulfills" (cf. *Pesikta Rabbati* 3:1). On the other hand, we read that "the righteous man lives through his faith" (Hab. 2:4), meaning that faith derives not from creativity but from a person accepting its presence in his life. This is a person's readiness to live with what God has given him. On this level, the act of faith is not a creative act. It is rather an act that derives

RELIGIOUS, POST-ZIONIST PEACE

The ideas above contain many practical implications, not only in terms of how we relate to our secular neighbors,[62] but also in relation to the other, the foreigner who dwells in our midst. The fact that the Arab, the Palestinian, lives here and sees this land as his beloved homeland (and the fact is this is indeed his beloved homeland) need not impinge on my belonging to this soil. His existence cannot harm my connection to this same strip of land that is also my homeland. This is the miraculous Land of Israel, wherein "all statements are received from heaven." From this perspective, we can perhaps attain a sense of kinship – a kinship that results not from abstraction and reducing people, cultures, and faiths to one-dimensional entities, but a kinship between others or even opposites.

"The Holy One, blessed be He, found no vessel that could contain blessing for Israel save that of peace."[63] Entering and settling this miraculous, wondrous land, and receiving the blessing from that vessel full of blessings, requires being prepared to speak multiple languages. Peace is the deepest meaning of the supernal holiness and contains opposites. Religious Zionism today certainly cannot achieve the peace it itself seeks. Therefore, it must decide to see its own radical potential and open up to the post-modern spirit, enabling it to find that which is hidden within the religious world and to find the mystical. Today, it is impossible to hold onto religion without its mystical core. Religious Zionism must become, as per the zeitgeist, religious post-Zionism.

Religious Zionism's response to cultural events within the State of Israel is fundamentally similar to the general ultra-Orthodox response to Zionism, that of absolute rejection and unequivocal invalidation. Religious Zionism recognizes the unresolvable contradiction between it and much of the reality of Israeli society. In truth, this recognition is an admission of failure on its part. The whole idea upon which Reli-

---

from the humility, self-nullification, and not-knowing, opening a person up to the possibility of cleaving to what he is, to what was granted to him, and to reaching oneness and personal identity.

62. See Rabbi Shagar, "*Tinok Shenishba*," in *This is My Covenant*, 97–161.

63. Mishna Uktzin 3:12.

gious Zionism was based was that it was possible to create a state which would blend all the different streams together. I must emphasize, I speak as a Religious Zionist who believes in this idea and sees it as a real path toward redemption.

This potential adheres to the fact that the basis of the religious mindset of Religious Zionist thinkers, the first and foremost being Rabbi Kook, has been the desire to create a new thinking or religious perspective that would know how to absorb within itself values which it traditionally has not contained. The possibility for innovation exists, and it stands ready and waiting for Religious Zionism. If it would just reach out and grab it, Religious Zionism could lead us toward the hoped-for redemption, the paradoxical peace that sees the other, the Arab, as belonging to the homeland, without giving up on the at-homeness of the homeland. This is how it will be possible both to see the intimacy within the foreigner and to find intimacy with the foreigner. This will be a new kind of harmony, the melody of the redemptive future.

Law and Love

Between the Love of the Land
and the Sovereignty of the State

THE SONG OF SONGS

Above all, the writings of Rabbi Abraham Isaac HaKohen Kook describe the Land of Israel as love. More specifically, they describe it as falling in love. His light, splendorous sentences are the poetry of a love-drunk lover, repeating himself again and again in almost every paragraph:

> In the Land of Israel the letters of our souls expand, they reveal a torrent…. The air of the Land of Israel manifests the refreshing growth of these letters of life, in their splendorous beauty, with pleasant niceness and joyous power full of the influence of holiness.[1]

Based on a draft written in preparation for a Yom HaAtzma'ut sermon in 5765 (2005). Edited by Yishai Mevorach and published in *On That Day*, 226–243. Like in "The Joke of the Megilla" (p. 145 above), in this essay, Rabbi Shagar relates to "The Disengagement Plan" from northern Samaria and the Gaza Strip, which was carried out a few months later.

When he immigrated to Israel, the man of God and former student of the Volozhin Yeshiva fell in love with the land and its pioneers. And, like a beloved revealing herself to her lover, the Land of Israel revealed its secrets to Rabbi Kook. In broad expanses that he had never known in his life in exile, in the time when he yearned for the land, Israel opened up before him. These expanses became primary aspects of his teachings: the ideas of all-inclusive unity, collectivity, idealism, holiness in nature, freedom, universalism, redemption, harmony, and ascending development. These are the love songs of his encounter with the land. The lover and the beloved reveal themselves to each other: "I am my beloved's and his desire is for me" (Song. 7:11).

A delightful world of grace illuminates and envelops the lover. Everything shines, is full of radiance, and is enveloped in wondrous harmony. He feels free and liberated. Not for nothing have the mystics of every generation described their mystical experiences in terms of falling in love, which is itself an experience of altered consciousness and of intense oneness, transparency, grace, and salvation: "Oh so much does the heart yearn to love everything, all beings, all of the works, all of creation."[2]

Rabbi Kook made this love the core of Religious Zionism. The love of the Song of Songs is a fundamental experience in the life of the Religious Zionist. The intimacy between lover and beloved that the Song of Songs projects is the intimacy of two who are connected to their environs. The setting of the Land of Israel is an integral part of this intimacy, occurring between lovers in the land's natural setting with all of creation involved in their love. This love absorbs the vistas of the land and the seasons of its year. The beloved in the Land of Israel is the *shulamit* whose hair "is like a flock of goats streaming down from the Gilead," whose nose is like "the Tower of Lebanon" looking down on Damascus, whose eyes are "pools in Heshbon," and whose neck is "like the Tower of David." Nature, time, the individual, and love, all come

---

1. Rabbi Kook, *Orot*, 12. There is a famous story about Yosef Ḥayim Brenner, who joined Rabbi Kook for the third meal of Shabbat, but left quickly, saying, "There is too much light there; I cannot stay."
2. Rabbi Kook, *Shemoneh Kevatzim* (Jerusalem, 2004), 366; vol. 3, §20.

together in this wondrous song. This combination forms the basis of Religious Zionism's spiritual world.

The Sages, who explained this song as a love song between the people of Israel and her lover, God, understood that this song depicts a different sort of religious language. This religious language is not exilic. It derives from a connected and deeply involved relationship with the land. In this language, nature itself becomes a different nature – a divine nature. This nature resonates with the poem of Hannah Szenes: "My God, / Let it never end / the sand and the sea / the churn of the water / the gleam of the sky / the prayer of man."[3]

LAW VERSUS LOVE

One of the places where Rabbi Kook's Song of Songs style manifested most clearly was no doubt in Gush Katif. This desolate piece of land encountered its lovers and began to bloom. In this reciprocal love story, the lovers are not distant and aloof from each other. Rather, the beloved reveals her love – the land blooms. This is how one of the lovers described the situation:

> For a generation we have been living in a magnificent settlement project in this beloved strip of land. The project was set up on virgin soil that had known no man since the creation of the world, and yet it miraculously responded to us, as if we were chosen, as if it knew how much we loved it.
>
> In the course of a generation, our souls have become connected to this beloved land, and to each other. With great effort and integrity, we have set up beautiful towns and splendid communities.... No evil and no impurity, only goodness and grace. Doors that have never been locked and open hearts are our symbols.... A place of Jewish and Zionistic pride, a place that is the dream of every proud Jew.... The spirit of man is what turned

---

3. Hannah Szenes, "A Walk to Caesarea," in *Diaries, Poems, Testimonies* (Tel Aviv: Kibbutz Hameuḥad, 1994), 221 (Heb.).

a barren desert into a blooming garden and a band of strangers into the most wondrous of communities.[4]

"I accounted to your favor the devotion of your youth, your love as a bride…in a land not sown" (Jer. 2:2). The Disengagement stands like a heavy cloud against this youthful love full of grace and trust. The state decreed the Disengagement upon this strip of land, painfully revealing the foundation of sovereignty, the violence that underlies its laws:

> What manifests itself as the law's inner decay is the fact that rule of law is, in the final analysis, without ultimate justification or legitimation, that the very space of juridical reason within which the rule of law obtains is established and sustained by a dimension of force and violence that, as it were, holds the place of those missing foundations. At its foundation, the rule of law is sustained not by reason alone but also by the force/violence of a tautological enunciation – "The law is the law!"[5]

More than anything, the Disengagement signifies the crime of the legislation of the law itself and the violence that it bears within it. It signifies the recognition that, in truth, violating the law is a less serious crime than making the law. The inner decay within the rule of law is expressed by the claim we constantly hear from those who support the disengagement law: this is the law, and the law is the law! And therefore, it must be respected! The legislation's arbitrariness strengthens the law's tautology, but it lacks any judicial wisdom. The legality of the process alone justifies it: the process is legal, it was confirmed and organized in the Knesset.

The law is justified not by ethics or judicial wisdom, but by the simple fact that the majority legislated it. The violence required to enact this law, removing people from their land, is not an extraneous remnant from the process of legislation. Rather, it is the very heart of law: the

4. Ami Shaked, Security and Military Coordinator of Gush Katif, Letter to Residents of Gush Katif, Nissan 5765/April 2005. The Hebrew version can be found at https://www.tora.co.il/parasha/meat/kdoshim_65.doc .
5. Eric Santner, *On the Psychotheology of Everyday Life*, 56–57.

violent claim that the law is law. This violence, "the fearfulness of the government,"[6] sprouting from deep within the very heart of sovereign existence which justifies itself with brute force, is what motivates the prophet Samuel to rebuke the nation by laying out "the law of the king" before them.[7]

The love of the land and the sovereign violence of the state thus clash tragically before our very eyes in the dilemma of law versus love. As Religious Zionists, we experience this confrontation incredibly harshly. Just as Rabbi Kook implanted love of the land within Religious Zionism, he similarly implanted the understanding and faith that the state is the greatest manifestation of, and pathway to, redemption: "Our state, the State of Israel, is the foundation of God's throne in the world."[8] According to him, this is a state "that bears within its existence the greatest idealistic content."[9] He saw the state as a necessary and decisive step in redemption, and his teachings about redemption deal with it and its purpose at length.

Faced with the Disengagement, it is impossible not to ask: Is the State of Israel really the beginning of redemption? Can it, or any state, really take part in salvation? The threat of exile hangs over the residents of Gush Katif, rooted in the forcefulness of the State, presenting us with the sharp contrast between the "idealistic content" full of light and love from the teachings of Rabbi Kook and the opaque and unmoving law of the State.

FROM LAW TO COMMANDMENT

Rabbi Kook undoubtedly recognized the violence hidden within the idea of the State, and he even wrote about it.[10] That being the case, what led him to teach that the State of Israel "is actually the greatest happiness of man"?[11] Is there a depiction of the state, "an ideal state," that does away with sovereign violence? One that describes a state where law does not

---

6. Avoda Zara 4a.
7. I Samuel 8:11–20.
8. Rabbi Kook, *Orot HaKodesh*, vol. 3, 191.
9. Ibid.
10. *Orot*, 14.
11. *Orot HaKodesh*, vol. 3, 191.

impinge on love? I intend to lay out here two possibilities for such a state, one that arises from the thought of Franz Rosenzweig, and one that can be derived from the teachings of Rabbi Kook himself.

What happens when the God who stands at the top of the pyramid is the one who justifies the rule of the king or the law? In such a case, the laws turn into commandments. Does this remove their violent sting? Considering Rosenzweig's principled distinction between a law and a commandment, yes:

> To me as well, God is not a law-giver. He is a commander. Only a person in his laziness devolves the commands…into laws – well ordered…without the urgency of being commanded, without the "I am the Lord."[12]

> The imperative of the commandment makes no provision for the future; it can only conceive the immediacy of obedience. If it were to think of a future or a forever, it would be, not commandment nor order, but law. Law reckons with times, with a future, with duration. The commandment knows only the moment; it awaits the result in the very instant of its promulgation.[13]

A commandment is not an instruction or a law. It does not support itself with external force, but rather receives its support from the fact that it is itself a holy act. The "command" aspect is an inherent part of this. For example, just as two objects in space bear a relationship to "the law of gravity" and act according to it, moving as part of their very existence rather than being forced artificially, so too there is an intrinsic, immanent connection between the commander and the commandment that cannot be severed. Just as gravity is not a function of the past, this connection is not a function of the past; rather it is an event happening in the present moment.

According to Rosenzweig, because commandment is a fundamentally unmediated relationship between two individuals, the heart of the

12. Franz Rosenzweig, *Selected Letters and Diary Excerpts* (Jerusalem, 1987), 326 (Heb.).
13. Franz Rosenzweig, *The Star of Redemption*, 177.

commandment is revelation. A person can perform the same actions as a commanded person, but "without the urgency of being commanded" he cannot encounter God through them: "In that moment, we only know the moment itself, and we know it with all the greatness of the divine-human substance of the commandment, from which we can say: 'Blessed are You'.... Only from the unmediated state of the commandments can we speak to God.... A person hears the voice of the commander only within the commandment."[14]

The law bears no relevance for those under its authority, it just attempts to force the past, or that which is written in a book, onto the present. In contrast, a commandment bears within itself significant meaning for the commanded. The commander and the commanded actively relate to and encounter one another. In other words, the commandment is the way the Torah organizes the falling-in-love of revelation. The commandment carries with it the ongoing revelation of the lover, God, to the Jew. The outcome of this is the statement, "Love me." "No third party can command [love] or extort it. No third party can, but the One can. The commandment to love can only proceed from the mouth of the lover. Only the lover can and does say: Love me!"[15]

A commanded person experiences the command as directed to him personally. Commandment is an experience that is lacking in the alienated law, anchored to the self-referential tautology and embodied in the law as the law. The sovereign does not address his subjects, but rather imposes laws upon them. What, then, would an ideal Jewish state, with commandments rather than laws, look like?

Let me clarify with an illustration. Imagine a driver at an intersection in the dead of night. There are no other drivers on the road, but the traffic light is red. The driver knows that no one is watching him, and he could safely drive through the intersection without fear of accident or getting stopped by the police. I know many people who, even in the middle of the night with no one watching, would not drive through a red light because of the religious framing of "*dina demalkhuta*" – "governmental law." From their perspective, crossing the intersection would

---

14. Rosenzweig, *Selected Letters and Diary Excerpts*, 336.
15. Rosenzweig, *The Star of Redemption*, 176.

be an *"issur,"* a religious prohibition. Just as they would never consider eating pig, even in a hidden room in the dead of night, so too they would not illegally run a traffic light. Divine law receives its applicability from its divine commander rather than its content; it therefore applies in all contexts. The commandment is not a function of content but of relationship. The same person stops at the red light not because of fear of the law. He stops because he feels an inner connection to, and identifies with, not the content of the action but the action itself – you don't drive when the light is red.

A state that replaces laws which rely on violent power to enforce their fulfillment with commands will lead, in psychological terms, to "release from the punishing pressures of the superego [that] is a form of grace...a grace *internal* to those rigorous imperatives...rather than one that suspends the law in its 'fulfillment.'"[16] For example, a father does not care for his children because of the law, but rather as a manifestation of his will and his freedom. He is driven by internal compulsion, not an external force which compels him. He finds this obligation in the very fact of being the father of his children, an obligation that is his very freedom.

Similarly, perhaps an ideal state would not collect income tax by compulsion, for example, but rather citizens would pay it as a commandment. Would a person who fills out the assessment for his income tax feel the same feelings that he feels when he gives charity to the needy? A person gives charity as part of his relationship with the needy individual, a relationship that is parallel to his relationship with the God who commanded him to give charity. Income tax would be paid from the place where a person forms an internal relationship with the state that requires the assessment.[17]

---

16. Santner, *On the Psychotheology of Everyday Life*, 109.
17. We might apply here the Talmud's statement that "God desired to give merit to Israel, therefore, He increased for them Torah and commandments" (Makkot 23b).

A STATE OF FALLING-IN-LOVE

Studying Rabbi Kook's teachings on redemption in depth and understanding what is so novel in them will enable us to learn about another possible avenue for sovereignty without violence.

Rabbi Kook's redemptive teachings do not just depict the End of Days or the spiritual greatness of the Land of Israel. They draw down lights. It is this act of teaching itself that draws out the lights of the Land of Israel. These are lights that, to a certain degree, did not exist in our world before their revelation; Rabbi Kook was the one who drew them into the world. Rabbi Kook's teachings create a different religious mindset that innovates beyond everything that preceded them: "religious Israeliness," and not just "religious Jewishness."[18]

Parenthetically, I would say that even with the difficult events that are threatening us and disturbing our Yom HaAtzma'ut celebration, we must celebrate this teaching of the redemption of the Land of Israel, a teaching to which we are bound and that is bound to us.[19]

In the deepest sense, Rabbi Kook's teachings drew down lights that did not just identify the process of redemption – they also enabled it. They blazed a path for the Jews from exile to the Land of Israel, one that was not simple and that many thought was impossible and undesirable. Redemption is not a historical-factual, material process. It is deeply connected to the specific teaching that lays out and enables the process.[20] Without the spirit that drives the process, providing its sensibility and its unique "light," the redemption will not happen, which is why Rabbi Kook's teaching is so vital for redemption.

What was the spiritual situation before Rabbi Kook's teachings? What was that "religious Jewishness" that we mentioned?

---

18. We can learn about the difference between Jewishness and Israeliness from the fact that there were Sages who wanted to hide away the Song of Songs which, as we saw, expresses the Land-of-Israel-esque relationship, which Rabbi Kook drew out, between man and God, and attempted to prevent its inclusion in the canon (see Mishna Yadayim 3:5).
19. See Rabbi Shagar, *On That Day*, 250 and on.
20. See Rabbi Shagar, *On That Day*, 143.

R. Elazar said: What is that which is written: "And many peoples
shall go and say: Come and let us go up to the mountain of the
Lord, to the house of the God of Jacob..." (Is. 2:3)? It is the God
of Jacob but not the God of Abraham and Isaac?

Rather, not like Abraham of whom it is written [that he
called the location of the Temple] "mount," as it is stated, "As it
is said on this day: On the mount where the Lord is seen" (Gen.
22:14). And not like Isaac of whom it is written [that he called
the location of the Temple] "field," as it is stated: "And Isaac went
out to meditate in the field" (Gen. 24:63). Rather, like Jacob, who
called it house, as it is stated: "And he called the name of that
place House of God [*Beit El*]" (Gen. 28:19).[21]

Jewish space is not a space connected to the earthly and external; it is a
space anchored within itself. The hasidic author Rabbi Yehuda Alter of
Gur describes this type of existence in his book *Sefat Emet*, when he talks
about "the inner point." Jewishness is not the mountain or the field of
Abraham and Isaac that are integral parts of the Song of Songs. Rather,
it is the at-homeness: "Jacob who called it a house." Jewishness resides
in the family, in "the children of Jacob" whose "bed was complete."[22]

Rosenzweig taught that Jewishness manifests as commitment
and being rooted in the covenant, both of which are the fundamental acts of Judaism. According to this definition, the Jewish exile is the
creation of a sheltered, a-historical family space that is not concerned
with surroundings or engaged in the rules of history.[23] The Jews "lack
the passionate attachment to the things that constitute the primary...
'objects' of other historical peoples and nations, attachments that ultimately constitute their vitality and endurance as peoples and nations:
land, territory, and architecture; regional and national languages; laws
[i.e., state laws], customs, and institutions."[24] Their land exists only as
a holy land for which they yearn. Their holy language is not their first

---

21. Pesaḥim 88a.
22. Song of Songs Rabba 4:7.
23. See Rabbi Shagar, *On That Day*, 176 and on.
24. Santner, *On the Psychotheology of Everyday Life*, 110.

language and not the language that they speak in their daily lives. Jewishness is bound up and connected only and entirely in itself: "Our life is no longer meshed with anything outside ourselves. We have struck root in ourselves"; "And so, in the final analysis, [the Jewish nation] is not alive in the sense the nations are alive: in a national life manifest on this earth, in a national territory, solidly based and staked out on the soil. It is alive only in that which guarantees it will endure beyond time, in that which pledges it ever-lastingness, in drawing its own eternity from the sources of the blood."[25]

The Jew being bound up in himself, and the nation in its very existence, creates a twofold relationship with the outside. Other nations and cultures either do not exist from a Jew's perspective, where the outside does not enter his horizon at all, or are brought inwards into the house or at-homeness via hospitality.[26] For example, the body either doesn't exist, in which case a Jew is not involved or bothered by it or it is ignored as irrelevant, or it is internalized as a medium for delighting in God, such as in the practice of "raising up the sparks" in hasidic worship. This is hospitality, where the "outside" ceases to play the role of "outside" and behaves like "inside" as part of the home.

The gaping difference between Jewishness and Israeliness is the difference between the images of the mother and the lover depicted in the Israeli love song of the Song of Songs.[27] The primary female image in the world of the Jew is the maternal-familial image: "Happy are all who fear the Lord, who follow His ways…. Your wife shall be like a fruitful vine within your house; your sons, like olive saplings around your table. So shall the man who fears the Lord be blessed…and live to see your children's children. Peace be upon Israel!" (Ps. 128:1–6). This is not the figure of the lover who descends from the hills of Gilead to see the flowering vines. To be sure, the fruitful vine and the olive saplings are present here, but they are organized around the familial table of the home.

---

25. Rosenzweig, *The Star of Redemption*, 304–305.
26. See Santner, *On the Psychotheology of Everyday Life: Reflections on Freud and Rosenzweig*, 116; Rabbi Shagar, *In the Shadow of Faith*, 106–111.
27. For a different understanding of these images, see Rabbi Shagar, *On That Day*, 123–127.

The image of the lover expresses revelation and the happiness of encounter, while the image of the mother expresses the womb, familiarity without encounter, in light of which no stranger is or could be. This difference is not simple. It demonstrates the innovative nature of the Song of Songs in the Jewish world and the boldness of Rabbi Kook's teaching: He returned us to the lover and the beloved, taking us out of the home and into the field, returning us to history. Not only do the lover and the beloved show themselves to each other, but the land also reveals itself to them. In strong contrast to how the exilic Jew steps away from all external connections to the world, they are enveloped in it and it in them.

The teachings of Rabbi Kook, then, return us to the outside world, to nature and to the land. We have a state just like we have bodies. The Jew no longer yearns for the land and grounds himself internally, but reaches the land and delves into its environment. Our original question thus returns in full force: does Rabbi Kook return us to the violence of the outside world, to the forcefulness of the body, to the compulsion of state institutions and the arbitrariness of law?

We could press further. Is Rabbi Kook's vision of redemption, the vision that returned us to nature and naturalness, the same as the Zionist vision of normalcy? Is it the vision of "the house of Judah like all the other nations" (Ezek. 25:8), a nation alongside other nations or a culture alongside other cultures? Is giving up Jewishness the same as normalcy? Furthermore, does not the lover, caressed by God's grace, prefer to escape from the world and delight in this love? Does not returning to the world contradict the love that gushes within him? Doesn't Rabbi Kook, the great lover, return us to this world? [28]

Rabbi Kook describes an abnormal redemption of falling in love, of man and nation "sick with love" where existence itself shines with a different light.[29] Existence itself shines with the light of falling in love. Rabbi Kook's utopia is a miraculous world, a world that shines with the

---

28. See Rabbi Shagar, "Grace and Rebellion," in *In the Shadow of Faith*, 43 and on. Regarding Rabbi Kook, see idem, "Then the God-Fearing Will Speak," in *The Time of Freedom*, 179–186.

29. On the views of Rabbi Yehuda Loew of Prague, the Maharal, and the *Sefat Emet*, who both greatly influenced Rabbi Kook, see Rabbi Shagar, *On That Day*, 193–199.

unending light of miracles. In this utopia, existence does not just look
different, it is different on an essential level. The state and its institutions
ascend and shine with a different light. Concrete, material existence
becomes mystical. Like the kabbalists, Rabbi Kook thinks that redemption is an ontological shift in existence, where the very material of the
world will change and be purified. The State of Israel, as the foundation
of God's throne in the world, is an ideal state that shines. At its center
lies not force but light: "Through the strength of Israel, their expansion
and the revelation of their lives, in whatever form this takes, the light of
the highest nothingness is revealed as concrete existence, and illuminates the whole world with the light of life, sustaining and improving
and elevating everything."[30]

I will attempt to sharpen this idea. The Land of Israel, as presented
in the Song of Songs, is the living background for the love of the lover
and the beloved; it is present in their love, which paints it with blazing
colors of beauty and desire. The land simply seems different, aromatic,
blossoming, loving, and full of plentiful waters from flowing rivers. In
Rabbi Kook's land, human life shines with the light of God's love and
divine vitality lies behind the growth and pleasure of all things.

The vessels through which the lover comprehends reality are different from those of a regular person, and these different vessels grant
reality a different meaning. However, this is not just a matter of understanding. Kabbala teaches that the vessels affect the light itself, enabling
it and shaping it;[31] the world of the beloved is really a different world.[32]

Just as a lover eating in the presence of his beloved experiences the
food differently, seeing the eating itself as a gesture of love and closeness,
so too did Rabbi Kook live in the Land of Israel in a constant Shabbat

---

30. Rabbi Kook, *Shemoneh Kevatzim*, vol. 2, 339; §319. Also see, ibid., 299; §189. In these
    words, Rabbi Kook departs from a central theme in the teachings of Ḥasidut – dis-
    covering the divine as the nullification of the world as opposed to its construction.
31. As we saw regarding Rabbi Kook's teachings about redemption.
32. ["The world of the happy man is a different one from that of the unhappy man."
    Ludwig Wittgenstein, *Tractatus Logico-Philosophicus*, trans. D. F. Pears and B. F.
    McGuinness (London and New York: Routledge Classic, 2001), 87, §6.43. –Hebrew
    Editor]

state, with his weekday meals being Shabbat meals. For him, the Land of Israel and the State of Israel were lit up with the light of Shabbat.[33]

Imagine a Shabbat-style state. I do not mean a state where no one works, where there are no police or banks, but a state where the days of the week shine like Shabbat. The cops will smile, the faces of the clerks will beam, and the storeowners will sing…. This is a state with love and grace, not force, at its center.

NEW LIGHTS

Rabbi Kook saw great purpose in the land and the Zionist institutions in his lifetime. In the continuing development of the state and its institutions he saw the lofty goal of a shining utopia, of a time when force will disappear and be replaced by love, solidarity, and brotherhood. This was how he experienced the beginning of redemption. He identified the Zionist settlement of the Land of Israel as part of a process leading to utopia. He was saw a certain degree of utopia had already taken place in the present, creating a feeling that it could come at any moment – that it is coming now, waiting just behind the door. Without this, Rabbi Kook's utopian redemption would be no different from the faith of every other Jew in an eventual Messiah.[34]

---

33. These words remind me of a debate that arose in a class when I was teaching Rabbi Kook's famous words on the holiness of eating: "The very essence of eating… and all movements and sensations of life are full of light and holiness" (*Shemoneh Kevatzim*, vol. 2, 271; §65). One of the students claimed that he wanted to eat an "ordinary steak" and not a "holy steak." This claim reveals the gap between Rabbi Kook's approach and that of *ḥaredi* Judaism. Ḥaredism does not seek to replace the outside world. It leaves a neutral world outside the Jewish home, and even when it is occasionally appropriated for the sake of holiness, its neutrality remains and the indifference towards it does not change. In contrast, Rabbi Kook's Land-of-Israel-esque demand is total: he desires to eliminate any neutrality of the outside, and to turn it into holiness despite its being "outside." How does this happen? Does a beloved who eats "ordinary ice cream" in the company of his beloved feel anomalous because of what the act represents? Is he interested in "ordinary ice cream" or in the act of eating ice cream with her, an act that turns into a deep gesture of love without overriding its ordinariness?

34. See Rabbi Shagar, *On That Day*, 140.

Can we also relate like this to the State of Israel as it is today without a fundamental change in how we think of utopia? In my opinion, we cannot. This is the hopeless situation that we are confronted with today and that we cannot deny.[35] Since the State of Israel does not scintillate light and love but force and law, how should we relate to it? Should we shrink away from understanding it as the beginning of redemption? Understanding the state as the beginning of redemption is what gives the state its meaning; it explains that what is happening is part of a utopian process. The utopia is already partially realized, with the process being well underway.

We must consider the present reality. We cannot get caught up in dogmas regarding redemption, deciding our interpretation of events in advance. It is possible that the events of our time demand of us, as the events of Rabbi Kook's time demanded of him, to construct new vessels and formulate new concepts in order to be able to properly grasp and understand them. The possibility of taking up Rabbi Kook's project of identifying the holiness in historical processes is now up to us to continue. Rabbi Kook stood before secular Zionism and taught about the possibility of elevating its holy sparks by formulating new religious concepts and by deeply, innovatively interpreting old concepts. The events taking place before our eyes demand no less.

The process of redemption may be different from how Rabbi Kook foresaw it, and we may not yet understand this process as it should be understood. Perhaps everything happening now can, and should, be

---

35. There are those who deny and attempt to ignore the chasm above which we are standing. For example, not too long ago I sat at a table at a bar mitzva celebration with two important Jerusalemite rabbis, a Kollel student from "*Har HaMor*" and a relative of *ḥaredi* appearance. The latter told us all woefully about how he had been a major in the IDF: "For thirty years I faithfully served the state, year in and year out, doing long stints of reserve duty, and here the state has gone and turned into a state like all the nations." He was referring to the ruling of the High Court on the topic of Reform conversions. He continued, asking: "Can anyone still believe that the state is the beginning of redemption?" The rabbis joined in angrily, lamenting the destruction of the religious councils and the *kashrut* system by the prime minister's son. The Kollel student did not take long to respond, spouting the normal line about delays in the process of redemption. The safety net is already spread out in case the Disengagement should actually happen.

understood in light of Rabbi Kook's famous words regarding the nullification of nationalism:

> With the Messiah, descendant of Joseph, the nation of Israel rediscovers its sense of nationalism. However, the ultimate purpose is not isolationist and elitist nationalism, but rather the attempt to unite all members of the world into one family, under God.... When the world needs to transition from nationalism to universalism, then the things that developed out of a narrow view of nationalism will need to be destroyed, for they demonstrate a corrupted and particularistic love. This is why the Messiah, descendant of Joseph, is going to be killed, and the true and lasting reign will be that of the Messiah, descendant of David.[36]

Considering these words, the process of redemption may not be held up at all. In fact, just the reverse – the redemption is happening even faster than Rabbi Kook could have foreseen, even faster than we normally would have thought. The rapid pace of the changes gives rise to the feeling of the loss of at-homeness which wells up within us even more forcefully due to the Disengagement Plan. Perhaps such crude destruction is progress. Perhaps post-Zionism is actually the killing of the Messiah, descendant of Joseph, to make way for the Messiah, descendant of David.

A person feels comfortable with the world and his usual understanding of it, so he feels violently shaken by drastic shifts that happen or could happen to him. However, he could see these changes as processes that announce the coming of the Messiah. A person feels, rightly, that his old world will be destroyed. Who knows what will be with the new one? What is its nature, and what will it bring with it? To this, the Sage R. Yosef responded in his famous statement: "He will come, but [I hope] I will not see him."[37]

Indeed, the Talmud depicts the "week" wherein the Messiah will come as consisting of harsh and terrifying events: "On Friday – dis-

---

36. Rabbi Kook, *Orot*, 160. Famously, Rabbi Kook identified the Messiah, descendant of Joseph, with the Zionists.
37. Sanhedrin 98b.

harmonies, on Saturday – wars, on Saturday night – the arrival of the Messiah."[38] The Maharal taught that the arrival of a new world of redemption is bound up with the destruction of the old, and therefore anarchy and war must precede the arrival of the Messiah.[39] The birthpangs of the Messiah in our day are opinion wars and cultural revolutions.

DISOBEYING FORCE

In conclusion, I want to say a few words about disobedience.[40] Disobedience appears specifically in the same place that we find the violent basis of the law. Disobedience is not disobedience to the law but to the forceful element that provides its foundation. In this context, justifying disobedience means accepting the position that the only response to the fundamental violence of the law is a corresponding act of force. Is that what we want, that force should overpower force? The true rebellion is not overpowering force, but rather abandoning it. The ability to abandon the game of force and violence is truly a messianic option. We do not dream of a time when the right power will win out, but for a time when power and might no longer make right at all. We seek the pleasure principle, and not the reality principle[41] – this is the true messianism.

The prophet, describing the arrival of the messianic king, used these images: "Rejoice greatly, fair Zion! Raise a shout, fair Jerusalem! Lo, your king is coming to you" (Zech. 9:9). As readers of this verse, we expect a monarchical appearance full of pathos and strength, but to our surprise all the shouting is simply for this: "He is victorious and triumphant, yet humble, riding on an ass, on a donkey foaled by a she-ass" (ibid.). The humble man riding on a donkey is the one who destroys the bow of war and speaks peace to the nations unto the ends of the earth: "He shall banish chariots from Ephraim and horses from Jerusalem; the

---

38. Ibid., 97a.
39. Rabbi Yehuda Loew of Prague, *Ḥiddushei Aggadot*, vol. 3, Sanhedrin, 204. See also Rabbi Shagar, *On That Day*, 204.
40. [Hebrew Editor's note: This is regarding the call by many Religious Zionist rabbis for IDF soldiers to disobey orders that have to do with removing settlers in the Disengagement Plan.]
41. See p. 211.

warrior's bow shall be banished. He shall call the nations to peace; his rule shall extend from sea to sea and from ocean to land's end" (v. 10).

Is the messianic process in which we are living capable of creating a religious *avant-garde* that is not politically right or center but left, that refuses to grab for power and calls us to rebel against force? Will a non-right Religious Zionist[42] political party arise that will truly be a prophetic party? I am not talking about a party like Meimad, with its bourgeois air of calm and its unconditional devotion to consensus, but about a party that will shatter the status quo of existing political options and lead us to new territory. Perhaps the path there is already being paved. The claims of the right against the Disengagement are essentially drawn from the humanistic discourse of the Israeli left.

In our situation, force inevitably triggers an opposing force, drawing itself into the constraints of force and wallowing in them. We must break this vicious cycle, as a step toward redemption:[43]

> For he has grown, by His favor, like a tree crown, like a tree trunk out of arid ground. He had no form or beauty, that we should look at him; no charm, that we should find him pleasing. He was despised, shunned by men, a man of suffering, familiar with disease. As one who hid his face from us, he was despised, we held him of no account. Yet it was our sickness that he was bearing,

---

42. Rabbi Kook emphasizes that the killing of the Messiah, descendant of Joseph, does not mean getting rid of nationalism but rather improving and renewing it: "There must also be a unique center, but the goal is not just the center; rather it is the way the center affects the larger whole" (*Orot*, 160).

43. This, too, is a form of battle, because it turns the gaze towards the other and reveals his violence. See also the words of Ami Shaked: "As a community, we have suffered one injury after another and the years of struggle have only brought out the best in us, and we are obligated to fight in a way fitting for our way of life, for our nature, for the goodness of our hearts and for our commitments to the fate of our community. Whatever our destiny may be, we must wear our garments white and our heads anointed. We are committed to a painful battle, one that will shake the nation of Israel in its nobility and its uniqueness, its concern for the collective despite the danger to our own project" (Security and Military Coordinator of Gush Katif, Letter to Residents of Gush Katif, Nissan 5765).

our suffering that he endured. We accounted him plagued, smitten and afflicted by God. (Is. 53:2–4)

Thus he shall judge the poor with equity and decide with justice for the lowly of the land. He shall strike down a land with the rod of his mouth and slay the wicked with the breath of his lips. Justice shall be the girdle of his loins, and faithfulness the girdle of his waist. The wolf shall dwell with the lamb, the leopard lie down with the kid; the calf, the beast of prey, and the fatling together, with a little boy to herd them. (Is. 11:4–6)

ADDENDUM: NON-VIOLENT PROTEST*

Every revolution is a process of shattering and descent, wherein we abandon the old world in advance of the arrival of a new, better world, though the transition may be quite difficult. For this reason, revolutions often contain violence, though I am not sure the violence is inevitable. History contains examples of non-violent revolutions, such as that of Mahatma Gandhi against the British Empire.

In the context of the Disengagement, I keep thinking that we must do something similar today. We must act with tolerance and non-violence, as per Gandhi. Our response today in the struggle around the Disengagement, just as in any public struggle, must account for the next possible step, which will depend on what happens now. Importantly, we are not just fighting for Gush Katif. We are locked in a deep struggle for the Land of Israel, and for the image and character of Israeli society in general. Violently refusing orders, as many leaders have suggested, just invites more violence and hatred. The Other Side, the *sitra aḥra,* draws its strength from exactly this sort of violence. Violence could even lead to the destruction of the state. However, if we respond non-violently, we will hold up a mirror to Israel society, reflecting the violence of the Disengagement. Perhaps this will lead it to consider what it has done and repent.

I am not saying that we should greet the evictors with hugs and kisses, but we must know how to act with restraint and non-violence. The moment when this response astonishes the other side is the moment when change can occur. This means that, from a certain perspective, we should have set up the march for the people exiting Gush Katif, not entering it. Imagine the rabbis and communities exiting Gush Katif in *tallitot* and with Torah scrolls. This march, though some might interpret it as submission, would hold up a mirror to Israeli society and reflect the violence of its own behavior. I believe that most Israelis are not chained to their hatred, so addressing them like this could create an unexpected change. It would demonstrate that the residents of Gush Katif and their supporters do not hate the people evicting them. This response may well be a form of exilic-ness, but this exilic-ness might be exactly what this moment needs.

---

* Based on lectures on *Likkutei Moharan* 22 delivered in 5765 (2005), edited by Netanel Lederberg and published in *Expositions on Likkutei Moharan*, vol. 1, 291.

Shavuot

The Folded Torah

DISPUTE FROM HEAVEN

> On the third day, as morning dawned, there was thunder, and
> lightning, and a dense cloud upon the mountain, and a very loud
> blast of the horn; and all the people who were in the camp trem-
> bled.... All the people witnessed the thunder and lightning, the
> blare of the horn and the mountain smoking; and when the peo-
> ple saw it, they fell back and stood at a distance. (Ex. 19:16, 20:15)

On Shavuot in 1805, Rabbi Nahman delivered a sermon discussing the
sounds of the giving of the new Torah, the sounds of revelation.[1] As with
many other sermons he gave, this sermon surreptitiously spoke about
Rabbi Nahman himself. Rabbi Nahman was tormented throughout his
short life by many harsh disputes over his spiritual path with those he
called "the elders of the generation."[2] These disputes plagued his path

---

Edited by Yishai Mevorach and published in *The Remainder of Faith*, 141–156 [He-
brew Editor's note: The term "Folded Torah" is influenced by Deleuzean philosophy,
which includes the idea of a "folded language."]

1. [Hebrew Editor's note: This sermon is consciously in dialogue with the Lurianic
    kavvanot for Shavuot.]

2. See Arthur Green, *Tormented Master* (Woodstock, Vt.: Jewish Lights Publishing,
    1992), 94–134; Rabbi Shagar, *In the Shadow of Faith*, 209–225; idem, *Expositions on
    Likkutei Moharan*, vol. 1, 122–139.

and scourged his followers. These "elders" denigrated him and marginalized his Torah. Interestingly, Rabbi Nahman often "invited" these disputes. His followers once heard him say: "Believe me, I have the power to make peace with the whole world, so that no one will dispute me, but what can I do? There are levels and palaces that a person can reach only by way of disputes."[3]

In the aforementioned sermon, based on a talmudic discussion of theodicy, Rabbi Nahman refers to himself as "a righteous person who suffers."[4] This term describes a person whose religious posture, or his quest for religious truth, keeps him from taking part in the norm and the religious establishment. Therefore, he "suffers" from exclusion and dispute, while in contrast "great righteous people prosper." As Rabbi Nahman remarked: "All of the great righteous people reached the high level they reached, *and stopped there*. I ... need constant dispute, *for I am always moving*, all the time, every second, from level to level. If I ever thought that I stood in the same place as I had the moment before, I would not want myself at all in this world."[5] In Rabbi Nahman's self-understanding, the disputes he underwent and his resulting suffering both signified and actually proved his supremacy as the righteous person of the generation – "the righteous person who suffers." The disputes against him expressed his singular uniqueness and provided him with the impetus for advancement and ascent.

In the context of Shavuot, Rabbi Nahman taught that the sounds of the giving of the Torah are the sounds of dispute, since they breach the status quo that preceded them. The sounds of revelation dispute and clash with what came before them. This is "dispute for the sake

---

3. Rabbi Natan of Nemirov, *Ḥayei Moharan*, "Regarding the Disputes Against Him," §10.
4. "Moses requested that the ways in which God conducts the world be revealed to him, and He granted it to him, as it is stated: 'Show me Your ways and I will know You' (Ex. 33:13). Moses said before God: Master of the Universe. Why is it that the righteous prosper, the righteous suffer, the wicked prosper, the wicked suffer?" (Berakhot 7a).
5. Rabbi Natan, ibid.

of heaven," which is greater than "a mindset of peace" that receives its spirit from heaven:[6]

> There is a *dispute that is for the sake of heaven*, which is a very great mindset (*daat*), *greater even than the mindset of peace*…. "A debate that is for the sake of heaven will ultimately be sustained" (Avot 5:17), meaning that it is really love…. This is the meaning of "Let us lift up our hearts with our hands to God in heaven" (Lam. 3:41). You must lift… the pulsing spirit that is in the heart, to the hands as mentioned above. This is the meaning of "to God in heaven," for this purifies heaven… for you must lift the hands, making them an instance of heaven…. For all statements are received from heaven, for all of the words are there, as the verse says, "God, your word stands forever in heaven" (Ps. 119:89). The words that are received from heaven are received via the thunders, an instance of "In heaven, God will thunder" (I Sam. 2:10), an instance of "God thunders marvelously with His voice" (Job 37:5)…. Accepting is primarily achieved through an instance of thunders, which is an instance of *a pulsing spirit*… for the pulsing spirit blows and disperses everything… this is an instance of thunders… and all words are received from there…. *You should not demean the one who receives, even if the halakha does not agree with him, for he received his words from heaven.* Thus, truly "these and those are the words of the living God" (Eiruvin 13b). The fact that the halakha does not agree with him – this is impossible to understand or comprehend… for "a righteous person (*tzaddik*) who prospers," this is the aspect of a *tzaddik* with whom halakha

---

6. Rabbi Nahman's great innovation here is setting dispute alongside peace, and perhaps even above it. This is in sharp contrast to the traditional Jewish ideal, stretching back to the days of the prophets, "For the work of righteousness shall be peace, and the effect of righteousness, calm and confidence forever. Then My people shall dwell in peaceful homes, in secure dwellings, in untroubled places of rest" (Is. 32:17–18). Rabbi Nahman, in the paradoxical manner he so loved, added that dispute is essentially peace, "for in truth this dispute is great love and peace." To fight and dispute are nothing less than acts of great love and peace.

agrees; "a righteous person who suffers," this is the aspect of a
tzaddik with whom the halakha does not agree.[7]

The revelation of the Torah appears as thunder from heaven: "Then the
Lord thundered from heaven, the Most High gave forth His voice – hail
and fiery coals" (Ps. 18:14). It is not a speech, but an event.[8] It is not an
idea, but the "pulsing spirit" which gives ideas their force. Revelation
neither strives for nor reveals truth – it creates it. Revelation, and the disputes that come with it, are an event that establishes a new truth which
will reign in the world, a new emergence of "halakha." Someone who
hears the sounds of revelation – who receives the Torah – will therefore necessarily stray from normative halakha, which reflects the given,
pre-existing situation: "This is the aspect of a *tzaddik* with whom halakha does not agree... and therefore... one ought not demean the one
who receives, even if the halakha does not agree with him."[9] The reason
you should not demean such a person is because his commitment to
truth is what leads him inexorably into disputes. Moreover, the thunder
of revelation hurls a person into disputes against his will, as someone
who merits to receive Torah is obligated to respond to it – he has no
other choice – and thus "one ought not demean the one who receives."
In essence, Rabbi Nahman teaches that even though the halakha does
not accord with this person, and many of the righteous and the sages of
the generation may attack him, it is ultimately incorrect to demean the
actions he took out of the thunder of receiving the Torah – "The fact that
the halakha does not agree with him – this is impossible to understand
or comprehend." Rabbi Nahman claims that his denigration indicates
more than anything else just how unjust that denigration really is. As
noted above, these disputes with him testified to his singular uniqueness, to the fact that he was a pioneer committed to the unique truth
which he had received.

---

7. Rabbi Nahman, *Likkutei Moharan* 56:8–10. Emphasis added.
8. [Hebrew Editor's note: Rabbi Shagar is using the terms "event" and "truth" in light
   of the thought of Alain Badiou in his book *Ethics: An Essay on the Understanding of
   Evil*. Rabbi Shagar's sermon "The Name of the Father" (p. 169 in this volume) treats
   these terms from a slightly different perspective.]
9. Ibid.

Thus, Rabbi Nahman teaches us that a person must be open to experiencing revelation, responding to it, as well as accepting the price of this response. The reason people do not experience revelation of truth is not because they seek but do not find it. Rather it is because they are never even open to its presence to begin with. They are not willing to pay the price of revelation. It is as Rabbi Nahman says at the beginning of his sermon: "For in truth, the Torah is constantly proclaiming and shouting and admonishing…just that he does not hear the call of the Torah's proclamation because of the concealments."[10] Attaining truth demands a sort of openness, rather than intellectual effort. You must be willing to set yourself free from all the typical ways of thinking and hear "the call of the proclamation." You must give sensitive attention to the thunder of the event. This sort of awareness leads to dedicating careful attention to the events through which God speaks to each person. When things resonate with a person, he can discover that they came to awaken and illuminate him in preparation for a new Torah.

It is hard for most people to accept these ideas for two reasons. First, people often rely on the fixed, stable orders of reality and these ideas disrupt those orders. Second, these ideas impose a much weightier responsibility upon a person. In the moment of revelation, the individual faces a critical juncture where he must decide whether to respond, and no one else can help him determine the correct choice. There is no sense in asking someone else in moments like this, since responding to revelation means being in a state of "the halakha does not agree with him." Any other person would simply respond that the "revelation" is nothing but a mistake, or even a sin. This is the most intensely personal situation, wherein a person cannot rely on anyone else. Therefore, when biblical figures like Abraham or Elijah the Prophet are disturbed by their revelations, and ask those around them what to do, the answer is clear: "Do not do it!" [11]

---

10. Ibid., 56:3.

11. [Hebrew Editor's note: Rabbi Shagar has in mind Abraham's decision during the Binding of Isaac, and his relation to idolatry as depicted in various midrashim. The reference to Elijah the Prophet denotes the prophet's encounter with the prophets of Baal on Mount Carmel, wherein Elijah sacrificed offerings on an altar outside the Temple, despite the biblical prohibition against doing so.]

From the perspective of the norm, every question has a clear answer. By contrast, a person who is open to revelation does not need to even ask a question. After all, he is facing a phenomenon which strikes him with astonishment. He is either disturbed by something specific or is inspired to really create something. This is the sound of the thunder, and this is what makes it a divine election, carrying with it divine certainty. In other words, the divine chooses to shine a light in a person's heart, conveying something that questions what he and those around him think is true and correct. The divine creates a challenge, and this itself is the answer. It is a self-evident reality, a reality that inspires a wonderment of chosen-ness in a person. Why did this thing awaken within me, rather than within someone else?! The Izbitzer Rebbe, Rabbi Mordechai Yosef Leiner, teaches that moments like this are moments of thunder, the very appearance of which in a person's heart indicate their certain force:

> The awakening of the heart … stirs wonder in the eyes of anyone who understands: why did his heart suddenly awaken with thunder and cacophony … ? How many thousands of souls came before him, and yet the question never arose within their hearts. From this awakening itself a person can understand that there is a creator who runs the world, for the passion that arrives in the heart … also only comes from what God, blessed be He, sent into a person's heart – if it was a natural occurrence, why didn't if happen to everyone in the world?[12]

SIGHING AND SCREAMING

Rabbi Nahman proceeds to teach that to attain the giving of the Torah and the hearing of thunders, a person must "refine the heavens" through sighing:

> To arrive at a debate that is for the sake of heaven, you must refine and purify heaven, so that it will not be an instance of "I clothe the skies in blackness" (Isaiah 50:3). *Purifying and refining heaven can be achieved through a true sigh.* For the heart has *a pulsing spirit …*

---

12. Rabbi Mordekhai Leiner of Izbica, *Mei Hashiloaḥ*, vol. 1, Tazria, *s.v. Ishah.*

and sadness of spirit prevents the spirit from pulsing properly. This makes the limbs heavy, for the pulsing spirit does not blow into them properly.... This is an instance of "sadness of the hands" (Genesis 5:29), for the primary damage caused by sadness of spirit is to the hands, as mentioned above. When the limbs are heavy, then they further weigh down the pulsing spirit, weakening it further.... This goes on until his soul departs, Heaven forbid. *But through sighing, he heals and revitalizes the pulsing spirit, and is saved from sadness of the spirit.* The pulsing spirit begins to blow again in the limbs properly, particularly in the hands. This purifies heaven, for the hands are an instance of heaven (*shamayim*) – fire (*esh*) and water (*mayim*) – an instance of the right and left hands... when the sigh purifies the hands – an instance of heaven... then it is an instance of debate for the sake of heaven.[13]

The "true sigh" that exits a person's lips is a departure and abandoning that precedes and parallels the thunder. In sighing, it is as if a person says, "I just can't anymore." A sigh does not convey any content or ideas, but rather purifies and cleanses, leading to a distinctly elementary state. Often, a person finds himself shambling through a reality defined by the crude, exhausting repetition of a limited set of options: "When the limbs are heavy, then they further weigh down the pulsing spirit, weakening it further. As a result of the limbs becoming heavier, it weighs further on the pulsing spirit. This goes on until his soul departs, Heaven forbid." The sigh comes and clears everything out, creating a state comparable to the feeling a person experiences after crying deeply. Thus, for example, Rabbi Nahman testified about himself: "For in the days of his youth... he would sometimes sigh, and afterward he would test himself to see if he could lift his hands, and he could not lift his hands. His body would really, truly break due to his sigh."[14] The person is emptied, breaking down to the point where his soul leaves him, and this opens him up to a spiritual revolution. He is now ready to listen anew, no longer stuck in the given and the known.

---

13. Rabbi Nahman, *Likkutei Moharan* 56:9.
14. Rabbi Nahman of Breslov, *Siḥot Haran* §167.

Based on this, Rabbi Nahman teaches that the sigh, or the groan, the "sounds of *oy vavoy*" always accompany beginnings. They are always present in the initial acts of spiritual creation by those who try to open new paths in their service of God. As he said in a teaching for the holiday of Shavuot 5569 (1809):

> This aspect...is very difficult and harsh. All service of God and repentance, *any act a person wishes to perform in the service of God,* must be preceded by many cries of "Oy vey!" and by groans and gestures – the strange motions those who fear God make in the course of serving God – in order for you to perform it. *This is primarily true at the start, when it is incredibly difficult,* for "all beginnings are difficult" (Mekhilta, Baḥodesh 2). You need many cries and groans before you can begin any beginning.[15]

To attain the giving of the Torah, a person must sigh a deep, thundering sigh that purifies the heavens from the clouds that block the sun's light. This is a precious sigh: "See how precious is the sigh and groan (the *krekhtz*) of a Jewish person, which provides wholeness in place of the lack."[16]

In another teaching, Rabbi Nahman teaches that *the scream* precedes and parallels the thunders of the giving of the Torah. In a time when the Torah is sealed, without any innovations, a time when "spiritual consciousness (*mohin*) has disappeared," a time that the kabbalists call "gestation" (*ibbur*), then "screaming is good for a person." Screaming is not a departure and abandoning like a sigh is. Rather, it means forcing energy into a constrained space – "From distress, I called out to God" – in the wake of which the breach and the birth take place – "God answered me and brought me relief" (Psalms 118:5):

> Sometimes the spiritual consciousness (*mohin*) and divine energy (*shefa*) are concealed, an instance of "gestation," (*ibbur*) at which

15. Rabbi Nahman, *Likkutei Moharan* II 4:2.
16. Rabbi Nahman, *Likkutei Moharan* 8:1. For more on the concept of the sigh, see Rabbi Shagar, *Expositions on Likkutei Moharan*, vol. 1, 92–99.

point screaming is good for a person, both in prayer and in Torah study, for the spiritual consciousness (*mohin*) have disappeared ... This is like a woman who is too exhausted to give birth, and when she crouches to give birth she screams seventy screams[17] ... then there is a birth ... and a person's shouts in his prayer and his Torah study, when the spiritual consciousness (*mohin*) withdraw and are in an instance of "gestation," (*ibbur*) these shouts are an instance of the shouts of the birthing woman.... *For you must shout in order to draw out... from concealment to revelation.* Revelation is an instance of birth ... when a person studies Torah and learns *a new idea*, this is due to the spiritual consciousness (*mohin*) and the intellect of this Torah and studying being in the aspect of "gestation" (*ibbur*) ... and then he must shout the voices mentioned above ... in order to draw out the spiritual consciousness (*mohin*) in an instance of birth.[18]

The letters of the Torah are dry. They say nothing new, only what is already known. While the words certainly convey information, a true encounter with the letters only happens when an event of understanding and meaning takes place, centering on enjoyment, not information. When the Torah is sealed in "the aspect of gestation (*ibbur*)," and the eruption of the scream breaks through the familiar and the known, it shatters the normal reading of the words and their typical meaning. The scream is the scream of the woman in childbirth, screaming seventy screams upon the birthing stool, after which the spiritual consciousness – the spiritual energies of comprehension and meaning – are born and lead to new ideas (*ḥiddush*). Something illuminates the person studying, and he cannot remain indifferent to it. This something opens the person up to new meanings and layers of understanding – he "learns a new idea."

---

17. Zohar III:149b.
18. Rabbi Nahman, *Likkutei Moharan* 56:7–8. Emphasis added. In the Lurianic system, gestation-*ibbur* is a lower period of consciousness before achieving the state of spiritual consciousness-*mohin*.

"All sounds: whether of crying out, or of sighing; whether the sound of the shofar, or the sound of song – they all are the concept of brazenness, as in (Psalms 68:34), 'Behold, He puts into His voice a brazen sound.'"[19] The sound of the scream, like all sounds and groans, embodies the erupting holy boldness that Rabbi Nahman saw as critical for a life of faith. These sounds are the "holy radicalness" necessary to break free from the stagnant and boring forms of faith and Torah that Rabbi Nahman called "false beliefs."[20] These beliefs are false by virtue of the way they bind a person, exhaust him, and close him off from a revelation of Torah and truth. A person must therefore scream against them and sigh in their face.

STUTTERING THE LANGUAGE

At this point, we must ask an important question about the idea Rabbi Nahman has set forward: if the Torah's truth derives from the singular event wherein it is revealed to the individual – and if getting stuck in its conventional meaning leads to boring, false faith – what does it mean to teach Torah to other people? What room is there for publicly expounding Torah, or worse, writing it down? Don't these actions lead to the reification of the vital, living Torah, reducing it to an empty dogma for those who read and hear it? Indeed, Rabbi Nahman teaches, "And, someone whose Torah study lacks *understanding and contains no new idea* should not expound it in public. For this Torah, which is ... an instance of gestation (*ibbur*) ... should nevertheless not be expounded as is. *For only things which are clear should be expounded.*"[21] According to Rabbi Nahman, a person is only fit to expound his Torah before an audience if this Torah has the power to inspire revelation and innovation in those who hear it. To clarify, it is not that the Torah conveys the content of a specific revelation. Rather, it is that the Torah itself brings the audience into contact with the infinite. When Rabbi Nahman speaks about "things which are clear," he is not referring to unambiguous instrumental knowledge or to ideas that are entirely illuminated. Instead, the clarity he has in mind is

---

19. Ibid., 22:4.
20. Ibid., 22:2, 55:6.
21. Ibid., 21:8. Emphasis added.

the self-evident posture of the person speaking the Torah. The person possesses a radiant inner conviction about the words he speaks. This conviction is itself his connection with the infinite.[22]

To explain: speech can function in many ways. It can inform, depict, instruct, imitate, etc. It can also function, as the Zohar says, as "horses of fire." The letters of the Torah are horses of fire, the vowel points are cavalrymen riding on the burning horses, and the musical notations are the weapons which the cavalrymen carry.[23] "Horses of fire" refers to what we might call "immanence of desire," in the language of Gilles Deleuze.[24] These are words that do not represent or indicate some meaning – they burn like horses of fire, they take place and sizzle. This is how Rabbi Nahman describes this desire:

> Sometimes, a person makes vowel points for the letters of the Torah … for the letters without vowel points are like a body without a soul, lacking any motion or activity… and the vowel points are love and yearning (*kisufin*), an instance of "silver (*kesef*) spangles" (Song of Songs 1:11) …. The vowel points enable the letters to join together and integrate, becoming yearning and desire.[25]

When speech carries within it these "horses of fire," then it is living, vital speech fitting to be spoken before publicly as Torah. It may even be fit for writing down in a book. This idea can help us understand Rabbi Nahman's own preferred method of expressing himself, reflecting his assertion that "the world has abandoned the sciences of grammar, and

---

22. See ibid., 64:5. The "clear language" about which the prophet Zephaniah speaks brings with it the melody, the song, and the silence that transcend speech, rather than informational-representational knowledge.

23. See R. Daniel Fisch, *Zohar Ḥadash* with *Matok Midvash* commentary, vol. 4 (Jerusalem: Mekhon Daat Yosef, 2002), 414.

24. My use of Deluezian terminology draws from the following sources: Ohad Zahavi, *A Logical Novel: Gilles Deleuze Between Philosophy and Literature* (Tel Aviv: Resling, 2005) (Heb.); Rafael Zaguri-Orli and Yoram Cohen, "Kafka's Monkey: An Introduction to the Book 'Kakfa: Toward a Minor Literature,'" in Gilles Deleuze and Felix Guattari, *Kafka: Toward a Minor Literature*, trans. Rafael Zaguri-Orli and Yoram Cohen (Tel Aviv: Resling, 2005), 7–23 (Heb.).

25. Rabbi Nahman, *Likkutei Moharan* 31:6, 14.

doesn't study it at all. For there is no need for grammar."[26] Rabbi Nahman's stuttered, disjointed, folded Torah is the farthest thing from "things
which are clear." If we evaluate Rabbi Nahman's teachings in light of the
Platonic concept of understanding, we find ourselves looking at heaps
of nonsense. Considering Deleuze's ideas, however, we might say that
Rabbi Naḥman challenges the classic Platonic concept of understanding,
which assumes correspondence between language and what it indicates
or represents. For both Deleuze and Rabbi Nahman, understanding
is not an inner light, but rather an encompassing light. It is not found
within the body of the word. According to Deleuze, understanding is
"on the surface" of the word and rests upon it.[27] Rabbi Nahman's Torah
"stutters the language, and leads a person outside it."[28] For the individual
who encounters it, Rabbi Nahman's language creates ideas and meaning
rather than purely representing them. What it creates is not the sense of
the words but the event that the words, the charging horses, themselves
create. This is the revelation that occurs when a person speaks Torah.
The person speaking opens a path to an event of truth. This takes place
in the encounter with the desire in the Torah, with the points of yearning and the pleasure within it.

The Torah exists in the effect that the words create. The correct
image for thinking about words of Torah is not a vessel that garbs light,
but a vessel that creates all kinds of movements of light. For this reason, it
is often impossible to determine what Rabbi Nahman is trying to convey
in his teachings, stories, and dreams, particularly if we attempt to apply
philological or semantic analysis. Rabbi Nahman is using words to *evoke*
feelings, ideas, and experiences. He uses language in an unusual way,
one which does not consider the grammatical sense of words. Instead,

---

26. Rabbi Nahman, *Siḥot Haran* §235.
27. Inner light and encompassing light are kabbalistic concepts. In this sense, the subject
who "takes pleasure in speech" does not reside "within" himself, but rather outside
on the surface, like encompassing lights. This is the meaning of a peculiar kabbalistic
assertion regarding the soul, from which emerges the subject and the revelation of
concrete reality that gives it pleasure. Kabbala asserts that the soul's root is not an
instance of "inner light" but rather an instance of "encompassing lights," which are
not found within the body itself but rather rest within the pleasure of its existence.
28. Cf. Zahavi, *A Logical Novel*, 18.

he uses words as "horses of fire" to enact a shift in whoever encounters them. In Deleuze's language, you have to "experience" Rabbi Nahman and his teachings, you must taste them[29] in order to understand them: "The more you explore them, the more you find wondrous, new tastes, sweet to the palate, and greatly illuminating for the eyes."[30]

For example, one of the words Rabbi Nahman uses most often is *"behinat."* This is often translated as "aspect of" or "instance of"– to the point where he once remarked "my Torah is entirely *behinot."*[31] Rabbi Nahman uses this word in order to string together an infinite chain of concepts and images, as can be seen in texts like the one with which we started: "Consequently, we receive the words from the hands (*yadayyim*), which are an instance of 'as God spoke through (*beyad*)...' which was said about Moses.... All the words that they receive from there – i.e., from the instance of hands, the instance of heavens, the instance of thunder – since they are received from heaven, one ought not demean the receiver."[32] The exact meaning of this word is hard to explain, but it creates the correct effect! It fits into the melody, the syntax, the stuttered rhythm – all of which are far beyond the word's content.

Torah that is fit to expound publicly is Torah wherein the language precedes the sense and creates it as an event. For this reason, Rabbi Nahman asserts that the *tzaddik's* words contain more than one meaning,[33] and he asks those who listen to him to find new ideas in his teachings, even if he never at all intended those ideas originally:

> Even an ordinary person, if he sits himself in front of a holy book and looks at the letters of Torah, he will be able to perceive new insights and wonders.... Then, one can see wonders [in the] new

---

29. Cf. The quote from Rabbi Nahman in Rabbi Natan, *Ḥayei Moharan*, "The Greatness of his Teachings and his Holy Books," §1: "The world has still not tasted me at all. If they would hear me speak even one teaching, with its melody and dance, they would all be totally and completely nullified."

30. Rabbi Natan, ibid., §23.

31. Ibid., §11.

32. Rabbi Nahman, *Likkutei Moharan* 56:9–10. Emphasis added.

33. Ibid., II 15

combinations. It is possible to perceive in the book something the author did not think of at all.[34]

TORAH OF THE MESSIAH

This tendency and form of expression in Rabbi Nahman's teachings is continuous with what various hasidic homilies – themselves characterized by broken, folded language – called "Torah of the Messiah." This is the Torah about which the rabbinic midrash says: "The Holy One, blessed be He, sits and expounds a new Torah which will be revealed in the future through the Messiah"; "Rabbi Avin bar Kahana said: The Holy One, blessed be He, says, 'A new Torah from Me goes forth' – a renewal of Torah from Me goes forth."[35] The redemptive Torah of the Messiah is the same Torah in which the music of Torah is revealed, with its roots in simple jest and pleasure. This pleasure derives from the mysteries of Torah: "In the future, 'Then our mouths will be filled with laughter' (Psalm 126:2) and 'A new Torah from me will go forth' (Isaiah 51:4) will be revealed, the meanings of Torah will be revealed in the future yet to come, in the Torah of the Messiah."[36]

The playfulness (and jest) in these homilies should be seen as that which "lacks nothing, constantly sustaining itself…a flow that issues from itself and returns to itself."[37] In light of what the kabbalists said about the personal play of the Infinite, blessed be He,[38] pleasure and jest should be seen as a lofty, supreme level. They are not some bourgeois experience that is moderate, refined, and contains within it a rational, sublimating representation of the energies that drive it. This is an anarchic, libidinal movement, which threatens the Platonic order of

---

34. Ibid., 281. And cf. 105.
35. *Tanna DeBei Eliyahu Zuta* 20; Leviticus Rabba 13:3. We should note that the term "new Torah" appears in the teaching we discussed above, *Likkutei Moharan* 56, at the end: "'When you bring a new grain offering to God' – this is an instance of a new Torah, a Torah of God, which is made through the aspect of *Malkhut*."
36. Rabbi Menachem Mendel Schneerson, *Torat Menachem: Maamarim Melukat*, vol. 1 (New York: Kehot, 2002), 298–299.
37. See Zaguri-Orli and Cohen, "Kafka's Monkey," 9–10.
38. Cf. Yosef Ben Shlomo, *The Mystical Theology of Rabbi Moshe Cordovero* (Jerusalem: Bialik Institute, 1986), 60–63 (Heb.).

representation, challenging its rigidity and enabling alternative readings of reality.[39] A Torah that centers around pleasure and jest is a Torah that reveals the most elemental reality. Connecting with it does not require any specific action or understanding, because it means connecting with the thing itself. The content you learn is nothing more than a vessel, a medium, for this pleasure-bearing connection. It is a vessel that creates lights and creative occurrences.

The pleasure of the Torah of the Messiah comes from its individualistic creativity: "No longer will they need to teach one another and say to one another, 'Heed the Lord;' for all of them, from the least of them to the greatest, shall heed Me – declares the Lord" (Jeremiah 31:34). The messianic Torah is a work of art, a personal creation that grants a person creative freedom. The purpose of the Torah and of the Messiah is to change the way the world operates. No longer will the world run according to the rules of cognitive discourse and justifiable truth. Imagination and aesthetics will reign as standards of truth. This Torah will enact a powerful shift within reality, bringing its dream layer to the fore. Thus, in the Torah of the Messiah, truth will be evaluated based on aesthetics, not on rationality. Torah study will focus primarily on new, original language games that reveal the love and pleasure of Torah. Unsurprisingly, therefore, Breslov's messianic figure appears full of song, creativity, and art whose creativity comes to fullest expression in his sermons.[40] Indeed, Rabbi Nahman taught that redemption is a song, the melody of the Land of Israel:

> But in the future, a new song will awaken which will be an instance of miracles … and this new song will awaken in the future … an instance of grace, for it enables the future renewal of the world, an instance of "Grace will build a world" (Ps. 89:3) … the renewal of

---

39. Cf. the distinction made by David Gurevich in *Postmodernism: Culture and Literature at the End of the 20th Century* (Tel Aviv: Devir Books, 1997), 40 (Heb.).
40. See Zvi Mark, *The Scroll of Secrets: The Hidden Messianic Vision of R. Nachman of Breslav* (Brighton, MA: Academic Studies Press, 2010).

the world is an instance of the Land of Israel ... then will awaken the song of providence and miracles.[41]

This is the song of the land of prayer, the land of hope that is open to all possibilities: "Prayer corresponds to miracles, for it is supernatural. Sometimes, the natural order necessitates one thing, whereas prayer overturns nature's course."[42] Thus, Rabbi Nahman's teachings carry within them this futuristic melody, wherein sense and reality do not dominate the word. Rather, the word creates sense and reality. Thanks to this melody, "vowel points are made for the letters so that they are animated and become vessels to receive good."[43]

---

41. Rabbi Nahman, *Likkutei Moharan* II 8:10.
42. Ibid., I 9:5. I would add that the Deleuzian way of thinking represents a possibility for coming into contact with this wondrous melody, which will certainly burst forth, the melody that will bring the Torah – and us with it – out of the confines of its exile.
43. Ibid., 31:13.

Face to Face

*"God spoke to you face to face on the mountain
from within the fire."*
(DEUT. 5:4)

INTRODUCTION

What is the meaning of revelation, which stands at the center of the experience at Sinai?

According to the Baal HaTanya (Rabbi Shneur Zalman of Liadi, 1745–1813) this question is particularly pressing when it comes to the content of revelation:

> The first thing to understand is the meaning of "the giving of the Torah," for our forefather Abraham fulfilled the whole Torah before it was even given...the verse says, "so that you will command your sons..." meaning that the Torah was something they received from their ancestors. Further, you must understand what it means that, during the Ten Commandments, God descended on Mount Sinai with thunder and lightning, and that the people's

Based on drafts written in 5758–5761, edited by Eitan Abramovich in preparation for the conference organized for the sake of Rabbi Shagar's recovery. Published on the website of the Institute for the Advancement of Rabbi Shagar's Writings (shagar. co.il).

souls left their bodies upon hearing each commandment, yet the commandments say, "Do not kill, do not commit adultery, etc.," and these are banal matters that are necessitated by human intellect itself.[1]

What value did the experience of Sinai add, if it only revealed things we already know? It seems that, as opposed to the things that occur in our regular existence, revelation is not defined by the content that it transmits. Rather it is defined by the very fact of revelation and the disruption of normal existence. According to the verse with which we began, revelation means the revelation of the face, wherein a person encounters God directly.

This makes the question of the relationship between the finite and the infinite quite urgent: what significance can revelation have if it must always be processed through human concepts and ideas? What connection could revelation create when the very idea of a connection is a human idea? Furthermore, Moses was told, "A man cannot see My face and live... you shall see My back but you shall not see My face." What then was the face that the Israelites saw from within the fire?

UNMEDIATED KNOWLEDGE

When Maimonides reads the first verse of the revelation as a commandment, this is how he explains its meaning:

> The foundation of foundations and pillar of wisdoms to know that there is a First Existent, that brought into existence everything that exists, and everything that exists, the heavens and the earth and everything between them, exists by virtue of the truth of His existence.... This is a positive commandment, as per the verse, "I am the Lord your God."[2]

"The fundamental term of faith is "the truth of His existence." From this true existence, all things receive their existence. The truth of existence

---

1. Rabbi Shneur Zalman of Liadi, *Likkutei Torah, Bemidbar* 12:3.
2. Maimonides, *Mishneh Torah*, Laws of the Foundation of the Torah 1:1–6.

is the assertion that God truly exists, while what we think of as existence does not necessarily exist. What we think of as existence is just a possible, incidental, existence, in contrast to the true existence that is a deeper layer than existence itself. In the revelation at Mount Sinai, the Jews encountered this layer, the truth of existence that transcends the existence with which we are familiar. This faith gives us our existence. Without it we lack substance – our lived existence is transient and deficient. Faith gives a Jew his place – he exists in God.

Already in Maimonides' depiction of Moses' request, he describes knowing the truth of existence as seeing a face:

> What did Moses want to comprehend when he asked: "Please show me Your glory"? He asked to know the truth of God's existence to the point of internalizing it in his mind, the same way you know a particular person whose face you saw and whose form has been engraved within your mind. This person is distinct within your mind from other men. Similarly, Moses asked that God's existence be distinct within his mind from the existence of other entities, to the extent that he would know the truth of God's existence as it is. God replied to him that a living person, body and soul, does not have the ability to comprehend this matter in its entirety. God revealed to him that which no man had known before him or would ever know afterward, until he was able to comprehend from the truth of God's existence distinctly in his mind, as a person is distinguished from other men when one sees his back and knows his body and his clothing. This is alluded to by the verse, "You shall see My back, but you shall not see My face."[3]

Knowledge of the face means knowledge of the essence, of unmediated recognition. In contrast, knowledge of the back, such as Moses merited, means the ability to understand characteristic movements. It allows us to internalize how walking, clothing, or writing reflect the individual's unique essence. Both types of knowledge involve some degree of

3. Ibid., 10.

unmediated contact with the essence. This is what distinguishes between them and the normal ways we talk about God, which connect with neither God's essence nor its reflection.

To use different language, we might say that unmediated knowledge is knowledge derived from direct recognition, distinct from theoretical, indirect knowledge. The difference between them is like the difference between getting an exact description from a matchmaker and directly encountering a partner. An unmediated encounter reveals "the thing itself," everything that escapes description. The unique aspect of a person is revealed only in such an encounter, while a description can always be applied to another person. According to Maimonides, the prophetic books only give mediated descriptions of God, teaching about God's existence rather than His essence.[4] The revelation at Sinai differed in this regard. It was only at Sinai that there was knowledge of God's unmediated presence. Only such knowledge can give faith its certainty because it is this knowledge that encounters reality, the divine entity itself. This is also what gives Mosaic prophecy its absolute quality.

This is the voice that Israel heard, "for hearing the voice without the mediation of an angel is called 'face to face.'"[5] Revelation of the face cannot be repeated. It is not an external, objective knowledge but an intimacy, an illumination, or in Maimonides' language, "the unity of knower, knowing, and known." Can we encounter God's face? Can we know God intimately, to the point of "if I knew God, I would be God"? As we said, already in the biblical text there is a contradiction between the description of the revelation at Sinai and the assertion that "a man cannot see Me and live." Indeed, the Sages said that the souls of Israel left their bodies and they had to be brought back to life.

The revelation creates a commandment to believe, but this belief "is not something expressed verbally. Rather it is something depicted in the soul when you believe in it as depicted."[6] Depicting it in the soul, rather than simply knowing it intellectually, gives reality to the faith that God really exists and is present. This knowledge is a connection to the

---

4. Maimonides, *Guide for the Perplexed* 1:46.
5. Ibid., 37.
6. Ibid., 50.

thing itself; it is the encounter with the face that Israel saw at Mount Sinai. As is clear from Maimonides' description of Moses' request, experiencing God's uniqueness lets you distinguish between the layer of what is common to others and the revelation of what cannot be conceptualized. This uniqueness is not a philosophical assertion to be affirmed. Rather it is a divine intimacy that is laid bare before the believer. This intimacy creates a person's intimacy with himself, the trust and calm of faith. Encountering the truth of existence grants a believer his own existence.

THE FORCE OF A COMMANDMENT

As mentioned previously, Maimonides, as opposed to all other early commentators, counts faith as a commandment. The statement, "I am the Lord your God," should therefore be read not as God's declaration presenting Himself, but as a command. However, Maimonides elsewhere taught that the commandments should be fulfilled for their own sake, meaning out of love. A commandment is not a law, enforced by violence, but it is also not a request, made from a position of inferiority. It is also not a declaration, which does not address the listeners present. In contrast, a command should be understood as the truth of God's existence turning toward the individual and toward the truth in him, "face to face."

The command is a distinct type of speech. When a person enters a room and presents himself before those present with the words, "I am Reuven," he is not reporting on or depicting something but creating with his words. However, such a person is not shouting into empty space. He needs the response of those present, for them to turn toward him in return – he needs their faces. If they turn away from him, he and his address remain incomplete, cut short and rejected. In the statement "I am," God turns toward man for man to receive God's kingship with love, for man to receive God's address and thus create Him as a reality.

The force of a commandment is not a force of violence. It does not use strength, but rather its force comes from its origin. The address comes from the truth of God's existence, from the depth of God's intimacy. Rosenzweig describes this as the lover's call, "love me."[7] In this address, the lover turns toward his beloved with his essence, and it is

---

7. Franz Rosenzweig, *The Star of Redemption*, 209.

impossible to ignore. This absolute demand does not attempt to shape the future, but simply happens in the present, in the moment of revelation. It therefore cannot be held onto and posited as law. In theory, it can be refused, but on the other hand there is no choice; if you do not accept it, the world will return to chaos.

RENEWING INWARDNESS, CREATING SPACE

The *Sefat Emet*, by Rabbi Yehuda Aryeh Leib Alter (1847–1905) of Gur, presents us with another approach to the revelation at Mount Sinai.

> For God created the world using the Torah. The inner vitality of all creatures is the primordial force from the Torah...but this inwardness (*penimiyut*) was created hidden. On the day of the revelation of the Torah, however, it was revealed and each thing attached to its root, as depicted in the verse, "face to face God spoke to you"...for then the all-enlivening power of the Torah was revealed...and the primary aspect of receiving the Torah is this revelation.[8]

We can understand the words of the *Sefat Emet* using Existentialist concepts. Initially, a person lives in a state of concealment and isolation. The vitality and meaning that rests in the world, what the *Sefat Emet* calls its "inwardness," is hidden from him. He therefore cannot escape his inauthentic existence, which is, practically speaking, a lack of existence. To escape this state, a person needs revelation, the disruption of this opaque existence and the revelation of reality. However, since we are talking about revelation and not an intellectual idea, the inwardness will eventually return to its concealment submerged in the world of facts and generalizations.

To maintain itself, revelation requires a space where it can occur, a plane which will replace the existing plane. The Torah fills this role, creating the space where reality can be revealed, the abode for holiness and the divine presence. The words of the Torah and the fulfillment of the commandments shape a world of holiness, the substance of which

---

8. *Sefat Emet, Bemidbar, Shavuot 5631, 22.*

transcends the day-to-day world of facts. This is the Jew's refuge from the alienation and estrangement of the outer world. It is here that he finds his place and his at-homeness. This is not the holiness of time, space, or any object. It is the holiness of speech, where the language itself becomes a holy language.

The revelation of the Torah does not require any special insight or deep understanding. It is readily available to every Jew who is involved in Torah for its own sake, conscious of the divine command. The Jew finds this revelation in the spoken words, in the open book, in understanding. As opposed to forms of understanding and experience that are an inner light – and which therefore vary from person to person – this light is an instance of "surrounding all worlds," beyond the emanated world, and it therefore shines on each person alike.

The *Sefat Emet* describes this revelation as a return to the beginning and as a source of renewal. When you first engage with something, you can encounter its substance clearly and directly. Eventually, routine and repetition conceal most things. Interactions dull and faces are no longer revealing, as if after many years of marriage. Revelation is the starting point, the openness to the concealed inwardness, renewing the connection from an old-new place. What is revealed and renewed is not some external object, but rather reality itself.

Even so, the revelation of reality is experienced first and foremost as *yirah*, as fear. As the Baal HaTanya explains in the continuation of the teaching with which we began: "The purpose of the Torah and the commandments is to reveal God's will within the lower world, as the verse says, 'God commanded us to follow all of these laws, to fear God.'"[9]

The fear that accompanies revelation is not fear of something, but rather a terror that overcomes a person without any clear cause. The fear arises when we discover the nothingness of existence, and thus expose the substantive reality behind our existence. Existence loses its material quality, its factual concreteness. It is spiritualized and appears as oneness and inwardness. This is the answer to the Baal HaTanya's question about the very human nature of the Ten Commandments: the revelation at Sinai does not grant human ethics support from an absolute and

9. *Likkutei Torah,* ibid.

transcendent source, but rather ethics itself appears as "nullified," as a revelation of the infinite. This revelation appears specifically in simple words and common statements.

This idea requires us to change how we think about the truth of revelation. Just like the creation of the world, as the creation of a space wherein reality is revealed, the revelation of the Torah cannot be evaluated based on external facts. The Torah is speech that creates rather than depicts or represents. The words construct their meaning, which is not evaluated based on how closely they adhere to reality but rather based on internal coherence, on being substantive and not artificial.

We can clarify this distinction by putting it in terms of the Baal HaTanya's distinction between forms of consciousness: *daat elyon*, "upper knowledge," and *daat taḥton*, "lower knowledge."[10] In lower knowledge, truth refers to speech matching reality, and the concreteness and stability of the fact grants speech its truth. In upper knowledge, truth refers to speech corresponding to its own inner reality. Speech receives its substance from its inwardness. The constructive speech of the Torah does not refer to external things. Such a speech instead comes from duality, from the objectified existence rooted in the *sefira* of *Malkhut*.

The Torah is a revelation of "I am who I am," speech that is one with itself and disrupts the familiar frameworks of existence. Of course, identifying the truth and revelation of the Torah is not a function of deep understanding or study. People other than just Torah scholars can therefore access it: "There is a bit of this in every Jewish soul...this is what we see practically with every Jew, when he learns any idea regarding God's immanence or transcendence, or the like...his soul is excited and he becomes entrenched in the idea and pursues it."[11] Every Jew can sense divinity and distinguish between holy and profane, between full and empty. Sometimes the simple Jew can do this better than anyone else. The divine in the Torah gives him great pleasure not because of the content, but because of what transcends it. This pleasure expresses his

---

10. See also Rabbi Shagar, *Faith Shattered and Restored*, 30.
11. Rabbi Dov Ber Schneurson, *Kuntrus Hahitpa'alut*, 58.

inner connection, his intimacy with the giver of the Torah who is present in it. It is the covenant that is the Torah.[12]

THE MYSTERY OF THE COVENANT

The covenant at Mount Sinai manifests most primally in the act of saying "we will do" *before* "we will understand." This is an order that is considered to be "the mystery used by ministering angels."[13] This mysterious idea – that understanding depends on doing – lies behind the familiar assertion that only someone who is part of the covenant can understand the Torah. However, we must clarify this assertion: what is the connection between comprehension, covenant, and deed? Why can study not stand on its own?

The Sages understood the Torah as God's covenant with Israel. Torah study primarily means partaking in that covenant. The Oral Torah, which the Sages called "the mystery," is the intimacy between God and Israel. The Sages expressed this in many homilies on their love of the Torah by using metaphors taken from marital life. A Jew finds his Jewish identity in the Torah, and through that his connection to God. That is how it was in the days of the Sages, and so it is today. Anyone devoted to the Torah experiences this, whether he is a student in yeshiva or a layman who gets up early to study a daily page of Talmud.

The bottom line of the halakha says that a person can fulfill the requirement to say the blessings on the Torah by saying the blessing of "Love," which is the second blessing of the twice-daily recitation of the *Shema*. After all, both the basis and the content of learning is love. This affects the form Torah study takes. Not every form of study can be covenantal, just as not every student can partake in the covenant. A non-Jew who learns Torah incurs the death penalty. This is not because he lacks the intelligence necessary to understand it. Rather, simply because he does not belong to the covenant, its meaning will not be revealed to him anyway. Even regarding an ignoramus the Sages taught, "One who

---

12. "Normally if a person takes an object home from the market, has he purchased its owners? But God gave the Torah to Israel and said to them, 'It is as if it is Me that you are taking.'" See Exodus Rabba 33:6.

13. Shabbat 88a.

teaches Torah in front of an ignoramus is like someone who has sexual relations with the ignoramus' fiancé in front of him," a sensitivity that reveals but a fraction of the intimacy of the scholar with his bride-Torah.

Some anthropologists claim something similar. Can a western researcher ever understand the culture of tribesmen living in an entirely different existential space? Simply translating the language and customs into another language is not enough. To understand the culture, you must live within it and be a part of it. The sense of texts and actions cannot be abstracted or described objectively. It derives from the cultural context and the way of life that they are rooted in. Therefore it must necessarily change in the transition to another culture. This was also the claim of the *Musar* masters against academic Talmud study, and this lay behind their demand that the study of *Musar* precede Torah study.

Regarding the Torah, the claim is even more far-reaching. Not only is there no Torah without covenant, but the Torah itself is the language or the speech of the covenant. Not only do you have to be a participant in the covenant to understand the Torah, but also the whole sense of it is just this revelation, the creation of the covenant through the learning. Here we return to an idea we mentioned previously about revelation: the Torah is not representation. It does not belong to the dualistic world and its meaning does not transcend it. The Torah does not describe the world of the covenant, but rather creates it. The covenant rests in and is realized by learning.

Accepting the yoke of heaven by putting "we will do" before "we will understand" is the only way to escape the external way of looking at things, the position that judges Torah by external criteria. Creating a covenant enables entrance into the world shaped by the Torah, a world that cannot be known before you enter it, a world in which holiness dwells. Some people want to use this to justify the casuistic style of learning. They claim that casuistry is like a work of art; a person should not evaluate it based on physical or philosophical truth, but also not just based on intellectual aesthetics. Freed from practical study and the exactitude of abstract research, the imagination can create the empty space necessary for the divine truth which is infinite and unbounded.

The covenant creates a different type of learning and understanding, shaping the personality of the student in its image. The Torah in its entirety is a revelation of the "I am," a speech that reveals reality rather than describes it. We measure its truth by its ability to be expressed. In fact, speaking Torah constructs it, without any dualism. A person does not know Torah just because they can compare it to other fields and identify similarities between it and some other meaning or value. A person knows Torah when they can speak it from the same place where it originated, when they can identify and unite with the intimacy it bears within it. "If I knew Him, I would be Him," and a person can only know Torah by "being it." You understand a sermon consisting of independent and constructive speech by deeply studying the words until you feel that you could have given the sermon yourself. This unity blurs the lines between discovery and creation. Thus the student understands, interprets, and creates all at the same time.

This changes the position of the student, as Rav Hillel of Paritch taught:

> "God spoke all these words to say, I am the Lord your God." The word "to say" seems redundant, for throughout the Torah the word "to say" is said to Moses as an instruction to convey the message to the Israelites...at the Ten Commandments all of Israel heard directly from God, so why was the word "to say" added?
>
> This all makes sense in light of "The Giving of the Torah" (*matan Torah*). This does not refer to the giving of the commandments of the Torah specifically, for they were given later at both Mount Sinai and the Tent of Meeting.
>
> Instead, the intent is that the capacity for Torah was given to each and every Israelite, enabling him to create by speaking the Torah and by performing the commandments, a revelation of "I am who I am" (this refers to God's essence and nature), causing it to dwell within the Israelite.... This is the meaning of "God spoke to say I am," for He drew these words into the souls of Israel so that each Israelite would be able "to say: I am," revealing "I am who I am" within his soul.[14]

---

14. *Pelaḥ Harimon, Shemot*, p.240.

In encountering and uniting with the divine speech that is in the Torah, the student receives its absoluteness, truth of existence, and inner unity that rests in the declaration "I am who I am." The ability to speak the speech of Torah, the word of God, frees a person from the incidental and the possible in existence and enables him to encounter reality.

REVELATION AND COMMANDEDNESS

Rav Hillel of Paritch's words raise another point regarding the covenant of "we will do and we will understand." Much has been written about the tension between the Israelites' putting "we will do" before "we will understand" and the Sages' understanding of the revelation at Sinai as "overturning (*kefia*) the mountain like a barrel." What is the place of compulsion – *kefia* – in revelation, when at its basis stands the absolute consent of "we will do and we will understand"?

We celebrate the giving of the Torah, not the receiving of the Torah. However, as we said, the acceptance of the yoke of heaven as expressed in the declaration, "we will do and we will understand," is critical. Without it, the revelation is just an unconvincing spectacle, a pyrotechnic display. To be convinced, you must be ready to be convinced.

If the Torah shapes the Jewish world, then there must be a process of consent that brings a Jew into this world, a moment when the Jew accepts it as his existence. Compulsory rules do not create a world. Ultimately, however, the flaw in freedom is inherent in subjectivity itself. The Tosafists expressed this distinction in their discussion of how a person who performs commandments while being commanded is preferable to someone who performs commandments without being commanded:

> The reason someone who is commanded is preferable seems to be because he is more concerned and distressed about accidentally transgressing than someone who is not commanded, who can simply forget about the commandment if he so chooses [lit., "he already has bread in his basket, so he can put this down if he desires"].[15]

---

15. Kiddushin 31a.

The greater value of "being commanded" thus derives specifically from the worry and distress a commanded person feels, which sustain the duality and distance between the person's finite human capabilities and the absoluteness of the divine command. The divine does not reveal itself as our natural, spontaneous impulses or as our inner nature. Even if the source of revelation is in a person's soul and inwardness, he still experiences it as transcending himself and his concepts. This is necessitated by the limited, split nature of human existence.

The duality in which we live prevents us from understanding free will as creating itself, as unaffected by any external context. Instead, we always perceive our freedom from the outside, and as such we see it as caught up in and responding to the causal frameworks in which we live. This sort of external perspective leads toward nihilism, as nothing in our existence can be meaningful in any absolute, non-relative sense.

In such a state, we develop a need to justify the unjustifiable, to make the external internal through duality-denying apologetics. The effort involved grants this process its meaning and makes a person stubborn and militantly heroic. It rarely achieves its goal precisely because it fails to be convincing. It feels forced, and thus only intensifies our nihilism. As the Tosafists taught, the path to freedom consists not in ignoring duality but in accepting it. A tension that is one with itself ceases to be tension.

Duality requires the compulsion and externality of revelation, but the individual chooses to accept them. The individual opens himself to being shaped. He gives up his hold on the way things are to enable the creation of the plane of holiness. The compulsion, accompanied by the fear of returning to the primordial chaos, reflects man's inability to create his own existence, and the fear of our familiar world crumbling away. In the affirmation "we will do and we will understand," a Jew enters a world he did not create, the rules of which are not tailored just for him, and only there can he feel holiness and achieve oneness. This is the meaning of the ability to say "I am who I am," which Rav Hillel of Paritch says was granted by the revelation of the Torah.

When inner truth reveals itself as an available option, man's freedom to choose himself, to accept himself as he is and where he is, reveals itself as well. When a person chooses that which is compulsory for him, he achieves inner oneness. The choice opens him up to the existence that rests within him. The "nullification" involved in putting "we will do" before "we will understand" lets a person hear the speech that creates the Torah, the letters whose roots start beyond conscious thought and surface meaning. The power of hearing creates a space for holiness, inspiration, and revelation.

The Three Weeks

The Destruction of the Home and the Renewal of Souls

THE DESTRUCTION OF THE HOME BEGINS AT BIRTH

A person experiences a recurring, drawn-out, and persistent trauma in life – the destruction of the home. This trauma, as various psychologists explain, begins with the moment of birth. The baby experiences leaving his mother's womb as a traumatic act, one which leaves scars on his psyche for the rest of his life. The womb is a person's first home. Just when he begins to feel at home there, he is forced to abandon it.

After his time in the womb, a time where he is part of his mother, as the rabbis said, "a fetus is the thigh of its mother,"[1] the person finds a new home in childhood. This early, foundational home will accompany him for the rest of his days. Childhood, even if not always happy, protects a person and grants him the shelter of home and parents. This shelter, as an existential and mental state of being, is different from a mature mindset. Therefore, we are constantly drawn to the unique

---

Based on a draft written in 5763 and a lecture delivered that year. Edited by Elhanan Nir and published on the website of the Institute for the Advancement of Rabbi Shagar's Writings (shagar.co.il).

1. Nazir 51a.

breath of schoolchildren.[2] In childhood, we live in a state of oneness with existence and with our family. As we mature, we cannot return to or re-attain this oneness. All that remains for us is longing and yearning.

Maturation necessarily involves detachment. At a certain point, a young person leaves home, gets married. Parents grow old, and they eventually die. This is the way of the world. For a time, the parents' spirit persists in the family's home. The parents' presence does not disappear immediately, but slowly the weeds of time grow up through cracks in the walls of the house and the walls of memory until it is destroyed and erased.[3]

This is the sin of Adam. By sin, I do not mean the sort of gluttonous trespass which we typically call "sin" in our world. By "sin," I refer to seeking independence through shattering the existing harmony and going in a different direction. Sin gave Adam freedom. Although he matured and left home, in leaving, he lost his home in the Garden of Eden. From that point on, he could no longer go home again. This is "the fiery ever-turning sword" (Genesis 3:24) which cannot be passed.

A person senses the destruction of the home in both personal and cosmic senses for a long period of time. I recently spoke with two men whose parents had died. Beyond the feelings of pain over the loss of a loved one, the conversation focused on the pain of losing "the home." Even mature adults who take responsibility for their lives and are totally independent feel that they have a home to which they can return. They have at least one place in the universe where they feel "at-homeness," where they smell the scent of home. When this home disappears, this adds to the pain of mourning, even though it is the natural way of the world.

When a person's home is destroyed, it leaves ineradicable scars on his personality. From that moment on, he moves through life in a

---

2. Shabbat 119b: "The world only exists because of the breath of schoolchildren."

3. [Hebrew Editor's note: In a diary entry written during his struggle with terminal cancer, Rabbi Shagar describes his experience regarding the persistence of his parents' spirit in their home, even after their deaths: "Yesterday, I was in the house of my parents, of blessed memory, who died not long ago. Only about 10 years. They are still present; my sister preserves their presence. I saw them there. The intimate objects: a keyring, a watch, a picture on the wall. I hope that excess rummaging will not profane this presence. What a person wove, spoke, gathered into a tangle over the years – these are the years of the days of his life."]

constant process of trying to deal with these scars. His life has changed, things will never be as they were. Longing for childhood will haunt him all his days. He will long for the protective shelter of his mother, for his father's gaze, and even for the conflicts he had with them. A degree of presence will still exist at first. As the books of Kabbala say, the departed does not leave this world entirely. Slowly, however, the ties come undone, and the home eventually disappears. Only particularly unique righteous people have a presence that lasts.[4]

DESTRUCTION OF THE JEWISH EXPERIENCE OF AT-HOMENESS

The kabbalists explained that the destruction of the Temple ultimately meant the destruction of at-homeness. This feeling disappeared, creating the fullest experience of the mourning that a person carries with him his whole life. Though a person must take care that this feeling does not expand to overwhelm his life, a mourning for this lost at-homeness still rests at the foundation of every human being. It is the same with the issue of exile. Exile is a national predicament, but it is also personal and cosmic with each person ultimately remaining alone.

Who lost their home in the destruction? With the Jews' home destroyed, we went wandering into exile. However, it was not only the Jews' home that was destroyed, but also the home of the *Shekhina*. The *Shekhina* was also expelled due to the sins of the Jewish people, and she too went into exile. The destruction of the home therefore causes the father (God) to expel the mother (the *Shekhina*) and to take apart the home entirely.

---

4. [Hebrew Editor's note: A more detailed discussion of this idea can be found in Rabbi Shagar's *hitvaadut* for the 19th of Kislev 5767, published in *We Will Walk in Fervor*, under the title "Your Nation Are All *Tzaddikim*." In particular, see this quote from p. 375: "This is truly one of the great wonders. Even when that righteous person leaves the world, his light still remains. It's not a natural occurrence, light without a body, without a vessel, without a garment…" and this quote from p. 359: "I would say that there are righteous people whose presence still persists in this world, and there are righteous people who, when they die, or perhaps slightly thereafter, disappear from the world – they no longer have any presence here. The Baal HaTanya certainly has a very strong presence, and very real…."]

The introduction to the *Tikkunei Zohar* goes even farther. Not only was the mother (the *Shekhina*) stripped of the walls that protected her, expelled, and sent into exile, but the father (God) even goes with her: "'Like a bird wandering from its nest, so is a man who wanders from his home' (Proverbs 27:8) – This is the Holy One, blessed be He."[5] This statement refers to our inability to live in a situation of intimate communication. This is direct oneness in the deepest sense of the word.[6] We live in a state of faces hidden and turned away, and our ability to come together as a couple suffers. The other does not accept me, nor am I open to the other accepting me or to the trust that this other radiates toward me.

God destroyed His very own home and now He walks with the community of Israel in its exile. It is as if the creator has returned to the state of seclusion and concealment that prevailed before creation. In the absence of God, the father, the entire home crumbles. The children transgress against the father, and He, in his anger, expels His children, sending their mother with them. When He expels the mother, His beloved, he essentially destroys His own home. Having destroyed His own home, the father too goes into exile.

THE EXILE OF THE RIGHTEOUS
AND THE TORAH AS A HOME

God and His *Shekhina* are not the only ones who sojourn, lost, in exile. The righteous person, the *tzaddik*, represents God and His *Shekhina* within the human realm, and thus goes into exile as well. As the *Tikkunei Zohar* continues: "'So is a man who wanders from his home' – who is this man? The righteous person, who goes wandering from his place.... For thus the rabbis established, that as long as the Temple is destroyed, it is decreed on the houses of the righteous that they should be destroyed, as well as that they should wander from their homes, for a servant should

---

5. *Tikkunei Zohar*, Introduction, 1b.
6. [Hebrew Editor's note: Rabbi Shagar discussed this issue on many occasions. See his final essay, "*Panim El Panim*" (different from the sermon titled "Face to Face" contained in this volume, p. 273), composed for a conference held in his honor and for the sake of his recovery on the eve of Shavuot 2007. It was published in *We Will Walk in Fervor*, 367–373.]

subsist in the manner of his master."[7] Existing in this world, the righteous person wanders and finds no rest. Both the righteous person and the *Shekhina* have no home. The restless impossibility of finding a home is an inherent part of the human and Jewish condition. The Talmud makes a similar remark about the decree on the houses of the righteous since the destruction of the Temple: "Rabbi Yoḥanan said as follows: From the day that the Temple was destroyed a decree was issued upon the houses of the righteous that they would be destroyed, as it is stated: 'In mine ears said the Lord of hosts: of a truth many houses shall be desolate, even great and fair, without inhabitant' (Isaiah 5:9)."[8] The righteous are condemned to exile in this world. They are condemned to a state of restlessness, to the destruction of their home, for "it is enough for a servant to be like His master."[9] Just as the master, God, has no place in the world because His house has been destroyed, so too the servant, the righteous so identified with their master, God, has no place or rest in this world.

This is the meaning of the trauma and mourning of the Three Weeks that commemorate the destruction. It is enough for a person to be like his master, and to feel the trauma of the destruction in the routines of his daily life. We all have homes, some place or another where we can rest our heads at night. However, on another level, we have no physical home. We exist in the world in a state of wandering. Our reality is a secularized reality of destruction characterized by a deep sense of abandonment and mourning.

However, the *Tikkunei Zohar* teaches that, in a sense, we do have a home even when in exile. This teaching refers to a house wherein people speak words of Torah: "Our rabbis established: any home where words of Torah are not heard will ultimately be destroyed."[10] In contrast, a house full of words of Torah fills with a reality that transcends destruction. Torah is the last form of at-homeness that remains available to us. Anyone who learns Torah can strongly feel that, on some level, the Torah enables us to escape. Life is full of confusions and disturbances, but we can still find calm respite in the Torah.

---

7. *Tikkunei Zohar* 1b.
8. Berakhot 58b.
9. Ibid.
10. *Tikkunei Zohar* 1b.

God's holy house left the physical world when the Temple was destroyed, but there is still one place where I can feel at home: a place where people speak words of Torah. The Torah, or in modern terminology, the text, is the Jew's home. I am not speaking metaphorically. Though we exist within physical space, there is also a mental space wherein we Jews feel sheltered, as if beneath the wings of the mother bird. This mental space is the Torah.

The Talmud says that "anyone who eats three meals on Shabbat will be saved from three painful experiences: the birth pangs of the Messiah, the judgment of *Gehinnom*, and the war of Gog and Magog."[11] What does this passage mean? There is a manner of existing (found particularly among the Hasidim) wherein we construct a virtual reality. It is specifically in this virtual reality that we feel sheltered from even the birth pangs of the Messiah.

Later, the *Tikkunei Zohar* quotes a homily about the commandment to send away a mother bird:

> Any home where words of Torah are not heard will ultimately be destroyed, while those in which words of Torah are heard are called "eggs," "young chicks," and "children." "Eggs" refers to the masters of Tanakh. "Young chicks" refers to the masters of Mishna. "Sons" refers to the masters of Kabbala. This is why it says, "If the mother is sitting over the fledglings or on the eggs, do not take" from them (Deut. 22:6). But regarding the masters of the Kabbala, it says, "do not take the mother together with her sons; ...those who make for her and for the Holy One, blessed be He, and fly with her to every place she flies."[12]

The mother is sent away from the masters of the revealed Torah, but she is not sent away from the masters of the hidden Torah. The masters of the hidden Torah are the ones who create a home for the *Shekhina*, a home for God, and they accompany the mother in all her hardships and wandering.

---

11. Shabbat 118b.
12. *Tikkunei Zohar*, ibid.

What is the exile which the author of the *Tikkunei Zohar* refers to here? He is speaking about a cosmic exile, a state of homelessness permeating all of reality. When reality itself has lost its at-homeness, the righteous person seeks to follow the *Shekhina* because of how deeply he identifies with her. The only place the righteous person can experience at-homeness is the Torah, specifically the Kabbala and even extending to Hasidism. Only there does he feel like he is a part of something larger than himself and take shelter in the soft at-homeness of the mother.

COMMEMORATING THE DESTRUCTION

At a certain point in time, a child leaves his parents' house. Even though he could physically remain there, and his parents are in no hurry for him to leave, mentally he just cannot live there any longer. Regardless of how their parents act toward them, children rightly feel that relying on their parents and living in their parents' homes makes them less independent. Despite this just need for separation, there is something tragic here, a cause for mourning. This new independence is bound up with the destruction of the old home. Even though the son rents an apartment with his friends, ultimately an apartment with your friends is not a home.

The Sages decreed that when a person plasters his home, he should leave one square *amah* unfinished.[13] Moreover, they decreed that a person is forbidden from "filling his mouth with laughter in this world."[14] I feel that these halakhic decrees reflect something very deep. Unlike the ascetics who decided to no longer drink wine or eat meat after the destruction,[15] we cannot live with the full strength and intensity of this mourning. The ascetics wanted to stop the world, to withdraw from everything – an experience manifest in the life of an individual when they stop engaging with the world and become incapable of doing anything at all. However, just as Rabbi Yehoshua said to those ascetics, life must go on. Giving yourself entirely over to mourning and letting it paralyze you is neither necessary nor desirable.[16]

---

13. Bava Batra 60b.
14. Berakhot 31a.
15. Bava Batra 60b.
16. "To not mourn at all is impossible, as the decree was already issued and the Temple

Though it is true that life must go on, there is always an internal feeling that wants time to stop. Think of the widow who feels her life has ended: her husband is dead and her children have left the nest. Even though she is in contact with her kids, as her dead husband would have wanted, she has no chance of experiencing any sense of wholeness or completion. The only thing that sustains her is to live continuously on memories. Similarly, the Jewish people do not live in the present. In some ways, going into exile meant going into memory, into the space of what once was. The nation's history froze at the destruction. There are no new souls being created and no new Torah. Jewish life happens in the past, in memory and perpetual yearning for the way things were in the time of their home, the Temple: "Build your house as it was initially, establish your sanctuary on its foundation. Let us see its rebuilding and let us rejoice in its mending. Return the priests to their service and the Levites to their songs and melodies. Return Israel to their shrine."[17] The nation's powerful connection to life in the present ceased when the *Shekhina* separated from the Holy One.[18]

Even if a person merits to build a home, that home will have a flaw in its essence. Like the unplastered corner in his home, some corner of his life will be unfinished. This is an essential matter, comprising the difference between something whole and complete and something cracked. To give a concrete example, imagine the difference between a car on the showroom floor and a car which the owners have already taken off the lot. The difference in price is drastic. This price difference is a result of our feeling that "new" also means "whole." Ever since the

---

has been destroyed. But to mourn excessively as you are doing is also impossible, as the Sages do not issue a decree upon the public unless a majority of the public is able to abide by it." Ibid.

17. From the Musaf liturgy for Sukkot, Pesaḥ and Shavuot.

18. [Hebrew Editor's note: Some saw this "freezing," which Rabbi Shagar here laments, as a good thing. For example, Franz Rosenzweig wrote that "The Jewish spirit shatters the bonds of historical periodization. Since it is eternal, and it craves eternity, it denies the omnipotence of time. It walks untouched through history." (Franz Rosenzweig, *Naharayyim: Selected Writings*, 69). However, Rabbi Shagar did not see eye to eye with Rosenzweig when it comes to Jewish history. For Rabbi Shagar, exiting history is a symptom of exile, and returning to history, to the possibilities of place, space, reality, even politics, are the first steps out of exile.]

destruction, the Jews feel like there is no wholeness in the world. Even if the world is remade new, there is a flaw in the very essence of reality that manifests the depth of our mourning over the loss of the Temple.

LOSS OF PASSION, SINGLEHOOD, AND THE REDEMPTION OF COUPLEHOOD

The post-destruction situation is much more dramatic than we have described it thus far. The destruction led to a loss of passion and a loss of inspiration: "Since the day the Temple was destroyed, sexual pleasure was taken away and given to transgressors."[19] As long as the Temple remained, there was no contradiction between passion and order (*tikkun*). After the destruction, passion began to appear as chaos and disturbance. It created a gaping chasm between eros and culture.

Elsewhere, the *Tikkunei Zohar* describes the destruction as a dried up river.[20] The river symbolizes abundance and passion. When the world shifted into a dried-up state, all passion and vitality disappeared. Sexuality, sensuality, and eros in the world disappeared as well. In this sense even Torah study has become dry, as the eros of wisdom and real holiness weakened and disappeared after the destruction.

The destruction returned God to a state of "singlehood," or to being in Himself. This was a return to the pleasure principle lacking any fullness, to an existence that is always lacking and never whole. Everything returned to a pre-creation state. This is a state where a "single" person is not just someone who has not found a wife but rather someone who lives a totally solipsistic life. Although such a person lives with a certain intensity, he can never break outside himself. Moreover, he will see any turn toward the other as harming or externalizing his inner life. Similarly, God existed before creation as the Hidden God, meaningful only unto Himself.

While the loneliness of the single person could certainly be seen as preserving their intimacy, at some point this self-preservation becomes a prison of conundrum and constraint. The ability to escape lonely isolation and move outwards is true redemption. The relationship between man and woman embodies this redemption in that they

19. Sanhedrin 75a.
20. *Tikkunei Zohar* §44, 82a.

no longer exist for themselves. As husband and wife, they have instead found a home in each other.

The Sages understood the wife as the embodiment of the home.[21] Just as the woman can accept a man, that acceptance must ultimately be reciprocated by the man. This acceptance is what grants the individual validation, a form of redemption. God created the world because He needed to find external validation for His existence. This is best expressed in the sentiment "there is no king without a nation."[22] The process works similarly between a man and woman in that the acceptance of the other validates the very fact of one's own existence. When the acceptance is true, correct relations develop between man and woman. At this point the subjectivity that was once trapped within itself and unable to achieve self-transcendence finally succeeds in stepping out of this state.

Let us return to the crumbling family discussed by the author of the *Tikkunei Zohar*. The sons transgressed, the children grew up, and they no longer accept their father. Personally, the father feels that they have betrayed him. Now more like strangers, they do not walk the path he wanted them to take in life. Although his lack of welcome in his own home is tragic, we must remember that this was also his fault. He did not accept the mother, was not the father figure his children needed, was singularly focused on his developing career, and generally did not communicate with his family. The painful aspect of this situation is that through it all, the father remains completely unaware that it is his fault. He is incapable of admitting culpability and directs his anger at the mother, claiming that his troubles are her fault and that she turned the children against him. This is a common phenomenon: as long as the children are small, something holds the couple together. However, when the children grow up, the glue that held the family unit together disappears. With the feeling of home dissolving, the couple ultimately divorces.

Interestingly, after the father drives away the children, he suddenly discovers the hidden connection he has with them and turns around to follow them into exile. This is the most tragic part of the entire story.

---

21. See, among other texts, Mishna Yoma 1:1: "'And he shall make atonement for himself and for his house' (Leviticus 16:6): 'his house' refers to his wife."
22. See *Keter Shem Tov*, part 1, §19.

Even though the father's sudden feeling of great love for his banished sons may mean that he cannot bear to part with them, all he can truly do to remedy their broken bonds is to be with them in their suffering.

RENEWAL OF SOULS, RENEWAL OF TORAH: RABBI ISAAC LURIA AND THE VILNA GAON

As noted above, the destruction is depicted as the drying up of a river and of divine abundance. Examining some of the words of Rabbi Isaac Luria in his particular language can help us clarify the meaning of this drying up:

> Through the coupling of *Hokhma* and *Bina*, angels and holy spirits come into being. Souls of supernal angels come into being, but we don't mean actual souls, but the light that pours into them to enliven them, as they said, "You keep them all alive" (Nehemiah 9:6) – you provide vitality to all of them. And this is constant… therefore they never separate, because they must provide sustenance and enlightenment to the supernal worlds for all time to give rise to new angels daily. Of course, there is also the coupling of *Tiferet* and *Malkhut*, and this is intermittent, and only on specific occasions.[23]

The world possesses a fixed, constant element of vitality and liveliness which enables a person to persist even in moments of dryness and thirst. This is the root of the coupling of *Hokhma-Abba* and *Bina-Imma* that gives birth to the souls of angels. Unlike the higher coupling, the lower coupling happens only intermittently. Comprised of the lower *sefirot Tiferet-Kudsha Brikh Hu* and *Malkhut-Shekhintei*, this lower coupling gives birth to *human* souls. This act is much loftier than the coupling of *Hokhma* and *Bina,* which creates new *angelic* souls each day. This is because the intermittent process of lower coupling takes place out of free choice and intent rather than the higher coupling's elements of necessity and compulsion.

---

23. Rabbi Isaac Luria, *Etz Hayim*, Gate of Rashbi's Sayings, 63b. See also the discussion of this distinction in chapter "The Name of the Father," pp. 181–186.

In order to clarify Rabbi Luria's intent when it comes to these two categories of interpersonal connections, we must distinguish between two different terms for the figure of the woman and her role in the family structure: "mother" and "lover." According to Rabbi Luria, the constant divine vitality corresponds to the woman as mother. Although this mechanical coupling derives from routine and from social norms rather than from passionate desire, without it the world would disappear. However, because this reality takes place constantly, it is not at risk of disappearing anytime soon.

The stable situation's constant vitality and abundance gives rise to angels, who are the fixed spiritual forces in the world. Conceptualized as the woman lover, human reality presents a stark contrast to this eternal state of the *sefirot* of *Ḥokhma* and *Bina*. From one perspective, human reality might be considered the lower of the two options. However, from a different perspective, it is the human soul through which divine power manifests in the world. This coupling of *Kudsha Brikh Hu* and *Shekhintei*, the revelation of abundance and the passionate desire at the heart of human existence, is what was lost in the destruction. Therefore, the souls that appear in the world after the destruction are no longer new souls, but rather old souls that act as combinations of souls that already existed and appeared in the course of history. On a deeper level, they have nothing new to say and no new perspective to offer. They are nothing more than different, recycled versions of the past.[24]

---

24. A new soul is a soul that has never appeared in reality. An example of something new would be Hasidism. Hasidism is not just one more variant of something that already existed, nor is it just a new method of Torah study. It is a new type of religiosity. Not only does the vessel change, but a new content and religiosity come to be. We can therefore think of the Baal Shem Tov as a new soul. The same thing is true in science. Einstein was not just adding on to Newton, he was starting an entirely new, different story. The scientific revolution created new vessels that draw down new lights.

[Hebrew Editor's note: In the essay, "Your Nation are All *Tzaddikim*" (see note 4 above), p. 353, Rabbi Shagar goes into greater detail about new combinations and also lists the Baal HaTanya as a new soul, saying, "Hasidism is entirely about creating couplings and putting together combinations. The Baal HaTanya, according to Chabad, was a new soul – novel combinations – a soul the likes of which the world had never seen."]

While Rabbi Luria laments the lack of renewal in the world of souls, the Vilna Gaon laments the lack of renewal in Torah. The Vilna Gaon views the Torah as a seismograph of sorts, accurately reflecting the deepest currents of reality. According to him, there are no more real innovations in Torah because of the lack of new souls. All that we have left is the capacity to reap the harvest from what those who came before us (specifically, the medieval authorities) have already written. This is what he writes:

> In this time we do not receive anything new in Torah such as we did in the time of the Temple, but rather only what we find written in the books of the medieval authorities. In contrast, in the time of the Temple, they would water the Torah.[25]

Innovating in Torah does not mean coming up with some novel idea, a *ḥiddush*, which is ultimately just a combination or rearranging of older, pre-existing elements. Innovating the Torah means renewing the Torah. During the time of the exile, the Torah functions like aftergrowth, sprouting from seeds already in the ground. However, in this case there are no new seeds. The mystical aspect, the inward or the inspirational, has disappeared from the Torah, and there is no way to innovate it. All that remains is to play with or switch out elements that are already there.

In this sense, the Vilna Gaon asserts that the destruction of the Temple was a destruction of the Torah. This is the part of the destruction that people see as metaphysical, or cosmic. Just as in the time of the Tanna'im and Amora'im, we lack a righteous person who could create new ideas. As such, there are no new souls. The world is arid and dry because the divine fertility has left it. Whereas Rabbi Luria views redemption as the creation of new souls, the Vilna Gaon sees it as the creation of a new Torah. Ultimately, the two are inseparable. When a truly new soul appears, it reveals and waters the new Torah, as the Vilna Gaon said."[26]

---

25. *Likkutim Betikkunei Zohar* 5b. [Translator's note: "water" here has much the same sense as it does when referring to "watering" plants or animals.]
26. For more on this, see Yosef Avivi, *The Kabbala of the Gra* (Jerusalem: Kerem Eliyahu, 1993), 36–42.

NEW SOULS

Rabbi Kook showed us that the return to the land meant the end of the exile. Because he showed us this, we were able to achieve stronger, bolder possibilities of Torah. I believe that it also made it possible for new souls to sprout up. The Sages said, "The son of David will not come until the souls from the body have been finished."[27] The old souls will be finished, and new souls will appear in their place. Today, I see novelties, people with all sorts of "combinations." I do not always understand these people. If you were to load their program on my computer, so to speak, it would just short the circuit. Perhaps these are new souls. Let us hope that these souls help the river flow stronger and help the passionate desire return. Let us hope that the couplings in the upper worlds and Torah innovations in this one will both be fruitful and creative. The father will then bring the mother back to the home, rebuild the home, and the sons will once again find a fitting place to rest in the world.[28]

---

27. Yevamot 62a.
28. This sermon originated during the Three Weeks in 5763/2003. Rabbi Shagar expressed these ideas even more sharply in his last *hitvaadut* in Kislev 5767/2006, just a few weeks before he was diagnosed with cancer:

    I truly think that today there are many new souls. Today you meet all sorts of guys with all sorts of new "combinations" "that our fathers never imagined" (Deuteronomy 32:17). The difference isn't just one of programming, it's in the computer chips themselves. The chips won't even load on my computer. I don't know how to comprehend them.

    Today we really see new souls in the religious world. I really think that this is one of the signs of the coming of the Messiah. It is written that in the time of the exile there are no new souls, everything is just a recycling of old materials. It's like when you meet someone and you feel that you've already met someone just like them. Someone once claimed that there are thirty-six types of people, and that you can catalog everyone accordingly. This is, generally speaking, true....

    On very rare occasions, you meet someone with a really new "combination," and it takes you by surprise. Initially, you don't know what to do with this "combination." Today, thank God, there are all kinds of new "combinations." I really feel this way. To put it in messianic language – as the Lubavitcher Rebbe loved to do – this is one of the characteristic signs of the redemption. In the religious world, I would compare it to my generation, when all the characters were boring and banal – everyone was the same. Thank God, today there are real novelties, real *ḥiddushim*, in the deepest, most original sense of the word. (Rabbi Shagar, *We Will Walk in Fervor*, 362–363)

The fonts used in this book are from the Arno family

Maggid Books
The best of contemporary Jewish thought from
Koren Publishers Jerusalem Ltd.